LABOR EDUCATION
IN THE U.S.:
An Annotated Bibliography

by

RICHARD E. DWYER

The Scarecrow Press, Inc.
Metuchen, N.J. & London
1977

Dedicated to

Mom, Dad and Janice

who have shown me so much love

Library of Congress Cataloging in Publication Data

Dwyer, Richard E   1946-
    Labor education in the U.S.

    Includes indexes.
    1.   Labor and laboring classes--Education--
United States--Bibliography.   2.   Labor economics--
Study and teaching--United States--Bibliography.
I.   Title.
Z5814. A24D95   [LC5051]   016. 3312'592'0973   77-21572
ISBN 0-8108-1058-1

TABLE OF CONTENTS

FOREWORD

This is the first attempt at tracing and cataloging the historical development of labor studies in the United States. The first section is an attempt to provide an overview as well as a three-stage methodological approach for the examination of the movement from its beginnings at the turn of the twentieth century to the present. The three stages, workers' education, labor education and labor studies thus set the format for an extensive though not exhaustive annotated bibliography. Journals and other sources spanning the period from 1914 to 1976 were searched and all relevant articles concerning workers' education, labor education, and labor studies were included in the bibliographic listing.

The bibliography is geared to buttress the arguments presented for the three stages of development in the field of the education of workers. Possibly more important, this work should be a major aid for the increasing number of scholars and researchers who are entering this field. For this reason, in addition to the traditional listings of books and articles, this bibliography includes ERIC listings and special sections for archival collections and oral histories. For the researcher, the index is the heart of the work; in addition to the usual subject index, an author index and a listing of journals searched are provided.

A work of this magnitude, which has taken the better part of three years, has not been a one person operation. I wish to thank several work-study students who searched out articles and jotted down notes for annotations. To Mark Sullivan, Joann Riggs, Barbara Israel, Steve Macfarlane, Sandra MacKouse and Thomas Menendez, my deepest thanks. Bernard Downey, librarian of the Rutgers University Institute of Management and Labor Relations Library, continuously encouraged me to complete and publish this work; to him I owe a great debt. Once again Janice, my wife proved to be an extraordinary helpmate.   In addition to typing the first draft of the entire manuscript, she was constantly by my side as we traveled from library to library searching out additional entries; without her this project would not have been completed.

Richard E. Dwyer

LIST OF JOURNALS

Adult Education
    Cleveland, Ohio: American Assn. for Adult Education, Oct. 1950-
autumn 1954, bi-monthly; Autumn 1954-present, quarterly.

Adult Education Bulletin
    Washington: Dept. of Adult Education, Nat'l Education Assn.
of the U. S. ; six times a year; June 1936-August 1950, vols. 1-
14.

Adult Education Journal
    Cleveland, Ohio: American Assn. for Adult Education, quarter-
ly, Jan. 1942-July 1950, vols. 1-9.

Adult Leadership
    Washington: Adult Education Assn. of the U. S. , monthly except
August, May 1952-June 1954; June 1954-present, monthly except
July and August.

Affiliated Schools Scrapbook
    New York: Affiliated Schools for Workers, Inc. , irregular,
1936-1939.

America; national Catholic weekly review
    New York: America Press, weekly from April 17, 1909-present.

American Federationist
    Washington: American Federation of Labor; since 1956 pub-
lished by the AFL-CIO; monthly from March 1894-present.

American Journal of Sociology
    Chicago: Univ. of Chicago Press, bimonthly from July 1895-
present.

American Labor
    N. p. : Communications Corp. , Inc. , monthly from May 1968-
present.

American Labor Monthly
    Monthly from March 1923-Sept. 1924, vols. 1-2 no. 6.

American Labor World
    Incorporated with the New York Union Printer. Published by
the American Federation of Labor, 1899-present.

American Labor Yearbook
    New York: Rand School of Social Science, annually from 1919-
    1932.

American Library Association Bulletin [Now American Libraries]
    Chicago: American Library Assn. (absorbed Adult Education
    and the Library, Jan. 1931; absorbed Public Libraries, March
    1957) 1907-present, monthly.

American Philosophical Society, Proceedings
    Philadelphia: American Philosophical Society, annually, 1838-
    present.

American Teacher [At times called American Teacher Magazine]
    Washington: American Federation of Teachers, ten times a
    year, 1912-present.

Ammunition   see   UAW Ammunition

Annals of the American Academy of Political and Social Science
    Philadelphia: American Academy of Political and Social Science,
    bi-monthly, 1891-1940, vols. 1-212.

Antioch Review
    Yellow Springs, Ohio: Antioch Press, quarterly, 1941-present.

Arbitration Journal
    New York: American Arbitration Assn., quarterly, 1937-pres-
    ent.

Brotherhood of Maintenance of Way Employes.   Journal [Now BMWE
Railway Journal]
    Detroit: Intern'l Brotherhood of Maintenance of Way Employes,
    monthly, 1892-present.

Bryn Mawr Alumnae Bulletin
    Bryn Mawr, Pa.:   Bryn Mawr Alumnae Assn., monthly, 1921-
    present.

Bulletin of the American Association of University Professors [AAUP
Bulletin]
    Washington: American Assn. of University Professors, quarter-
    ly, July 1915-present.

Business and Government Review
    Columbia: Business and Public Administration Research Center,
    Univ. of Missouri, bi-monthly, 1960-present.

Business Week
    New York: McGraw-Hill, weekly, 1929-present.

Butcher Workman
    Chicago: Amalgamated Meat Cutters, Butcher Workmen Educ.

& Benevolent Assn. , 1911-1914, vols. 1-4.   New series begun
monthly, 1915-present.

The Carpenter
   Washington: United Brotherhood of Carpenters and Joiners of
   America, monthly, 1881-present.

Catering Industry Employee
   Cincinnati: Hotel and Restaurant Employees and Bartenders International Union, monthly, 1890-present.

Catholic Digest
   St. Paul, Minn. :   College of St. Thomas, Catholic Pub. Center,
   monthly, Nov. 1936-present.   In 1936 titled Catholic Book and
   Magazine Digest.   From Dec. 1936 to Nov. 1937 title was
   Catholic Digest of Catholic Books and Magazines.

Catholic Educational Review
   Washington: Catholic University of America Press, monthly,
   September-May, 1911-present.

Catholic Mind
   New York: America Press, monthly, 1903-present.

Catholic School Journal
   Milwaukee, Wisc. :   Bruce Publishing Co. , monthly except July
   and August, 1901-present.

Change
   New Rochelle, N. Y. :   Educational Change, Inc. , monthly, with
   double issues July/August and Dec. /Jan. , 1968-present.

Changing Education
   Washington: American Federation of Teachers, AFL-CIO; quar-
   terly, 1967-present.   In August 1971 it merged with American
   Teacher.

Christian Century
   Chicago: Christian Century Foundation, weekly, with some ex-
   ceptions, 1900-present.

College and University
   Washington: American Assn. of Collegiate Registrars and Ad-
   missions Officers, quarterly, 1925-present.

Common Ground
   N. p. :   Common Council for American Unity, summer, 1940 to
   autumn, 1949.   Vol. 1-10.

Commonweal
   New York: Commonweal Publishing Inc. , biweekly, Nov. 12,
   1924-present.

Crisis
New York: Crisis Publishing, Inc., official organ of the
NAACP, monthly, 1940-present.

Current History
Philadelphia: Current History, Inc., monthly, September, 1914-
present. Formed by the union of Current History and Forum
and Events.

Dissent
New York: Dissent Publishing Corp., quarterly, winter, 1954-
present.

Education
Indianapolis: Bobbs Merrill, quarterly, 1879-present.

Education and Training
London: A. B. E. Publications, monthly, Feb. 1959-present.
Title varies.

Education for Victory
Washington: U. S. Office of Education. Replaced School Life
during World War II; March 3, 1942 to June 20, 1945; Vol. 1-3.

Educational Administration and Supervision
N. p.: Warwick and York, Inc., bi-monthly, 1915-present.

Educational Forum
Urbana: Kappa Delta Pi, Univ. of Illinois, quarterly (Nov. -
May), 1938-present.

Educational Record
Washington: American Council on Education, quarterly, 1920-
present.

Educational Review
New York: Doubleday Page & Co., monthly, except July and
August, 1891-1928. In 1928 it merged into School and Society.

Educational Review   see   University of South Florida Educational Review

Educational Screen [Now AV Guide: The Learning Media Magazine]
Chicago: Trade Periodicals, Inc., monthly, except July and
August, 1922-present.

Educational Trends
Evanston, Ill.: n. p., January 1932 to July/August 1941; Vol.
1-9.

Electrical Workers' Journal [Now IBEW Journal]
Washington: Intern'l Brotherhood of Electrical Workers, monthly, Aug. 1914-Dec. 1947. From 1893-1914 published as Electrical Worker.

Federal Employee
 Washington: National Federation of Federal Employees, monthly, July 1917-present.

Film Forum Review
 New York: Institute of Adult Education, Teachers College, Columbia University (in Cooperation with National Committee on Film Forums), quarterly, Vol. 1-3 no. 4 spring, 1946 to winter 1948/49. Thereafter merged into Adult Education Journal.

Fortune
 New York: Time, Inc., monthly, Feb. 1930-present.

Free Labour World
 Brussels: Intern'l Confederation of Free Trade Unions, monthly, 1950- .

Frontiers of Democracy
 N.p.: Progressive Education, monthly Oct. 1934 to Dec. 15, 1943; Vol. 1-5 published under the name Social Frontier. Vol. 6-10: Frontiers of Democracy.

Fundamental and Adult Education
 New York: Unesco, 1949-present. Oct. 1949-April 1952 known as Fundamental Education.

Harvard Business Review
 Boston: Graduate School of Business Administration, Harvard Univ., bi-monthly, 1922-present.

Harvard Educational Review
 Cambridge, Mass.: Harvard University, Graduate School of Education, quarterly, 1931-present.

Higher Education
 Washington: Higher Education Div., U.S. Office of Education, Federal Security Agency, semi-monthly, Jan. 1945 to June 1964; Vol. 1-20.

Highway
 London: Workers Education Assn., monthly, 1908-present.

IUD Digest [IUD Agenda]
 Washington: Industrial Union Dept. of the AFL-CIO, monthly, 1965-present.

Industrial and Labor Relations Review
 Ithaca, N.Y.: New York State School of Industrial and Labor Relations at Cornell Univ., quarterly, Oct. 1947-present.

Industrial Education Magazine
 Formerly Manual Training Magazine, monthly, Oct. 1899 to Nov. 1939; Vol. 1-41.

Industrial Management
　　Des Plaines, Ill.: Industrial Management Society, monthly,
　　1952-present.

Industrial Relations
　　Berkeley: Institute of Industrial Relations, Univ. of Cal. at
　　Berkeley, three times a year, Oct. 1961-present.

International Labour Review
　　Geneva; Washington: International Labor Organization, monthly,
　　Jan. 1921-present.

International Molders' and Allied Workers' Journal
　　Cincinnati: International Molders' and Allied Workers' Union,
　　1863-1907 known as Iron Molders' Journal; 1908-1940 known as
　　International Molders' Journal; monthly, Jan. 10, 1894-present.

Irish Monthly
　　Dublin: n. p., July 1873 to Sept. 1954. Vol. numbers irregu-
　　lar. 1873-1874 known as Irish Monthly Magazine; industrial
　　issues in 1873 known as Catholic Ireland.

Journal of Adult Education
　　Cleveland, Ohio: American Assn. for Adult Education, quarter-
　　ly, Feb. 1929 to Oct. 1941; Vol. 1-13 No. 4.

Journal of Education
　　Boston: Boston University, quarterly, 1875-present.

Journal of Educational Sociology [Now Sociology of Education]
　　N. p.: Payne Educational Sociology Foundation, Inc., monthly,
　　Sept. to May; Sept. 1927 to fall, 1963; Vol. 1-37 No. 1.

Journal of Electrical Workers and Operators see Electrical Workers' Journal

Journal of General Education
　　University Park: Pennsylvania State University, quarterly, 1946-
　　present.

Journal of Higher Education
　　Columbus: Ohio State University Press, bi-monthly, Jan. 1930-
　　present.

Journal of Negro Education
　　Washington: Howard University, Bureau of Educational Research,
　　quarterly, 1932-present.

Journal of Reading
　　Newark, Del.: Intern'l Reading Assn., 8 times a year, Oct.
　　through May, 1957-present.

Journal of the National Education Association [Now Today's Educa-
tion]

Washington: National Education Assn., 1911-1951; Vol. 1-40.
Name changed to NEA Journal in 1951, bi-monthly, Sept-March,
1951-present.

Journal of the American Association of University Women [AAUW
Journal]
  Washington: American Assn. of University Women, 1906-1964;
  Vol. 1-57.

Junior College Journal [Now Community and Junior College Journal]
  Washington: American Assn. of Junior Colleges, monthly, Sep-
  tember-June and bi-monthly Dec.-Jan., 1930 to present.

Justice
  New York: International Ladies Garment Workers' Union,
  weekly or semi-monthly, Jan. 1919-present.

Labor Age
  N.p.: Intercollegiate Socialist Society, Oct. 1913 to March,
  1933; Vol. 1-22. Vol. 1-7 published 1913-1919 as Intercollegiate Socialist; 1919 to May 1921 as the Socialist Review; and
  1921 to 1933 as Labor Age.

Labor and Nation
  N.p.: Inter-Union Institute for Labor and Democracy, quarterly,
  Aug. 1945 to March 1952; Vol. 1-8.

Labor Education Viewpoints
  Morgantown, W.Va.: Local 189, AFT, AFL-CIO, irregularly
  from 1959 to 1968; South Bend, Ind., quarterly, spring 1970-
  present.

Labor History
  New York: Tamiment Institute, quarterly, 1960-present.

Labor Information Bulletin
  Washington: U.S. Dept. of Labor, Sept. 1934 to April 1953;
  Vol. 1-20.

Labor Law Journal
  Chicago: Commerce Clearing House, monthly, 1949-present.

Labor Studies Journal
  N.p.: University and College Labor Education Assn., three
  times a year, May 1976-present.

Labor Today
  N.p.: Labor Today Publishing Co., quarterly, June 1941 to
  May 1942; Vol. 1-2 No. 3.

Labor Today
  Detroit: independent rank and file organization, bi-monthly,
  1962-present.

Labour Education
  Washington: International Labor Organization, Workers' Education Branch, three times a year, June 1964-present.

Labour History
  Canberra, A. C. T.: Australian Society for the Study of Labour History, twice a year, Jan. 1962-present.

Library Journal
  New York: R. R. Bowker, semi-monthly (Sept. -June), monthly (July-Aug), 1876-present. Vol. 1 known as American Library Journal.

Life and Labor
  N. p.: National Women's Trade Union League, monthly, except summer, 1911 to Oct. 1921; Vol. 1-11 No. 8.

Life and Labor Bulletin
  N. p.: National Women's Trade Union League, irregularly, Aug. 1922 to Feb. 1923 and then again April 1933 to June 1949.

Lithographers Journal [Now Graphic Arts Unionist]
  N. p.: Amalgamated Lithographer of America, quarterly, June 1915 to 1964.

Locomotive Engineers Journal [Now Locomotive Engineer]
  Cleveland, Ohio: Brotherhood of Locomotive Engineers, monthly, 1907 to 1957; Vol. 41 to 93. Volumes 1-40, 1867-1906, published under various titles.

Machinist Monthly Journal
  Washington: International Assn. of Machinists, monthly, 1889 to 1956; Vol. 1-68.

Management Record [Now Conference Board RECORD]
  New York: National Industrial Conference Board, monthly, Jan. 1939-present.

Monthly Labor Review
  Washington: U. S. Dept. of Labor, monthly, July 1915-present.

Nation
  New York: Nation Co. , weekly, except bi-weekly in July and August, 1867-present.

National Municipal Review
  New York: National Municipal League, monthly, except August, 1912-1958.

Nation's Schools
  Chicago: McGraw-Hill, monthly, 1928-present.

New Jersey Adult Educator
    Trenton: Association for Adult Education, annually, 1970-
    present.

New Republic
    Washington: New Republic Inc., weekly, 1914-present.

North American Review
    Cedar Falls, Iowa: North American Review Press, quarterly,
    May 1815 through winter 1939, 1940; Vol. 1-248.

Opportunity
    New York: National Urban League, 1923-winter 1949; Vol. 1-
    27.

Personnel Administration
    Washington: Society for Personnel Administration, bi-monthly,
    1938-present.

Personnel Journal
    Santa Monica, Calif. : Personnel Journal, Inc., monthly, May
    1922-present. From 1922-1927 known as Journal of Personnel
    Research.

Phi Delta Kappan
    Bloomington, Ind. : Phi Delta Kappa Inc., monthly, Sept. to
    June, 1915-present.

Proceedings of the Council on Social Work Education
    New York: Council on Social Work Education, annually, 1953-
    present.

Proceedings of the Industrial Relations Research Association
    Madison, Wisc. : Industrial Relations Research Assn., annually,
    1948-present.

Proceedings of the National Council of Social Work see Proceedings
of the Council on Social Work Education

Proceedings of the National University Extension Association
    Washington: National University Extension Assn., annually,
    1915-present.

Progressive Education
    N.p. : Progressive Education Association (1955-1957 by the
    John Dewey Society), April 1924 to July 1957; Vol.
    1-34.

Public Affairs
    Halifax, Nova Scotia: Institute of Public Affairs, Dalhousie Uni-

versity, August 1937 to winter 1953; Vol. 1-15.

RWDSU Record
New York: Retail, Wholesale, Department Store Union, monthly, 1954-present.

Railway Clerk/Interchange
Rosemont, Ill.: Brotherhood of Railway, Airline, Steamship
Clerks, Freight Handlers, Express, and Station Employees,
monthly, 1900-present.

Railway Maintenance of Way Employee   see   Brotherhood of Maintenance of Way Employes. Journal

Religious Education
New Haven, Conn.: Religious Education Assn., bi-monthly,
1906-present.

Review of Educational Research
Washington: American Educational Research Assn., quarterly,
Jan. 1931-present.

Saturday Review of Education [Internal monthly part of Saturday Re-
view/World, now Saturday Review]
New York: Saturday Review, Inc., weekly, 1924-present.

School and Society [Now Intellect]
New York: Society for the Advancement of Education, bi-weekly,
Oct-May, 1915-1965; Vol. 1-93.

School Life
Washington: U. S. Office of Education, August 1, 1918 to pres-
ent on a monthly basis with the exception of February, 1942-
October, 1945 when it was replaced by Education for Victory.

Sign
Union City, N. J.: Passionist Missions, Inc., monthly, Aug.
1921-present.

Smith Alumnae Quarterly
Northampton, Mass.: Smith College Alumnae Association,
quarterly, 1909-present.

Social Education
Washington: National Council for the Social Studies, seven
times a year, Jan. 1937-present.

Social Forces
Chapel Hill: Univ. of North Carolina Press, four times a
year, Nov. 1922-present.

Social Frontier
N. p.: Progressive Education, later known as American Educa-

tion Fellowship, Oct. 1934 to June 1939. Later known as Frontiers of Democracy.

Social Research
New York: New School for Social Research, quarterly, 1934-
present.

Social Work Today
New York: independent rank and file coalition, March/April,
1934 to May 1942.

Socialist Review
N. p. : Socialist Party, U. S. A. , Jan. 1932 to spring, 1940; Vol.
1-7.

Southwestern Social Science Quarterly [Now Social Science Quarterly]
Austin, Texas: Southwestern Social Science Association, quarterly, June 1920-present.   From 1920-March 1923 known as
Southwestern Political Science Quarterly; June 1923 to March
1931; Southwestern Political and Social Science Quarterly.

Speech Teacher
New York: Speech Communication Assn. , four times a year,
1952-present.

Survey
N. p. : Survey Associates, bi-weekly; Vol. 1-68, 1897-1932;
Vol. 85-88, 1949-May 1952.

Survey Graphics
Published 1921-1948; merged with Survey in January 1949.

Teachers' College Record
New York: Columbia University, Teachers' College, quarterly,
1900-present.

UAW Ammunition
Detroit: United Automobile, Aircraft, and Agricultural Imple-
ment Workers of America, monthly from April 1943-present.

University of South Florida Educational Review
Tampa: College of Education, Univ. of South Florida, semi-
annually, 1962-present.

Vassar Quarterly
Poughkeepsie, N. Y. : Associate Alumnae of Vassar College,
quarterly, May 1926-present.   Formerly Vassar Alumnae Magazine.

Wellesley Quarterly
Wellesley, Mass. : Wellesley College Alumnae Association,
quarterly, Vol. 1-39, 1916-Nov. 1954.

Wilson Library Bulletin
Bronx, New York: H. W. Wilson Co., monthly (Sept-June), 1914-present. Vols. 1-13 No. 10 known as Wilson Bulletin Index.

Woman's Press
New York: Young Women's Christian Assn., Vol. 1-16, 1907 to August 1922 entitled The Association Monthly; from Sept. 1922 to Dec. 1950 known as Woman's Press.

Woodstock Letters
Woodstock, Md.: Jesuit Seminary Guild; from the Woodstock Conference in Baltimore, Maryland, 1926-present.

Workers' Education
New York: Workers' Education Bureau of America, irregularly, 1921 to 1936.

World Association of Adult Education Bulletin
N.p.: World Assn. of Adult Education, July 1919 to Nov. 1931; June 1935 to Feb. 1946.

World Tomorrow
Jan. 1918 to July 26, 1934. Vol. 1-17. Merged into Christian Century.

INTRODUCTION*

A cursory examination of the literature in the field of the education of workers indicates that three separate terms have been used to describe this movement in the United States. The terms workers' education, labor education, and labor studies have gained widespread usage in chronological sequence. The first term, workers' education, described the movement from its permanent beginnings in the first decade of the twentieth century until the 1940's; the second term, labor education, began to be used in the late 1930's and became the predominant term used to describe the movement after World War II; the third term, labor studies, was first used in the late 1960's and is presently gaining acceptance among practitioners in the field. Throughout the literature these terms have been used almost interchangeably with little consideration of the possible differences in their meaning. Such usage has confused not only outsiders but also students within the field.

The core of the problem is more than a question of semantics. A careful examination of the literature leads one to believe that three distinctive historical periods accompany the three distinctive terms. For a different position see Linton (#1398), Rogin and Rachlin (#1828), Carlson (#1106). The three periods differ in curriculum content, student body, and the basic objectives which were sought. Granted, these periods are not mutually exclusive. There is some overlapping, but the major trends in the movement change significantly enough to warrant an effort to describe the three distinct periods. Even though the popularized usage of the particular term does not exactly fit the historical period designated to it, the designation will assist the student of the subject to categorize issues and time periods. By defining the particular emphasis of each distinctive period, the student will be able to understand not only the historical development of the movement, but also the cord of commonality which links the present stage of the movement with the previous two. One of the major difficulties with tying the terminology to the historical period is that the term does not span the historical period it is meant to describe. For example, what is described as labor education began in the late 1930's, but the term, labor education, did not gain wide acceptance until after World War II. This can be explained by the "time lag" theory. That is to say that the basic objectives of the movement changed to meet social

*Reprinted by permission from Review of Educational Research. Copyright © 1977 by The American Educational Research Association.

and political changes, but the previous nomenclature, workers' education, held on for some years to come.

One thing is certain. What is happening today in the area of labor studies can be traced directly to the workers' education movement of the first decades of this century. Many changes have transpired in these seventy odd years, but the overall goal remains the education of the working class.

WORKERS' EDUCATION

The term workers' education was brought to the United States from Great Britain where it was and still is used to describe the movement for the education of workers. In the United States, workers' education had its beginning in the first decade of the twentieth century. In 1901 Walter Vrooman, an American and one of the founders of Ruskin College in England, approached the American Federation of Labor (AFL) Executive Council asking for its endorsement for a Ruskin College in the United States. This request was refused. In 1906 the Rand School of Social Science was formed in New York City by the Socialist Party. The objective of this school was to provide workers with the type of broad education required to create a new social order based on socialism (Gray (#1826), p. 54). In addition, the Rand School provided educational services for the International Ladies Garment Workers Union (ILGWU) and the Amalgamated Clothing Workers of America (ACWA) until these unions established their own education departments in 1917 and 1919 respectively. The first decade of the century also saw the birth of the Women's Trade Union League which was largely devoted to the task of educating working women as to their rights as citizens and to conveying the need for trade unions on the job (Foner, P. History of Organized Labor in the United States. v. 3. New York: Intern'l Pub., 1964, pp. 228-32). Like the previous two attempts, this educational effort was largely ignored by the leadership of the AFL. With the end of World War I, central labor bodies perceived the need for broad-based educational programs, and during the 1920's over 300 labor colleges dotted the United States.

The decade of the twenties was a boom time for workers' education in the United States, with 1921 the most outstanding year of the decade. In that year the University of California expanded its extension program to include a program specifically geared for workers; the Bryn Mawr Summer School for Women Workers in Industry opened its doors to one hundred working class women; and Brookwood Labor College initiated its two-year resident program at Katonah, New York. The Workers Education Bureau of America (WEB) was formed in New York City in 1921 by concerned men and women for the purpose of coordinating workers' education services conducted under trade union auspices. As the decade proceeded, schools for workers were established at Barnard College, the University of Wisconsin, the Southern Summer School which was held at various college campuses throughout the South during its twenty-

five year existence, and the Vineyard Shore School located in West
Park, New York.   With the exception of the latter, these schools
were conducted in the summer months on a college campus.   In
1927, the summer schools of Bryn Mawr, Barnard, and Wisconsin
joined together to form the Affiliated Summer Schools for Women
Workers in Industry to coordinate recruitment and fund-raising efforts.   The Southern Summer School, however, maintained only in-
formal ties with this organization.

A brief examination of these schools which provided educational services in the first period, termed workers' education, will
provide an understanding of the movement as it began in the United
States.   Each of the three specific time periods which comprise the
movement for the education of workers will be delineated; the objectives, curriculum, student body, duration of classes, and the finances and administration of the programs will be scrutinized to determine the distinctive characteristics of each period.   An examination of the educational activities for workers in the aforementioned
areas will provide an understanding of the movement known as workers' education when it began in America.

Basic Objectives

The Rand School and the Workers School of the Communist
Party, later known as the Jefferson School, characterized the most
striking example of the basic objectives espoused in the period
termed workers' education.   These two workers' schools were ad-
ministratively under the control of political parties which called for
radical change in the social structure of the United States.   The
basic objective of these schools was to raise the consciousness of
the working class and to prepare them to assist in bringing about a
change in the social order.

At the other extreme, the summer school for women workers
conducted by Wisconsin State University recognized the role of workers' education in bringing about social change, but disclaimed any
direct relationship between the school and collective social action.
In October 1925, at an advisory committee meeting, the purpose of
the school was stated as, "primarily to offer to women of limited
opportunity a chance for further study adapted to their needs.   Any
impetus to social reform which may come out of the school will be
secondary and largely individual" (Schwarztrauber (#1563), p. 39).
Another summer school located on the campus of Bryn Mawr College was founded with the belief that social change was imminent
and that workers of the future were to see international and industrial peace and the reign of reason in the economic world.   The
preparation of women workers to contribute to these forces in a
democratic way was the goal of its educational endeavors (Schneider
(#710), p. 63).   The director of this school and later of the Affiliated Schools for Women Workers, Inc., felt that workers, from the
basis of new facts discovered in classes, should assume responsibilities leading to various forms of social action (Smith (#1052), p.
83).

The first president of the WEB, James Maurer, contended that "the basic purpose of workers education is the role of an intelligent guide to a new social order ... and the ultimate liberation of the working masses" (#1049, p. 12). The director of another independent worker education project, A. J. Muste of Brookwood Labor College, "could see the inadequacy of 'pure and simple trade unionism' as an instrument of social change" (Hansome, (#1669), p. 59). Muste incorporated his beliefs into the basic objectives of Brookwood Labor College.

Even the educational programs conducted under the auspices of trade unions had as their basic objective the reordering of the social system. Louis Lorwin (The Women's Garment Workers, New York: B. W. Huebsch, 1924.) characterized the educational program of the ILGWU as not merely wanting to turn out "educated men and women in the ordinary sense, but to touch the hearts and minds of members and mold them into intelligent conscious union men and women ... [who] strive for the reconstruction of society" (p. 494). A similar objective was expressed by the secretary of the ILGWU education department when she described workers' education as "a movement for special education ... which will enable the workers to accomplish their special job which is to change economic and social conditions so that those who produce shall own the product of their labor" (Cohn (#13), p. 10).

In 1941, Mark Starr, education director of the ILGWU and former teacher at both Brookwood Labor College and Bryn Mawr Summer School for Women Workers in Industry, remarked that the ultimate goal of workers' education had been to play "an important and creative role in replacing rugged individualism by some sort of democratic collectivism ... education for a new social order" (#1684, p. 90).

One of the most comprehensive discussions of workers' education, by Arthur Gleason (#28, p. 5), sums up its basic objective.

> The heart of workers' education ... the class, financed on trade union money, the teacher a comrade, the method discussion, the subject the social sciences, the aim an understanding of life and the remolding of the scheme of things. Where that dream of a better world is absent adult workers' education will fade away in the loneliness and rigor of the effort.

The various groups which sponsored workers' education programs in the 1920's filled the ideological spectrum from radical political parties to the much more conservative state universities. For this reason alone it is evident that although the basic objective of the vast majority of the workers' education programs was a change in the social order, each program (depending upon its ideological persuasion) defined the methods of achieving the new social order and the final form it would take in a different manner.

Curriculum

In order to prepare workers for their role in the trade union and society in general, workers' education programs focused on providing a broad understanding of the social and economic dimensions of the world in which they lived. An examination of the course titles of workers' education classes shows very little deviation from traditional educational programs. What distinguishes workers' education from more traditional education is not so much the subjects themselves, but rather it is the course content which is unique. In short, it is not the form but the substance which made workers' education distinctive. A workers' curriculum typically included a course in American history. However, the content of the course would examine the contributions of working men to the development of the nation rather than the more traditional study of military, political, and industrial heroes.

For the most part, the curriculum of the workers' education period was based on the social sciences. The University of California's workers' education program in 1921 reached 250 students in six classes with two of these classes being termed vocational education courses. These two classes in blueprint reading drew more than one half of the students. This trend continued and it was not until 1928 that the director, John Kerchen, could report that the demand for vocational education had ceased and the entire workers' education curriculum was now based on the social sciences (Daniels (#804), pp. 38-41).

At the 1924 annual convention of the National University Extension Association (NUEA), Spencer Miller, Jr., secretary of the WEB, in response to a question on the character of courses demanded by workers, answered:

> Most of the courses that have been demanded by the workers' classes and colleges have fallen in the field of social science. I would say, as a result of inquiries conducted for the Workers Education Bureau and also for the U.S. Bureau of Education, that the popular courses are those in history, economics, and problems in the labor movements....
> In addition to this course of social science, there has been a great deal of interest in courses in psychology and literature, with particular emphasis placed recently on social psychology... (#826, p. 20).

Similarly, the Workers' Bookshelf of the WEB had a policy that it would "contain no volumes on trade training nor books which give short cuts to material success. The reasons which will finally determine the selection of titles for the Workers' Bookshelf will be because they enrich life, because they illumine the human experience, and because they deepen men's understanding" (#827, p. 45).

A. W. Calhoun, a teacher at Brookwood Labor College, felt

that the environment in which workers live and work has determined that their education should be extensively in the social sciences. In addition the belief was expressed that although the social sciences constitute the basis of workers' education, attention should be given to a comprehensive culture covering the whole range of human interests (#111, p. 7). Although the curriculum of the various summer schools joined together in the Affiliated Schools for Women Workers in Industry varied slightly, the social sciences formed the backbone of the program (Smith (#750), pp. 127-145; Schwarztrauber (#1563), p. 42).

As for the union-sponsored educational programs, Jack Barbash states that the ILGWU and ACWA gave predominantly humanistic emphasis to their programs (#1476, p. 7). The education directors of both of these unions, Mark Starr (#1684) and J. B. S. Hardman (#1670), respectively support Barbash's claim. In addition to these courses in the social sciences, the summer schools for workers offered courses in the fine arts. Vineyard Shore's curriculum contained music, art, and dramatics (#826, p. 142). The Pacific Coast School for Workers introduced an "Appreciation Hour" as part of its curriculum. "One week of the four-week summer school was devoted to the four areas of music, poetry, drama, and painting" (Hanson (#1126), p. 147).

Student Body

As for the student body in the period known as workers' education, Bryn Mawr Summer Schools for Women Workers had a policy of recruiting one-half of its students from union ranks and the other one-half from unorganized workers (Smith (#750), p. 6). The first year of the Wisconsin School for Workers only 9.8 per cent of the students were organized. It was not until 1932 that organized workers outnumbered unorganized workers at the Wisconsin Summer School for Workers (Schwarztrauber (#1563), p. 60).

The policy statement of the University of California's workers' education program stated:

> It shall be the aim and purpose of this department to provide an educational medium through which those persons engaged in manual labor may cooperate with the members of the teaching staff of the University of California and develop courses of instruction that treat particularly those problems that chiefly concern labor.... The term 'Labor' as used in this statement shall in no way be construed as to include organized labor exclusively but should include all interested workers, organized or unorganized. (Daniels (#804), pp. 37-38).

A major concern of the NUEA was that it could not offer workers' education programs solely to organized workers. Such programs would have to be open theoretically to the general public (#824). In addition those schools conducted by political parties,

YWCA's and settlement houses were open to all workers. Even the
student body of the labor colleges sponsored by local central labor
bodies were comprised of both organized and unorganized labor
(Miller, S. The University and the American Worker. New York:
Workers' Educ. Bureau, 1922, p. 14).

Of course those workers' education programs administrative-
ly controlled by trade unions such as the ILGWU and the ACWA limited their student body to their own union members. Brookwood
Labor College also limited its students to trade unionists or those
who espoused trade union principles (De Caux, Len. Labor Radical.
Boston: Beacon, 1970, pp. 100-105).

The student body, regardless of union affiliation was recruited as individuals and not as union members. The schools did not
go to a union and expect that union to provide students. Rather the
students were recruited as individuals through such organizations as
churches and YWCA's. At short courses sponsored by the WEB all
attendees were recruited on an individual basis. The same was
true with Brookwood, the Affiliated Schools, and the University of
California, as well as the trade union schools conducted by central
labor bodies.

Duration of Classes--Administration--Finances

An added characteristic of workers' education can be found in
the length of the programs. Workers' summer schools lasted from
four to eight weeks; Vineyard Shore and Brookwood's curriculum
lasted for one and two years respectively. With the exception of
Barnard which was a commuter school with a student body based in
New York City, all of these schools were considered long term and
residential. Even those schools which were not residential in nature,
such as the labor colleges conducted by the central labor bodies and
the winter program of the University of California Workers' Education Program, conducted their courses one night per week for an
average semester of sixteen weeks.

Finally, the bulk of educational programs for workers were
administered independently of organized labor. Although some international unions were actively engaged in education, they were in the
distinct minority. The AFL did not have an education department
until 1954 when it officially incorporated the WEB to function as its
education department.

Financial contributions for workers' education in the period
from 1921-1938 tend to emphasize the independent nature of workers'
education. Of the approximately four million dollars spent in this
period, trade unions contributed one and a half million dollars, and
of this, one-half was donated to independent workers' education projects leaving only $750,000 spent on trade union sponsored workers'
education (Schneider (#710), p. 25). The bulk of these monies ex-
pended by trade unions were for programs developed after 1935.
These programs were conducted mainly by CIO unions, not the older

AFL unions. Working students were able to attend long-term residential workers' education programs because the independent educational institutions provided scholarships covering the entire cost of the school to all of the participants. Another factor which enabled the student-worker to take time off from work was that many of the schools were conducted during the summer months when many industries were in a slack time and the workers were laid off.

The period described as workers' education spans from the first decade of the twentieth century to the middle 1930's. Its basic characteristics include: 1) education for social change; 2) a curriculum based primarily on the social sciences; 3) a student body consisting of both union and non-union students, individually recruited; 4) courses which tended to be of a lengthy duration; 5) financing and administration of workers' education was generally, although not exclusively, independent of the organized labor movement.

LABOR EDUCATION

The initial movement away from the objectives and curriculum of the workers' education period occurred in 1929 at the annual convention of the WEB. In the previous year, the AFL had censured Brookwood Labor College and the college supporters were incensed with the WEB's lack of support for Brookwood in the controversy. The central issue at the convention was a constitutional amendment which would insure AFL control over the policies of the WEB. James Maurer, president of the WEB, announced that he was forced to resign his position because of certain distressing trends in the American workers' education movement. The same issues which distressed Maurer also heralded the end of workers' education and the beginnings of labor education. These issues included: the denial of the purpose of workers' education as an intelligent guide to a new social order and a proposed change in the WEB constitution which would take away the right of representation on the executive board of the WEB from all groups except the AFL and international unions.

With the advent of the 1930's other events occurred which continued the changing emphasis from workers' education to labor education. As has been shown, prior to this time, the AFL gave only perfunctory support to workers' education. The labor movement made no serious financial commitment, leaving it to socially-minded intellectuals to finance educational endeavors for workers. "In the United States, perhaps more than elsewhere, well meaning liberals and radicals with access to bankrolls and foundation grants have started various forms of labor colleges and workers education committees" (Starr, (#1684), p. 89). Thus with the inception of the Depression, the labor movement was more concerned with survival than with the frills of education. The interests of the "angels of mercy" changed as a result of lower incomes, and as the Depression became more severe, the mortality rate of labor colleges and workers' institutions increased.

While workers' education in the early period seemed to be an individual effort of educating individual workers, the Depression ended many of these endeavors. By 1939, Brookwood Labor College had ceased to exist, and both Vineyard Shore and Barnard had become casualties of the Depression. Almost all of the labor colleges sponsored by central labor bodies in cooperation with nearby colleges had by this time also closed their doors. For example, two labor colleges which for a time were supported by the Garland Fund were forced to close during this period, Seattle Labor College in 1932 and Portland Labor Temple in 1938.

The 1930's ushered in the passage of a flood of labor legislation. The most important was the National Labor Relations Act which, in fact, legitimized the American labor movement. This rash of governmental regulations added to the growing complexity of labor management relations, and thus made utilitarian labor education an imperative for survival. Finally, the rise of the Congress of Industrial Organizations (CIO) in 1935 and the upsurge of union membership which swelled the ranks of CIO unions to 3.7 million by 1937, provided labor education with a student body untrained in the laws which governed industrial relations and in the daily operation of the union organization.

By the end of the decade, the administration of education for workers had changed. As mass production industries were organized (CIO), provisions were made for educational programs as part of the general process of organization in establishing these unions (Ware (#1581), p. 6). Thus educational departments were established in such new unions as Automobile, Rubber, Steel, and Textile Workers. Older unions such as the United Mineworkers and the International Association of Machinists began to devote themselves seriously to labor education (Douty, A. American Workers' Education in Action. Paris: Economic Cooperation Administration, 1950 (mimeo), p. 1).

It was also in this decade that the federal government began to support financially a program for workers' education administered through the Works Progress Administration (WPA) under the direction of Hilda W. Smith. Unemployed teachers were hired and instructed in the techniques of teaching workers. Between 1933 and 1943 the WPA workers' education program reached one million workers in thirty-six states. In the 1940's many state govenments followed the example already established by Wisconsin and California in financing programs for the education of workers through their respective state universities.

Basic Objectives

The characteristics of the second period termed labor education are distinctive from the former period labeled workers' education. The basic objectives of labor education were more immediately utilitarian than those of workers' education. While workers' education was attempting to bring about a new social order, labor education focused on the practical needs of the trade union movement.

The objectives of the education department of the UAW, CIO from its inception in June 1936, through the early 1950's bore directly upon the maintenance of the union.   From 1936 through the Second World War, the maintenance of the union was expressed through two concerns--the importance of leadership training and the need for membership loyalty to the union (Linton (#1398), p. 40). Even after Walter Reuther had solidified his political position in the union, and Brendan Sexton was appointed educational director, the major concern of regional education departments was on educational programs which would make the worker a more effective union member in the narrow sense of the term (Linton, (#1398), pp. 187-197).

The basic objectives of other trade unions at the time closely paralleled those of the UAW.   Agnes Douty prepared a survey of labor education conducted by American trade unions for the Economic Cooperation Administration.   She discovered that although the American labor movement was divided among several major federations and a number of large independent unions, there was not enough difference in the general scope, character, and content of their educational programs to justify separate treatment of each federation.   As for the basic objective, Douty discovered that the "emphasis in labor education has been placed on training members in the functional, day to day aspects of collective bargaining" (American Workers' Education in Action.   Paris: Economic Cooperation Administration, 1950 (mimeo), p. 3).

This modification of the emphasis in the education of workers was evidenced not only in the labor education conducted by trade unions, but those universities which had been involved in workers' education also began emphasizing utilitarian education based on immediate trade union needs.

The shift in the primary objective of the School for Workers at the University of Wisconsin is documented by Alfred P. Fernbach in a study done for the NUEA (#1498, pp. 9-11).   Fernbach contended that as organized labor began to take increasing interest in the school the focus of the objectives shifted to more utilitarian subjects.   It was Professor John R. Commons, chairperson of the university committee for the school, who was chiefly responsible for this shift in emphasis.   He insisted, in line with his belief that collective bargaining was essential to harmonious industrial relations, that the School for Workers should meet the practical needs of organized workers.   The twentieth anniversary brochure of 1944 substantiates this shift when its statement of objectives for the school included: "Here arises the chief function today of the School for Workers.   It makes itself available at the point of the workers most immediate needs--those growing specifically out of his role in union-management relations" (Fernbach (#1498), p. 15).

State universities which were commissioned to begin labor education programs during the decade of the forties received lofty

charges which in reality meant that the education should revolve
around the labor-management agreement. The fundamental objectives of the New York State School of Industrial and Labor Relations
(Cornell) was to promote the understanding of industrial and labor
relations, more effective cooperation among employers and employees, and general recognition of their rights, obligations and duties under the laws pertaining to industrial and labor relations in
New York State (Day (#1491), p. 225). The fundamental objective
for the Rutgers Labor Education Program was ostensibly the same
as for Cornell, "to promote harmony and cooperation between management and labor" (Public Laws 307, Statutes of the State of New
Jersey, 1947).

Even the WPA workers' education service had a narrow objective. The administrator of the WPA, Harry Hopkins, said of the
project:

> This phase of adult education is designed to meet the spe-
> cial needs of wage earners who have little formal school-
> ing. Its chief purpose is to stimulate an active intelligent
> interest in the economic and special problems of the times,
> and to develop a sense of responsibility for their solution.
> In contrast to the broader curriculum scope of adult educa-
> tion, topics of study are for the most part confined to in-
> dustrial and labor problems of particular concern to the
> workers (Cook and Douty (#1488), p. 86).

These utilitarian objectives inherent in labor education were
also expressed on the international scene by the International Labor
Organization's (ILO) Workers' Education Branch. A resolution
adopted in 1950 by the International Labor Conference stated that the
basic objective of labor education was "to promote opportunities for
workers to be educated in order to enable them to participate more
effectively in various workers' movements and to fulfill more ade-
quately their trade union and related functions" (The Role of the University in Workers' Education. Geneva: Intern'l Labor Org., 1974,
p. 9).

Curriculum Content

This basic objective can be seen more clearly by examining
the curriculum in labor education programs of the period. The educational program of the United Automobile Workers concentrated on
summer schools and night classes with such subjects as: parliamentary law, public speaking, current events, collective bargaining,
leadership training, grievance procedure, and contract interpretation.
(Linton (#1398), p. 45). The UAW was not alone. The Amalgamated
Clothing Workers of America conducted correspondence courses
through their union newspaper. The four subject areas covered were
1) problems of collective bargaining; 2) labor in American history;
3) the CIO, and 4) economics of the garment industry ("Our Union
University." The Advance. April, 1938, pp. 24-25). By the late
1940's the typical labor education course sponsored by the CIO

usually lasted from three to ten days and was located at
a church, YMCA, or on a college or university campus.
Union members lived at the institute. Most common were
courses which included public speaking, how to read and
negotiate a contract, how to serve as a shop steward and
increasingly specialized work in history and economics
(Eby (#1717), p. 188).

AFL affiliates also educated to preserve the union structure.
Mark Starr, educational director of the ILGWU explained that "classes in parliamentary law and public speaking enable members to run
their meetings and unions properly" (#1242, p. 248). The Paper-
makers Union provided an excellent example of education for organizational imperatives. The union severely limited its educational
activities to only shop steward training. Without apology they de-
clared, "The program described is not of education but of training.
Union officials do not take responsibility for making up the deficiencies in the general education of the membership" (Brooks and Allen (#1324), p. 399).

The WEB's policy changed drastically after James Maurer resigned as president in 1929. The new philosophy was stated by
George W. Perkins, late vice president of the AFL. "The purpose
of workers education is to enable the individual to get the best possible in life regardless of the system we live under" (Hansome
(#1669), p. 63).

Following the 1929 change in philosophy, the WEB instituted
courses of a more utilitarian nature. WEB activity increased after
the passage of the Norris-LaGuardia Act and the National Industrial
Recovery Act. Spencer Miller could report to the 1934 AFL convention that forty-five labor institutes were conducted in twenty-seven
states, or one every ten days after the passage of the National Industrial Recovery Act   (#269, p. 234). Each of these educational
programs focused on the interpretation of national legislation. As
more and more "labor bills" passed Congress, the need for secondary leaders to be informed about the implications of the new laws
became mandatory. So, as the Wagner Act, Social Security Act,
and Fair Labor Standards Act were passed, those concerned with
educating organized labor concentrated on preparing the secondary
leadership to function within the new legal guidelines.

Not only did those educational programs directly related to
the labor movement become more utilitarian, but the university labor education programs focused their attention on "bread and butter"
courses as well. At the University of Wisconsin School for Workers, the stress was laid particularly on training workers for the
collective bargaining relationship. "By the 1940 summer school the
utilitarian courses in the school increased dramatically" (Schwarztrauber (#1563), p. 119). Collective bargaining problems and techniques, time and motion study, and the economics of the particular
industry were the most requested courses.

In 1950, Irvine L. H. Kerrison, first director of the Rutgers University Labor Education Program, conducted a study of university labor education programs. One conclusion was that "demand is growing throughout the labor movement for instruction in utilitarian 'tool' subjects like collective bargaining, public speaking, parliamentary procedure and time study" (Kerrison (#1516), pp. 4-5). Even the politically oriented schools had switched their curriculum to reflect the utilitarian "bread and butter" courses. In the last decade of its existence, the Rand School had lost much of its radical character and instead concentrated on cooperation with unions in supplying educational services largely limited to the "tool subjects" (Starr (#1687), p. 75). Carolyn Ware, in her two studies of labor education, found the same curriculum as did Kerrison (#1582, p. 59).

The federal government-financed workers' education programs provided courses which were of a utilitarian nature as well. The WPA Workers' Education Program contained subjects which "ranged from literacy to the creative arts," but its major area of concentration "included a high portion directly related to effective unionism" (Rogin and Rachlin (#1828), p. 21).

Student Body

The composition of the student body and the recruitment method used also differed from the workers' education period. The trend was now toward a student body composed largely if not totally of organized union members, who were most often recruited through their union rather than on an individual basis. Not only was the student a union member, but in most cases he was in a lower level leadership capacity such as shop steward, committeeman, or business agent.

In her study on patterns of workers education, Florence Henley Schneider termed the labor education period training for trade union service. Her findings showed that not only was the course content in the tool subjects, but also that the target population was union officers, shop chairmen and business agents (#710, p. 29).

By 1937, the School for Workers at the University of Wisconsin had experienced a shift in the student body. Now any applicant was admitted regardless of educational background (previously the applicant had to have a deprived educational experience), provided he had two years of industrial experience in his immediate background and was actively engaged in the labor movement or expressed a desire to prepare for such activity. Workers who were not members of labor unions were not excluded at first, but their numbers declined rapidly. In 1941, the School for Workers conducted institutes sponsored exclusively by unions and this eliminated non-union participation (Fernbach (#1498), p. 10).

As would be expected from such an upsurge in union-sponsored labor education, student bodies were recruited from the ranks of the membership. The student body in WPA courses was recruited

for the most part from unions and organizations of the unemployed
(Rogin and Rachlin (#1828), p. 21).

Duration of Classes--Finances--Administration

During this labor education period a change in the duration of
classes was also witnessed. The majority of students in the workers' education period attended classes in residence during the summer from six to eight weeks and in some schools for a year or
more. Their expenses were paid by scholarships provided by private contributors, rarely by their unions. In the later period of labor education, 1935-1965, the duration of courses had been greatly
reduced to short institutes and summer schools of from one to two
weeks in length (Fernbach (#1498), p. 13). The Harvard Trade Union Program cut back its year-long resident program to thirteen
weeks of residency.

In addition to the cutback in time for the residency programs,
the semester-long night courses which had been the hallmark of the
labor colleges were shortened. Wisconsin's year-long program between 1937-1939 ran courses for a fifteen week semester, but had
the program continued they were anticipating three ten-week semesters to encourage the students to finish the course (Fernbach
(#1498), p. 11).

The financing and administration of labor education programs
also changed from the period of workers' education when a great
number of programs were conducted independently of organized labor. During the second half of the 1930's, labor education programs
were chiefly financed and administered through two separate sources
--the federal government, under the auspices of the WPA, and the
trade union movement under the auspices of the education department
of the individual national union. After this decade, and with the demise of the WPA, the federal government ceased to be a viable factor in labor education. Labor education through the trade union continued to develop, and after World War II many states began financing and administering labor education through the extension divisions
of their state university.

The period described as labor education spans from the middle of the 1930's to the 1960's although labor educators were calling
for a broadening educational scope as early as the 1950's. The basic characteristics of this period include: 1) education to meet the
immediate organizational needs of the trade union movement; 2) a
curriculum based on technical courses; 3) a student body composed
solely of trade unionists recruited through their unions; 4) courses
of short duration, i.e. week-long summer schools, weekend conferences and shorter semesters; and 5) programs financed and administered either by the federal government, through the WPA, state
governments through the extension division of the state university, or
the trade union movement.

Some of the distinguishing characteristics of workers' education and labor education have been noted by practitioners in the past. In her essay (#1126), Alice Hanson maintains a difference in course content between what she calls "tool" courses and "background or foundation courses."

> The Workers' Education Movement has adopted a handy nomenclature to distinguish between classes directly related to such specific requirements as public speaking, parliamentary law, time-motion study, etc. and classes like history, government, or literature. The first are known as "tool" courses, the second "background" or "foundation" studies (p. 138).

Jack Barbash takes Hanson's description one step further by delineating a distinctive change in emphasis in the course content between the two periods.

> The tremendous upsurge of unionism in the New Deal period and afterward gave a new direction to workers' education. From a humanistic tone it veered sharply to a "bread and butter" emphasis. The change was understandable. Suddenly, many unions found that they could no longer rely on long experience as the major training medium to meet their pressing needs for manpower competent in the skills that it takes to keep a union functioning efficiently (#1476, p. 138).

Eleanor Coit, in an essay on workers' education (#1115), also saw a change in the curriculum content, but in addition she lamented the change from long-term projects to short courses.

> Earlier emphasis was put on long-term projects in the summer schools, and it was with reluctance that shorter-time institutes and special projects were even considered. Today as unions set their own educational departments, and as the necessity grows for workers to be prepared on specific questions in order to function in government committees and in other community affairs, the resident schools have somewhat changed their form ... they now organize short courses for unions, and plan leadership training projects to prepare leaders to meet new demands (p. 155).

More recently, Lois Gray developed an historical overview for labor education by using an era delineation much like the one developed in this study. Gray proposes that the era termed workers' education was a period where the objective of education was social reform. The 1930's also provide Gray with a change in emphasis. She develops two distinct objectives for the period described as labor education in this study. The 1930's saw labor education for unionization while in the 1940's the emphasis shifted to industrial relations. Written in 1966, Gray's article implicitly notes the beginnings of the labor studies period, although she does not use that term when she states that the role of the universities in labor education had led to experimentation with the broadening of its content and methods (#1826, pp. 53-66).

Transition Period

In the post World War II era, the United States witnessed a great deal of labor-management unrest. Many states created institutes of labor-management relations in the extension division of their universities to promote harmony between the parties in the bargaining process. Although these university labor education programs offered mainly utilitarian "bread and butter" courses, it was only a matter of time before they began experimenting with liberalizing the curriculum and attempting to provide course progression. As universities engaged in increased labor education activity, utilitarian objectives and course content were supplemented with more liberal education.

As early as 1948, labor education practitioners both inside and outside the university were urging the profession to expand its objectives. Although Kermit Eby, education director of the CIO, recognized the need for utilitarian courses which centered in the labor-management relationship he believed that labor education should broaden its scope; "since labor has taken on the mantle of social, political and economic leadership, it must provide workers with information and explanations of problems affecting the entire national life." Hence Eby concludes, "the purpose of workers' education programs should be to train the individual worker and potential leader, not only how to function in a labor-management situation, but also how to be effective in the community and the society in which he lives" (#1717, p. 185).

From his 1951 survey, Kerrison was encouraged by a few institutions which offered a wide range of courses for labor. "The variety indicates that attempts are being made both to meet workers' actual and concrete needs as trade unionists and to develop a widening interest which may eventually involve the workers' consideration of every aspect of world economic, social, and political life" (#1516, p. 67).

The major emphasis of labor education programs focused on "bread and butter" subject matter when the Inter-University Labor Education Committee (IULEC) was formed in 1951. The goal of the IULEC was to expand the curriculum of labor education especially in the area of international affairs. The basic objective of labor education as seen by the IULEC was:

> the improvement of the workers' individual and group competence and the advancement of his social, economic, and cultural interests, so that he can become a mature, wise, and responsible citizen, able to play his part in the union and in a free society and to assure for himself a status of dignity and respect equal to those of other groups and individuals (Mire (#1532), p. 17).

In 1956, after the IULEC grant had expired, Joseph Mire, former executive secretary of the committee, could report, "within the last few years ..., there has been a noticeable broadening of the scope of programs, particularly with a view [to] including programs on international affairs, community participation and health problems" (Mire (#1531), p. 793).

Through the experience of the IULEC, it was demonstrated that given the proper care, professional competency and general cooperation, labor and non-labor agencies could work together to mutual advantage in the field of labor education. Therefore, with the expiration of the IULEC grant in 1956, another central agency, the National Institute of Labor Education (NILE), was established for the effective promotion and development of cooperative labor education projects.

Although the suggestions for broader curriculum content and the development of a systematic progression in curricula developed out of the IULEC, it was NILE that began extensive experimentation in these important areas. Grants were secured through the NILE for such long-term labor education programs as the UCLA's Liberal Arts for Labor Program, the labor leadership series conducted by the University of Chicago, and the University of Indiana's residential course for steelworkers.

In 1961, Freda H. Goldman chaired a symposium on Liberal Education for Labor in the University, which was published by the Center for the Study of Liberal Education for Adults. In the introduction she wrote: "A number--admittedly not large--of labor educators have become convinced that workers need education which goes beyond the narrow utilitarian ends of the traditional bargaining and management courses that still comprise the bulk of labor education in this country" (Reorientation in Labor Education. Chicago: Center for the Study of Liberal Education for Adults, 1962, p. 1). Throughout this book, labor educators wrote of the various experiments being conducted to provide a liberal education for workers; many of these had been sponsored under NILE. Anne Gould spoke of the University of California's program, Liberal Arts for Labor; Irvine Kerrison spoke of Rutger's Union Leadership Academy and the Trade Union Certificate Program; finally Emery Bacon told of the Fourth Year Institute, the World of Ideas, sponsored by the United Steelworkers.

Commenting on this last year of the Steelworkers summer school, Bacon stated the main objectives of this program were "1) to stimulate participants to think critically about themselves as individuals and members of an industrial society; 2) to open possible areas of creativity and 3) to develop an understanding of the values by which men live" (#1771, p. 46). Kerrison writes of a thirst "for education which permits one to take stock of his way of life and encourages ... self mastery of the whole man" (#1803, p. 51).

In this transitional period from circa 1950 to 1967, it must be remembered that the main objective and basic course content remained utilitarian in nature. At the conference on Liberal Education for Labor previously mentioned, Russ Allen, then education-director of the Industrial Union Department of the AFL-CIO stated, "Liberal education as such is of little interest to the American Labor Movement." (#1313, p. 61). As the 1970's approached, the shift from labor education to labor studies progressed slowly.

LABOR STUDIES

Near the end of the decade of the 1960's, events occurred which began to expand the basic nature of labor education and develop the third period entitled labor studies. It was at this time that many state universities were again made aware of ethnic differences, and students demonstrated to include in the curriculum such disciplines as Black Studies and Hispanic Studies. Some labor educators on university campuses began to recognize the need for a credentialed discipline which examined not only ethnic differences, but more broadly defined class differences. As a result, the study of work, workers, and their organizations became a credit-bearing discipline named labor studies.

This same decade also produced an immense interest in credentialization. Standards of employment in our technological society increasingly demanded a college education, and for the most part workers and their children had been denied access to colleges. The college degree became a screening agent that sorted applicants for jobs into different positions. Therefore, there arose a need to provide workers, and particularly trade unionists, with an educational program that would be not only relevant, but also would provide them with the necessary credentials.

Society continued to grow more complex in all areas, and newly emerging labor leadership had to be educationally equipped to deal with these complexities in the collective bargaining relationship.

> Contract language today is far more complex and varied in intent, meaning, interpretation, and application at the local bargaining unit level where the day to day responsibilities of making the contract work place an ever increasing burden of responsibility upon the shop steward, committeeman, and local union officers on the plant floor, or at the initial stages of the grievance procedures of the United Automobile Workers and every other international union (Hutton, C. Objectives--Proposals, Policies, and Guidelines for the Associate Degree in Labor Studies Program. Detroit: UAW Educ. Dept., n.d. (mimeo), p. 4).

The American worker could no longer be an isolationist in his thinking. Oil embargoes and multi-national corporations were forcing him to be concerned with foreign policy and international labor re-

lations. Workers were concerned about automation, distressed by
large-scale unemployment, and puzzled by runaway inflation. They
began to look to education as the road to a better, more effective
union, greater on-the-job satisfaction, and a richer community life
(Levine (#1806), p. 99).

The movement for the education of workers had taken another
step forward. No longer did labor educators solely accept the episodic hit and miss short course which lacked continuity with possible future educational endeavors. It was now recognized that organized workers needed, as well as deserved, the same educational
opportunities afforded the rest of society. Farmers had long en-
joyed access to a full array of educational opportunities, ranging
from cooperative extension to degree-granting agricultural colleges.
Businessmen had long had the opportunity to earn a degree in business administration, sales management, or personnel administration.
With this new emphasis on credentialization labor education found itself entrenched in the non-credit university extension operation.
The strategy for developing degree programs was to use the base
established in the extension division to reach out to the degree-
granting programs of the university and establish degrees in labor
studies. Surrounding community and state colleges were also approached with proposals for establishing these degree programs.

This third period, labor studies, is not nearly as easily defined, dated, or delineated as the previous two periods. In the examination of the previous periods, the advantages of historical hind-
sight are of immeasurable assistance. Today, this labor studies
period is still taking shape and attempts to explain its historical
relevance at times becomes mere prognostication.

In the late sixties, both universities and unions moved to expand their labor education offerings to include degree-granting programs. The first was the University of Massachusetts which in
1965 began a masters degree in labor studies. With the beginning
of the 1967 academic year, Rutgers University offered a bachelor of
arts degree with a major in labor studies in its evening college.
In October 1967, the UAW initially proposed to three community colleges in the Detroit area, and the community college in Flint, Michigan, that they broaden their curricula to include an associate arts
degree in labor studies. In 1972, the UAW again increased its efforts to set up labor studies degree programs in community colleges
within proximity of large concentrations of its members. Today,
associate arts degrees in labor studies are available in New Jersey,
Connecticut, California, Kentucky, Maryland, Illinois, Indiana, and
Missouri because of direct union initiative.

Other unions have also become involved with credential programs. District Council Thirty-Seven of the American Federation
of State, County, and Municipal Employees sponsors a degree-
granting college at its own union hall in conjunction with New Rochelle College. In 1971, the AFL-CIO established a Labor Studies
Center which can now issue a college degree on an external basis

through the University Without Walls of Antioch College.

University labor education programs which are affiliated with
the University and College Labor Education Association (UCLEA)
are assisting community and state colleges in their states to establish labor studies programs.   For example, the Rutgers Labor Education Program has assisted several state and community colleges
in New Jersey such as Essex County College, Middlesex County College, and Ramapo State College in the establishment of their labor
studies programs.

Educational offerings for workers, especially trade unionists,
are expanding on the college campuses.   Membership in the UCLEA
has expanded from twenty-four to forty schools in the last five
years; at the present time many community and state colleges are
seeking admission.   A recent survey conducted by Lois Gray indicated that the number of institutions of higher education offering ma-
jors in labor studies had increased from eleven to thirty-one over
the past year.

Basic Objectives

George Boyle, president of the UCLEA, outlined the following
objectives for the education of workers: "The field of adult labor
education cannot be exclusively remedial nor exclusively vocational.
It must also be directed to the broader needs of workers to know and
understand the world in which they live (#1714, p. 280).   Boyle continued by saying that labor education must prepare the labor leader
to have "the breadth of vision and universality of a Modern Renais-
sance Man" (p. 292).

At a 1974 meeting on universities' roles in workers' education, sponsored by the ILO, the participants developed objectives
which broadened the traditional ILO objectives of workers' education.
For these practitioners, workers' education was "a means by which
the trade unions could help the worker deal with his problems in his
role as a producer, consumer, and citizen.   In effect, this definition embraced that group of goals which generally come under the notion of 'quality of life' " (The Role of the University in Workers'
Education.   Geneva: Intern'l Labor Org., 1974, p. 9).

University labor education programs have tended to have broad
liberal goals set forth in brochures summarizing their programs.
The objectives of these programs are "aimed at helping the worker
to become 1) a better individual; 2) a contributing member of his
own union group; and 3) a participating citizen in his community"
(Levine (#1806), p. 94).   The UAW has the same basic objectives in
their efforts to establish associate degrees in labor studies.   Their
three-fold objectives are the following: 1) to provide a broader understanding and perspective of economic, social, and political problems of our society and the role which unions and workers should
play in it;   2) to provide educational opportunities for individual
growth and advancement; and 3) to equip members of labor organi-

zations with technical skills needed to exercise their union and civic
responsibilities, especially those arising in urban areas (Hutton, C.
Objectives--Proposals.... Detroit: UAW Educ. Dept., n.d. (mimeo),
p. 4).

Helmut Golatz, in describing the concept of labor studies,
stated:

> The Department of Labor Education has discovered that its
> own perspective was too limiting. It now recognizes that
> the study of labor transcends the collective bargaining
> nexus and spills over into the psychological, sociological,
> and political dynamics of world-wide phenomenon. Thus,
> labor is no longer perceived as one aspect of industrial
> relations; instead, industrial relations is viewed as one of
> several areas on which the labor presence impinges.
> Thus Labor Studies emerges as the integrating principle of
> a new body of knowledge among the social sciences, the
> focus of which is the examination of the total labor effort
> according to the insights of the various traditional disci-
> plines. Hence, also the change in name to that of the De-
> partment of Labor Studies (Labor Studies at Pennsylvania
> State University, Annual Report of Activities, July 1,
> 1973-June 30, 1974, p. 2).

The objectives of the Rutgers University Labor Studies Program is
to offer students (workers) an opportunity to learn about the nature
of work, those who work, and the organizations they create to advance and defend their interests. Its main focus is on the current
aspects of a worker's life; the political, economic, and social problems faced by workers, and the present day response of workers'
organizations to many of these problems.

Curriculum Content

The objectives expressed here describe a union member or
leader who is committed to a democratic society, vigorous in his
sense of justice, competent in his knowledge and understanding of
political, social, and economic problems, and eager to contribute
to the general welfare as well as to the special interest of his class
(Levine (#1806), p. 98). Neither the utilitarian tool courses offered in the labor education period nor the more liberal courses of
the transition period could prepare trade unionists to meet these
goals. The episodic nature of the courses in these periods made it
impossible for the student to be presented with a systematic sequence that would lead to a breadth of knowledge. The new trend in
labor studies is adding to the extension program degree-offerings in
the liberal arts which can provide this breadth. The sequence provided as one moves from the associate arts degree to the doctorate
provides the opportunity for a continuity of learning.

The major courses in labor studies are offered with an emphasis in the social sciences, and as a result one does not earn a

technical or professional degree but rather a liberal arts degree.
The major courses in labor studies are aimed at providing working
men and women students with a theoretical background of their life
experiences as well as equipping them with an understanding of the
practical tools utilized by workers and trade unions to improve working conditions.

Courses in the degree program do not concentrate on the
techniques of trade unionism.   That is, a course is not solely concerned with the techniques of bargaining or how to process a grievance.   Such a course is rather concerned with the history and philosophy of collective bargaining or the grievance procedure.   This
is not to say that the techniques are not covered, but rather they
do not make up the entire course.   If that were the case, the
courses would be the tool courses of the labor education period with
the simple addition that they would now be credit-bearing.

If a labor studies service is to provide the educational opportunities for organized workers to approach the objectives outlined,
a wide range of programming must be available.   The convenience
and flexibility of short courses, discussions, conferences, and summer schools offered by the extension division cannot be abandoned,
but rather, must be strengthened.   Built upon this base, degree
programs provide a systematic progression in the learning experience.   The pyramid concept developed by Kerrison and Levine
(#1518) with certain modifications is applicable here for clarification.

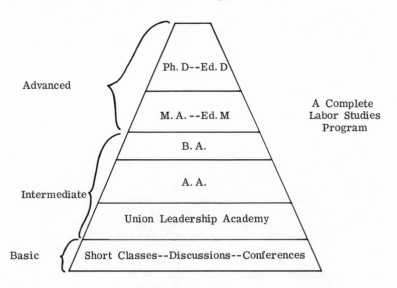

Advanced

Ph. D--Ed. D

A Complete
Labor Studies
Program

M. A. --Ed. M

B. A.

A. A.

Intermediate

Union Leadership Academy

Basic

Short Classes--Discussions--Conferences

The extension courses are necessary to meet any trade union's need
on a short notice, while the more long-term courses provide an indepth progression of educational opportunities.

Student Body

The composition of the student body in the labor studies period and the recruitment procedure duplicate those found in the previous two stages. In the extension division, the main concern continues to be trade unionists recruited through their union. Now added
to this group are organized members of minority groups especially
Black and Hispanic. For the most part, this continues as under labor education.

In the degree program, once again the trade unionist is the
major concern. However, for these programs he is recruited as an
individual, reminiscent of the workers' education period. This program also embraces the sons and daughters of trade unionists as
well as those individuals who are ideologically committed to the labor movement (Brameld, T. Workers' Education in the United States.
New York: Harper & Row, 1941, p. 290). In addition some students from management enroll in the program to learn about workers and the labor movement.

Duration of Classes--Finances--Administration

The length of courses in this stage of development cover a
wide range--from one day discussions to a program leading to a doc-
toral degree in labor studies.

One of the most essential aspects of any attempt to educate
workers in the labor movement is to have a close working relationship between the university and the labor movement. In the labor
education period when university involvement was confined to the extension division, it was learned that a consulting committee comprised of trade unionists was essential (Mire (#1532), p. 178). This
group advised the program on course offerings, staffings, recruitment, and aided with lobbying.

Likewise, in the labor studies era, the trade union consulting
committee is essential. In the labor studies program in the extension division, there is no substantive change in this committee.
However, when one deals with an academic program or department,
problems arise. Academic freedom, departmental, and college au-
tonomy encroach upon the consulting committee. To solve any possible problems in this area, one university assigned sub-committees
of its existing Trade Union Consulting Committee to work with the
various academic programs. In this manner, the original Trade
Union Consulting Committee in the extension division became a sound-
ing board for the academic programs as well.

This period described as labor studies began in the mid-

	Basic Objectives	Curriculum	Student Body and Recruitment	Duration	Finances	Administration
A	Education for Social change	Social Science based, with Economics, and English the most prevalent courses	Consisted of both Trade Unionists and Non-Trade Unionists recruited mainly as individuals	Relatively long term eight week resident summer schools; one and two year resident programs	Liberal sympathizers, some Trade Union support	Independent of AFL or Linked to the AFL through the Workers Education Bureau
B	Education for organizational imperatives	"Tool" courses e.g., Shop Steward Training, Grievance Handling, and Parliamentary Procedure	Strictly Trade Unionists recruited through the Union apparatus	Short term courses and conferences, week long summer schools	Trade Union funds, federal government through the WPA, state governments through universities; after W.W. II some foundation grants IULEC	First decade predominantly by CIO Unions; WPA; next two decades large university influx
C	Education for the "whole" person	Liberal Arts based in the Social Sciences; in addition the non-credit extension program offers "Tool" courses	Extension: Trade Unionist mostly with some civil rights activists recruited through their organizations. Degree: open to all recruited as individuals	Extension Programs; predominantly short term degree programs of rather long duration one year or longer	State governments through the state university federal government and foundation grants	Predominantly institutions of higher learning; however some unions have recently begun Labor Studies Degree programs, AFL-CIO Labor Studies Center, DC-37 College

sixties. Its basic characteristics are: 1) education for the "whole" person; 2) a curriculum based on the social sciences examining workers and their organizations; 3) a student body consisting of organized, unorganized, and young students recruited individually and through unions, depending on the program; and 4) programs of courses which are comprehensive enough to provide short courses as well as long-term comprehensive educational degree programs.

Labor studies, like university labor education before it, must be viewed as a university's service to and for the labor movement. The one major change that is evidenced in this latter stage is that the service has been broadened to make available all aspects of higher education to trade unionists.

Opposite: Periods: A. Workers' education 1900-1935. B. Labor education 1935-1965. C. Labor studies 1965- .

BIBLIOGRAPHY ON WORKERS' EDUCATION

PHILOSOPHY AND GOALS

1. Adler, Felix. "Ideal Workers' Education." Workers' Education. XII (January, 1935), 2.
   The key goal of workers' education should be to provide the worker-student with knowledge as raw material. With this new knowledge, students will draw conclusions from which they can make decisions that will affect their daily lives.

2. Adult Education vs. Workers Education. Fourth Annual Conference of Teachers in Workers' Education at Brookwood, February 18-20, 1927.
   A discussion of the meaning and scope of adult education and workers' education in the United States, as well as in various European countries.

3. Allen, Devere. "Political Action and Workers' Education." What Next in Workers' Education? Seventh Annual Conference of Teachers in Workers' Education. Katonah, N.Y.: Brookwood, 1930, 53-57.
   A call for an independent labor party to be organized as the political tool of the workers' education movement.

4. Beard, Charles. "The Role of Labor Education." Proceedings of the Second National Conference on Workers Education, 1922. New York: Workers' Education Bureau, 93-97.
   The role of workers' education in the United States is to teach workers the virtues of democracy.

5. Berg, Jacob. "Educating Labor for Leisure." Journal of Adult Education. III (June, 1931), 278-282.
   The major role of adult workers' education must be the inculcating in workers the ideals of creative living. In this effort, workers' education has been a failure. To rectify this problem, workers' educators must begin educating labor to consider work as a means of attaining leisure.

6. Brophy, John. "Miners' Problems and Workers' Education." Proceedings of the First National Conference on Workers' Education, 1921. New York: Workers' Education Bureau, 65-67.
   The goal of workers' education is to provide workers

with ideas which can be translated into power. Workers' education, therefore, can assist miners in solving many of the problems with which they are confronted.

7. Brunson, H. L. "Workers' Education--What Is It?" International Molders Journal. LX (April, 1924), 201.
    Through an examination of the principal aims and objectives of the movement, the author attempts to define workers' education.

8. Bugniazet, G. M. "The Need for Workers' Education." Workers' Education. III (November, 1925), 12-15.
    The need to combat personal ignorance as well as the ignorance workers have within and without the labor movement is the major goal of workers' education. For this reason the author issues a call for all workers to become involved in workers' classes.

9. Cohn, Fannia. "Education Aids Working Women." Labor Age. Vol. XVII (January, 1928), 12-13.
    The most outstanding tool which women have at their disposal in their fight for equalization is the workers' education movement. The author maintains that it is the function of workers' education to find precisely what the problems of workingwomen are through studies that such classes should conduct.

10. _____. "Educational and Social Activities." American Federationist, XXXVI (December, 1929), 1446-1452.
    The major goal of workers' education is to provide the worker with the necessary tools so that he can participate in social and economic change. The worker will gain such an opportunity when his education is geared to changing his environment.

11. _____. "Ideology of Workers' Education." In Harry W. Laidler and Norman Thomas, eds. Prosperity. New York: Vanguard Press, 1927, 257-263.
    The ideology of workers' education should reflect the worker's background and should act as a unifying source with the labor movement. Such an ideology should be cognizant of the worker's desire for power and encourage him to function in an organized group.

12. _____. "The Near Future of Workers' Education." The Journal of Electrical Workers and Operators. XXV (September, 1926), 428, 465.
    The author maintains that the immediate task of the workers' education movement should be to train the entire trade union population in workers' classes in the aims and development of the union and in such new areas as banking, research, life insurance and publicity.

13. _____ . "New Year Thoughts. " Justice.   January 5, 1923,
    10.
         After describing the merits of the workers' education
    movement, the author examines its relationship in develop-
    ing a new workers' consciousness.

14. _____ . "What Can Workers' Education Do for Working Wo-
    men?" Workers' Education.   II (August, 1924), 11-13.
    Also in Justice.   August 29, 1924, p. 10 and International
    Molders Journal.   LX (November, 1924), 671-672.
         Since men have been the barrier to keeping women out
    of trade unions, workers' education can show both men and
    women that equal wages and protection have the effect of
    strengthening the movement for all members regardless of
    sex.

15. _____ . "Why Workers' Education Should Be Under Trade
    Unions. " The Locomotive Engineers' Journal.   LVII
    (March, 1923), 202.
         Using the precept that the political and economic struc-
    ture of western civilization must be re-adjusted, the author
    maintains that the greatest influence to this re-adjustment
    is education.   The trade union movement should invite the
    university personnel to help them build their own workers'
    education institutions.   The author feels that the workers'
    education movement should not be wholly entrusted to other
    groups.

16. _____ . "Workers' Education Aims at Power. " Labor Age.
    XVI (November, 1927), 9-10.
         The author lists the ideas and ideals which workers'
    education must present if it is to do battle with the uni-
    versity-trained executives of management.

17. _____ . "Workers Education--Its Importance. " Workers'
    Education.   II (November, 1924), 20-22.   Also in American
    Federationist.   XXXL (November, 1924), 878-880.
         Since education is considered by the author to be equal
    to power, the trade union movement is in a position to be-
    gin meeting its members' intellectual needs, thus assisting
    them to increase their power.

18. Cox, Rachael Dunaway.   "Are Adult and Workers' Education
    the Same?" Woman's Press.   XXIX (December, 1935),
    540-542.
         Examines the similarities and differences between work-
    ers' and adult education.

19. Cummins, Earl E.   " Workers' Education in the United States. "
    Social Forces.   XIV (May, 1936), 596-605.
         Examines the philosophy that motivates the workers'
    education movement.

20. Curoe, Philip R. V. "A Real Opportunity for Our Colleges."
    Educational Review. LXIV (December, 1922), 420-425.
         After examining the philosophy of workers' education,
    the author discusses how colleges can participate.

21. Day, J. F. "Education and Labor." Journal of Educational So-
    ciology. IV (March, 1931), 434-442.
         Discussion of the reasons for and benefits of workers'
    education.

22. Farley, R. P. "Educational Principles for Labor." The Loco-
    motive Engineers Journal. LVII (March, 1923), 177.
         Traditional colleges in both the United States and Great
    Britain have failed to meet the needs of labor. The author
    examines the educational principles of the Workers' Educa-
    tion Association of Great Britain and attempts to apply these
    principles of education to the American labor movement's
    educational endeavors.

23. Fenton, Frank. "Democracy in Industry and Education." Pro-
    ceedings of the First National Conference on Workers' Edu-
    cation in the United States. New York: Workers' Educa-
    tion Bureau, 1921, 89-92.
         A worker-student explains what he thinks are the most
    important objectives in workers' education.

24. Fichlander, Alexander. "Workers' Education: Why and What."
    Socialist Review. X (April-May, 1921), 49-50.
         The author answers the question "why workers' educa-
    tion?" by examining what should and should not be taught in
    workers' classes.

25. Frey, John P. "Democracy in Education." International Mold-
    ers Journal. LXIV (July, 1928), 388-390.
         The author attempts to determine what education should
    be provided for adult workers.

26. _____. "What the Labor Movement Expects of Workers' Edu-
    cation." Workers Education. II (August, 1924), 9-10. Al-
    so in Justice. VI (August 15, 1924), 10.
         Delineates what should be the role of workers' educa-
    tion. Going beyond those areas covered in traditional edu-
    cational institutions, workers' education must provide work-
    ers benefits that will meet their practical needs.

27. _____. "Workers' Education." Justice. April 13, 1923,
    p. 11. Also in International Molders Journal. LIX (July,
    1923), 394-395.
         Only through workers' education will the workers be able
    to abolish industrial injustice.

28. Gleason, Arthur. "Workers' Education." International Molders
    Journal. LX (December, 1924), 739-744. Also published

in a pamphlet entitled Workers' Education. New York:
Workers' Evaluation Bureau, 1927.
   A definition and description of workers' education examining the control, objectives, teachers and curriculum
in the field.

29. Goff, Mary. "Introducing the Pupil to the Class." Proceedings
   of the First National Conference on Workers' Education in
   the United States. New York: Workers' Education Bureau,
   1921, 94.
      A student provides her perspective on the aims and
   goals of workers' education.

30. Green, William. "Education and Industrial Peace." Workers'
   Education. III (May, 1925), 4-9.
      According to the author, the labor movement is enter-
   ing the third stage of its development. In this stage education would play a leading role in disseminating information
   concerning the labor movement to the general populace.

31. _____. "Education and the Labor Movement." International
   Molders Journal. LXI (May, 1925), 257-260.
      An examination of the role of education in enhancing a
   worker's ability to obtain a better life. This is the text of
   Green's address to the 1925 WEB Convention.

32. _____. "Union Education." Workers' Education. II (June,
   1934), 1-2.
      The president of the AFL outlines how he feels the
   workers' education movement should develop.

33. Hanchett, David Scott. "Labor Education and the Industrial
   Community." Proceedings of the National Conference of Social Work. 1922, 346-351.
      A discussion of the various purposes and objectives of
   workers' education as described by the various groups involved in the movement.

34. Hardman, Jacob B. S. "Class Consciousness as a Factor in
   Labor Education." Proceedings of the First National Conference on Workers' Education in the United States. New
   York: Workers' Education Bureau, 1921, 122-125.
      The basic objective of workers' education should be the
   raising of class consciousness of the worker-student.

35. Hedges, M. H. "The Function of Workers' Education. The
   Place of Workers' Education in the Labor Movement. Fifth
   Annual Conference of Teachers in Workers' Education. Katonah, N.Y.: Brookwood, 1928, 5-8.
      A discussion of the function of workers' education as
   that which is to develop and aid the labor movement in the
   performance of its function.

36. _____. "Workers' Education a Basis for Hope." Justice.
    October 15, 1926, 6.
        The goal of workers' education must be the development
    of intellectual capabilities in workers to bring about mean-
    ingful social change.

37. Hendley, C. J. "Obstacles in the Way of Labor Education."
    Proceedings of the First National Conference on Workers'
    Education in the United States. New York: Workers' Edu-
    cation Bureau, 1921, 102-108.
        An examination of the problems confronted by a teacher
    in a workers' education class.

38. Herstein, Lillian. "Realities in Workers' Education." In
    Hardman, J. B. S., ed. American Labor Dynamics. New
    York: Harcourt Brace, 1928, 377-382.
        A warning against allowing workers' education to be-
    come a cultural arts program or an escape for intellectuals
    rather than a movement which must be flexible, changing
    and developing according to the changes and development in
    American industry.

39. Hill, Robert T. "New Forces for Liberal Education." Educa-
    tional Review. LXV (January, 1923), 14-15.
        Believes that workers' education must provide the work-
    er-student with a non-vocational liberal education.

40. Hillman, Harry. "The Engine of Workers' Education." Pro-
    ceedings of the First National Conference on Workers' Edu-
    cation in the United States. New York: Workers' Educa-
    tion Bureau, 1921, 95.
        A short paragraph from a student on what he believes
    the aims of workers' education should be.

41. Hogue, Richard W. "Status of Workers' Education." Survey.
    LIII (December 15, 1924), 343.
        Through a criticism of the present status of workers'
    education, the author examines what should be the objectives
    and format of the movement.

42. _____. "The Value of Our Own Education." Labor Age.
    XIII (May, 1924), 12.
        Organized labor must take the responsibility of educat-
    ing its rank and file membership because traditional educa-
    tional institutions have been effectively closed to workers and
    their children.

43. Hopkins, Prince. "Education or Dogmatic Training." Labor
    Age. XIII (April, 1924), 20-22.
        A warning to those beginning their own school for work-
    ers concerning the differences between education and dogmat-
    ic training.

44. Jacks, Lawrence P. "Breadwinning and Soul Saving." Journal
    of Adult Education. I (February, 1929), 5-10.
          A philosophical discussion concerning the role of educa-
    tion, the nature of work, and the responsibilities connected
    with workers' education.

45. _____. "Education for Leisure." Workers' Education. VI
    (June, 1929), 1-4. Also in American Federationist.
    XXXVI (June, 1929), 725-728.
          A challenging philosophical article calling for the labor
    movement and those involved in workers' education to strive
    for the highest educational goals.

46. Kallen, Horace M. Education, the Machine, and the Worker.
    New York: New Republic Inc. 1925, 204 pp.
          An extensive examination of the underlying preconcep-
    tions of workers' education.

47. Kehoe, William F. "Value of Workers' Education." Proceedings
    of the First Annual Conference on Workers' Education in the
    United States. New York: Workers' Education Bureau, 1921,
    63-64.
          A statement of the Educational Committee of the New
    York State Federation of Labor in support of the concept of
    workers' education.

48. Kerchen, F. L. "The Service of Workers' Education to Labor's
    Cause." American Teacher. XII (December, 1927), 22.
          A short article in which the author attempts to show the
    significance of workers' education to the labor movement.

49. Kerchen, John L. "Challenge of Workers' Education." Ameri-
    can Teacher. XV (September, 1930), 15.
          An examination of the challenge workers' education pro-
    vides for workers to exercise the fundamentals of thinking.

50. _____. "Workers' Education in an Abundance Economy."
    Workers' Education. XI (September, 1934), 31-32.
          This article points out that the goals of workers' educa-
    tion must be expanded to include more than economics.

51. Lever, E. J. "Workers' Education Is Practical." Workers'
    Education. III (November, 1925), 15-16.
          The goals of labor education must be broader than just
    helping the individual, it must be geared for the advance-
    ment of the entire labor movement.

52. Lindeman, Eduard C. "Adult Education: A Creative Opportunity
    for Libraries." Workers' Education. II (February, 1925), 6-17.
          Cites a philosophy for creating a new world and how in-
    dividuals can participate in such an undertaking. Since edu-
    cation plays such an important role in creating the new
    world, the author examines the role which can be played by li-
    braries.

53. _____ . "Making Labor Education Educative." In Harry W.
Laidler and Norman Thomas, eds. Prosperity. New York:
Vanguard Press, League for Industrial Democracy, 1927,
249-257.
    Implores teachers in workers' education to explore the
opportunities for a higher level of creativeness in the educational movement.

54. MacTavish, John M. "The Aim of Workers' Education." Justice. V (April 20, 1923), 10.
    Claims the aim of workers' education should be to cre-
ate a working class consciousness which reflects the dignity
and importance of manual work.

55. Mann, Charles R. "Education for More Than a Job." Journal
of Adult Education. I (February, 1929), 53-56.
    Discusses the aims of modern American education and
its meaning for workers' education.

56. _____ . "Workers' Education." Workers' Education. VI
(September, 1929), 1-4. Also in American Federationist.
XXXVI (September, 1929), 1102-1105.
    An examination of the differences between education for
intellectuals and education for workers which will prepare
them to function in society.

57. Maurer, James H. "Forty Years in the Labor Movement."
Proceedings of the Second National Conference on Workers'
Education in the United States. New York: Workers' Education Bureau, 1922, 104-109.
    Public schools cannot provide the educational needs of
workers. Only workers' schools can develop a working
class consciousness.

58. _____ . "Labor Day Reflections." Workers' Education. II
(August, 1924), 8. Also in Justice. (August 29, 1924), 10.
    The author stresses the importance of workers' educa-
tion to assist the worker, his union and society in general
rather than education for the worker's personal advancement.

59. _____ . Labor's Demand for Its Own Schools." Nation.
CXV (September 20, 1922), 276-278.
    The need is for labor education to be developed at all
levels of society. While at the same time, the author calls
for the creation of labor schools to balance the input of
management in existing schools today.

60. _____ . "The Pressing Need of Labor Education." Proceedings of the First National Conference on Workers' Education
in the United States. New York: Workers' Education Bureau, 1921, 75-77.
    The aim of workers' education in the midst of a crum-

bling industrial system should be to educate workers for a
new social order.

61. Maytos, Jennie. "Working Girl and Labor Education." Pro-
    ceedings of the First National Conference on Workers' Edu-
    cation in the United States. New York: Workers' Educa-
    tion Bureau, 1921, 95-96.
        A student's perception of the aims of workers' classes.

62. Meiklejohn, Alexander. "American Labor and Adult Education."
    Workers' Education. XII (January, 1935), 3-6.
        The thesis of this article is that for democracy to sur-
    vive, workers must have the benefit of adult education.

63. Miller, Spencer, Jr. "Adult Education and the Industrial Work-
    er." Journal of Adult Education. I (October, 1929), 382-
    387.
        The author examines the effect of certain labor prob-
    lems such as mechanization and leisure on the worker and
    the implications of these problems for workers' education.

64. _____. "Adult Education and the Workers." American Fed-
    erationist. XXXVII, (April, 1930), 477-482. Also in
    Workers' Education. VII (April, 1930), 5-10.
        A definition of workers' education which states that it
    is a process which prepares workers to cope with the rap-
    idly changing society.

65. _____. "Labor and the Challenge of the New Leisure."
    Harvard Business Review. XI (July, 1933), 462-467.
        The chief goal of workers' education should be slanted
    more toward cultural and humanistic activities which are
    concerned less with making a living and more with making
    a life.

66. _____. "The Need of Education for Labor." Journal of
    Educational Sociology. V (April, 1932), 508-512.
        An examination of the reasons why workers' education
    is a positive social force.

67. _____. "Workers' Education as a Social Force." Workers'
    Education. XI (September, 1934), 32-34.
        An examination of the reasons why workers' education
    is a positive social force.

68. Mufson, Israel. "The Vitalization of Workers' Education."
    In Harry M. Laidler and Norman Thomas, eds. Prosperity.
    New York: Vanguard Press, League for Industrial Democ-
    racy, 1927, 245-249.
        The major concern of workers should be an understand-
    ing of the changes taking place in industry. Workers' edu-
    cation must have as its aim the enlightenment of workers
    in this vital area.

69. _____ . "Where Are We Heading For?" Labor Age. XIV
(December, 1925), 5-7.
If workers' education is made an intimate part of the
activities of the union, then it can provide a practical educational experience for the union member.

70. _____ . "Wings or Microscopes." Survey. LIV (September
15, 1925), 635, 645.
A criticism of the concept of workers' education for
"culturizing." The article underscores the idea that the
education should relate itself to the workers' jobs.

71. Mumford, Lewis. "Re-Educating the Worker." Survey.
XLVII (January 7, 1922), 567-569.
A philosophical critique of workers' education.

72. Muste, A. J. "What Does Workers' Education Mean for Education?" American Teacher. XI (November, 1926), 3-4.
The article contends that workers' education can provide three functions. First, it can make real the theory
that education is for all people at all times. Second, it can
end the notion that education is simply preparation for life.
Third, it can also end the notion that manual labor and cultural education do not mix.

73. _____ . "What's It All About?" Labor Age. XIII (April,
1924), 1-4.
The fundamental aim of workers' education is to assist
the members and officers of workers' organizations to ren-
der more efficient and intelligent service to their organization.

74. _____ . "Why Workers' Education?" World Tomorrow. XII
(January, 1929), 28-30.
Workers' education must allow the worker-student to
think freely and critically so that the working class will be
able to take control of its own destiny and build a new social order.

75. _____ . "Workers' Education in the United States." World
Tomorrow. VI (December, 1923), 368-369.
This article lists the aims of the movement entitled
workers' education.

76. _____ . "Workers' Education Today." Labor Age. XX (October, 1931), 14-16.
An examination of the industrial worker in the midst of
the Depression and the implications for workers' education.

77. _____ , Spencer Miller, Jr. and B. W. Barkas. "Symposium
on Goals of Workers' Education." The Journal of Electrical
Workers and Operators. XXV (September, 1926), 430-469.
Three authors present their views of what the ultimate

goal of workers' education is. Their thoughts range from understanding the world of industry economically and socially, to the development of a program which will enable labor to direct the great energy forces at work in America, to creating a new commonwealth.

78. O'Connor, Julia. "Can Education Serve the Labor Movement?" Workers' Education. III (May, 1925), 11-12.
     An examination of why the worker needs education more than any other citizen and an explanation of why the union should call on the workers' education movement to satisfy its needs.

79. Randall, H. K. "Why Workers' Education?" New Republic. XXVIII (November 16, 1921), 351.
     An explanation of the opinion that separate educational institutions for workers in addition to regular schools and colleges will become biased.

80. Russell, Harry. "Training of Labor Leaders." Proceedings of the First National Conference on Workers' Education in the United States. New York: Workers' Education Bureau, 1921, 88.
     A student explains why he thinks workers' education is important.

81. Saposs, David. "Some Underlying Factors in Workers' Education." Justice. (April 13, 1923), 11.
     After examining the purpose and function of workers' education, the author suggests the use of correspondence courses.

82. Schapiro, Sarah. "What I Learned in a Workers' Class." Proceedings of the First National Conference on Workers' Education in the United States. New York: Workers' Education Bureau, 1921, 86-88.
     A student explains what benefits she received from a workers' education course.

83. Schlossberg, Joseph. "The Labor Union as an Educator." Proceedings of the First National Conference on Workers' Education in the United States. New York: Workers' Education Bureau, 1921, 70-74.
     The author examines the aims and goals of workers' education calling for the creation of a new society.

84. Shafer, Robert. "Working People's Education." North American Review. CCXIV (December, 1921), 786-794.
     A claim that workers' education will be nothing but propaganda as long as it remains separate from the public educational agencies.

85. Silverstein, Louis. "Workers' Education: Its Social Conse-

quences." World Tomorrow. VII (September, 1924), 274-276.
A discussion of the differences between the aims and procedures of workers education and workers' education.

86. Snyder, George W. "Old and New Education." Proceedings of the First National Conference on Workers' Education in the United States. New York: Workers' Education Bureau, 1921, 92-95.
A student examines the aims and goals of workers' education.

87. Sproger, Chris. "The Value of Workers' Education." Proceedings of the First National Conference on Workers' Education in the United States. New York: Workers' Education Bureau, 1921, 84-86.
A student, noting the inadequacies of public education, calls on workers' education to show workers that they have had an input into the history of society.

88. Sullivan, John. "Aims of Workers' Education." Proceedings of the Second National Conference on Workers' Education in the United States. New York: Workers' Education Bureau, 1922, 86-88.
The aims of workers' education should be to equip workers to face the challenges of the world in which they live.

89. Trowbridge, Lydia J. "Education--An Adventure." Life and Labor Bulletin. III (October, 1924), 3.
The author examines workers' education, the need for it, the value of it, and how unions are using it.

90. Troxell, John P. "Toward a New Organizing Technique." American Federationist. XXXIV (January, 1927), 52-54.
A call for the education of all union members so that they can assume the role of organizers in the field.

91. Tubbs, Easton V. "Equalizing Educational Opportunities." Workers' Education. VII (September, 1930), 1-5.
The author gives suggestions as to how to equalize educational opportunities for all social classes.

92. Wander, Paul. "The Function of Education in the Labor Movement." American Labor Monthly. I (May, 1923), 81-91.
An examination of the role and function of education in the labor movement. The author examines the role of education in the entire spectrum of labor activities from bread and butter unionism to radical unionism.

93. "What Do I Want from Workers' Education?" Workers' Education. V (January, 1928), 1-8. Also in American Federationist. XXXV (January, 1928), 94-101.

A symposium of worker-student opinions concerning workers' education.

94. Woll, Matthew. "AFL and Workers' Education." Proceedings of the Second National Conference on Workers' Education in the United States. New York: Workers' Education Bureau, 1922, 113-116.
    A speech calling for cooperation between the labor movement and the WEB.

95. Wooten, Barbara F. "Making Democracy Safe for the World." Journal of Adult Education. II (June, 1930), 284-288.
    The author maintains that a specialized form of adult education is needed for industrial workers. The goal of this educational endeavor must be the extension of democracy.

96. Workers' Education at the Crossroads. Sixth Annual Conference of Teachers in Workers' Education at Brookwood, February, 1929. Katonah, N. Y.: Brookwood, 1929, 22-24.
    The conference proceedings centered on the basic nature of workers' education comparing resident and nonresident programs. Other sessions dealt with the AFL and workers' education and foreign examples of workers' education programs.

97. Zukoffsky, H. "Education and the Class Struggle." Proceedings of the First National Conference on Workers' Education in the United States. New York: Workers' Education Bureau, 1921, 89.
    A short explanation of why the author as a student felt that workers' education was important.

CURRICULUM AND METHODS

98. Barghoorn, Fred. "Tips on Teaching Current Events." The Affiliated Schools Scrapbook. I (June, 1936), 4-5.
    The article provides hints for teaching current events in a workers' class.

99. Barkas, Benjamin. "Workshop Economics as Taught in Philadelphia." The Promotion and Maintenance of Workers' Education. Third Annual Conference of Teachers in Workers' Education. Katonah, N. Y.: Brookwood, 1924, 48-60.
    An examination of how a teacher in workers' education should go about preparing a class for worker-students.

100. Bascom, Lelia. "Correspondence Course." What Next in Workers' Education? Seventh Annual Conference of Teachers

in Workers' Education. Katonah, N. Y. : Brookwood,
1930, 30-31.
    An examination of the role of correspondence courses
as a teaching method in workers' education.

101. Bauerman, G. F. "The Public Library and Workers' Educa-
    tion." Workers' Education. VI (July, 1929), 1-4.
    An examination of the role that public libraries can
play in workers' education.

102. Blanshard, Paul. "Open Forum." Proceedings of the Second Na-
    tional Conference on Workers' Education in the United States.
New York: Workers' Education Bureau, 1922, 158-162.
    A discussion of the use of the open forum as a meth-
od to stimulate workers' interests in classes.

103. _____. "Popularizing Workers' Education." Proceedings
    of the First National Conference on Workers' Education in
the United States. New York: Workers' Education Bureau,
1921, 109-112.
    A discussion of how to advertise workers' education
classes in order to sell education to the worker-student.

104. Blechschmidt, Richard. "Value of Recreation in Workers'
    Education." Mass Education for Workers. Second Annu-
al Conference of Teachers in Workers' Education. Katonah, N. Y. : Brookwood, 1925, 7-9.
    A description of the various types of recreation which
a worker can be involved in and the need for recreation in
all workers' lives.

105. Bowerman, George F. "The Free Public Library: It's Possi-
    bilities as a Public Service Agency." American Federa-
tionist. XXXIII (May, 1926), 378-384.
    After explaining the services which the public library
can offer, the author discusses actual incidents of workers'
education classes receiving assistance from libraries.

106. _____. "The Public Library and Workers' Education."
    American Federationist. XXXVI (July, 1929), 846-849.
    The author urges the workers' education movement to
take greater advantage of the services of public libraries.

107. Brainard, Theodore. "Conferences .. What For?" Labor
    Age. XVIII (March, 1929), 14-15.
    The author lambasts the use of large conferences as
a method of teaching in workers' education.

108. Budish, Jacob M. "Mass Education." Survey. XLVI (June
    25, 1921), 441-442.
    A philosophical discussion of the use of certain tech-
niques in mass education.

109. _____. "Methods of Mass Education." Survey. XLVI
      (September 16, 1921), 678-679.
           A discussion of the various educational methods which
      workers' education could utilize in mass education of work-
      ers.

110. Burnham, Grace. "Methods of Health Education." Proceed-
      ings of the Second National Conference on Workers' Educa-
      tion in the United States. New York: Workers' Education
      Bureau, 1922, 167-170.
           A discussion of the concept of a workers' health bur-
      eau and how it would help workers.

111. Calhoun, Arthur W. "The Psychological Basis and Background
      of the Social Sciences." Conference of Teachers in Work-
      ers' Education. Katonah, N.Y.: Brookwood, 1925, 7-12.
           A discussion of how workers' education should not nec-
      essarily be restricted to professional training in the labor
      movement, but should encompass the social sciences as its
      nucleus of study.

112. _____. "The Social Significance of Dramatics." Workers'
      Education. IV (May, 1924), 18-20. Also in The Promo-
      tion and Maintenance of Workers' Education. Third Annual
      Conference of Teachers in Workers' Education, February
      19-22, 1926. Katonah, N.Y.: Brookwood, 1926, 35-36.
           This article cites reasons why dramatics can be an im-
      portant teaching device in workers' education.

113. Cannon, John D. "Place of the Film in Labor Education."
      Proceedings of the First National Conference on Workers'
      Education in the United States. New York: Workers' Edu-
      cation Bureau, 1921, 67-70.
           A discussion of the use of films in workers' classes.

114. Carter, Jean. "Labor Drama." Journal of Adult Education.
      VII (April, 1935), 179-182.
           An explanation of the experimentation taking place in
      the area of labor dramatics as an educational method.

115. _____. "A Traveling Library for Workers." Wilson Li-
      brary Bulletin. X (February 1936), 396-7.
           The author delineates the need for library materials to
      be disseminated among workers' study groups.

116. _____ and Hilda Smith. Education and the Worker Student.
      New York: Affiliated Schools for Workers, Inc., 1934, 69p.
           A pamphlet written to explain to groups of educators
      interested in workers' education methods.

117. Christenson, Edith. "Impression of an Observer in a Class in
      Trade Union Problems." The Affiliated Schools Scrapbook.
      I (June, 1936), 6-7.

Acting as a participant-observer, the author provides hints for teachers in workers' classes.

118   Cohn, Fannia.   "Method and Approach in a Discussion of the Economics of the Garment Industry for Young Workers." Workers' Education.   XIV (April, 1937), 12-15.
A presentation for prospective teachers in workers' education on the types of educational methods which can be used in workers' classes.

119.   _____ .   "Social Drama--A technique for Workers' Education."   Workers' Education.   XII (October, 1935), 11-15.
A call for the use of drama as a teaching method in workers' education classes.   Included in the article is a sample dialogue of a labor play.

120.   Colby, Josephine.   "Written English."   Conference of Teachers in Workers' Education.   Katonah, N. Y.:   Brookwood, 1925, 59-64.
An examination of some of the important points in the teaching of English to workers.

121.   Commons, John R.   "The Laboratory Method in Workers' Education."   Workers' Education.   IV (August, 1926), 1-7. Also in International Molders' Journal.   LXII (October, 1926), 580-583.
An examination of how to get knowledge.   The method used most often and the worst for producing results is the "hand me down" method of someone imparting knowledge; an acceptable way of gaining knowledge is through the use of the research method; the best way is for the student to discover knowledge for himself.

122.   Copenhower, J. R.   "What Subjects of Study Are of Most Practical Value to the Workers?"   Proceedings of the First National Conference on Workers' Education in the United States.   New York: Workers' Education Bureau, 1921, 81-82.
From a worker-student point of view, the author explains what subjects are most worthwhile.

123.   Cosgrove, Lloyd M.   "The Development of a Workers' Demand."   The Promotion and Maintenance of Workers' Education.   Third Annual Conference of Teachers in Workers' Education.   Katonah, N. Y.:   Brookwood, 1926, 21-25.
An examination of the problem of interesting trade union officers in a program of education.

124.   _____ .   "Methods of Pedagogy in Workers' Education." Proceedings of the First National Conference on Workers' Education in the United States.   New York: Workers' Education Bureau, 1921, 100-102.
An examination of the role of the teacher in a workers' education class.

125. Dana, Harry W. L.   "The Lecture Method."   Conference of
     Teachers in Workers' Education.   Katonah, N.Y.:   Brook-
     wood, 1925, 48-49.
          A short description of the advantages of the lecture
     method.

126. _____.   "The Place of Literature in Mass Education."
     Mass Education for Workers.   Second Annual Conference
     of Teachers in Workers' Education.   Katonah, N.Y.:
     Brookwood, 1925, 76-81.
          A three-pronged rebuttal against those who maintain
     that literature classes in workers' education are wasteful,
     less important than other topics, and are "sissy" courses.

127. _____.   "Query on Mass Education."   Mass Education for
     Workers.   Annual Conference of Teachers in Workers'
     Education.   Katonah, N.Y.:   Brookwood, 1925, 81-82.
          A brief exposition of some of the very fundamental
     questions involved in the matter of mass education for
     workers.

128. Daniels, Margaret.   "The Humanizing of Knowledge."   Mass
     Education for Workers.   Second Annual Conference of
     Teachers in Workers' Education.   Katonah, N.Y.:   Brook-
     wood, 1925, 45-47.
          A call for the use of psychoanalysis in workers' edu-
     cation classes.

129. _____.   "Psychology and Workers' Education."   Proceedings
     of the First National Conference on Workers' Education in
     the United States.   New York: Workers' Education Bureau,
     1921, 117-118.
          An examination of the methodology used to teach psy-
     chology in a workers' class.

130. _____.   "Whom Shall We Educate?"   Labor Age.   XVI
     (July, 1927), 20-21.
          A suggestion that students in workers' classes be homo-
     geneously grouped, placing those students with more ad-
     vanced training in one class, and those students who need
     more basic training in another class.

131. Dent, Mary C.   "The Retention of Support--How Not to Do It."
     The Promotion and Maintenance of Workers' Education.
     Third Annual Conference of Teachers in Workers' Educa-
     tion.   Katonah, N.Y.:   Brookwood, 1926, 40-42.
          A list of don'ts for running a successful workers' edu-
     cation program.

132. Engel, Bernard.   "The Education the Workers Want."   Proceedings
     of the First National Conference on Workers' Education in the
     United States. New York: Workers' Education Bureau, 1921,
     83-84.
          The author cites those courses which are of the most

practical value to the workers from a student's point of view.

133. Falkowski, Edward. "Mickey Tries Education." Labor Age. XVI (August, 1927), 18-19.
A report of one attempt and failure to establish an on-going workers' education program in an anthracite mining town.

134. Fichandler, Alexander. "The Discussion Method." Proceedings of the Second National Conference on Workers' Education in the United States. New York: Workers' Education Bureau, 1922, 162-164.
A call for more discussion in workers' education classes in order to increase worker participation.

135. _____. "The Discussion Method." Conference of Teachers in Workers' Education. Katonah, N. Y.: Brookwood, 1925, 49-50.
An outline in which the advantages and disadvantages of the discussion method are detailed.

136. _____. "How Labor Classes Operate." Labor Age. XI (April, 1922), 3-5.
A description of the organization, teachers, and methods used in workers' education classes.

137. _____. "How to Teach a Class of Workers." Proceedings of the First National Conference on Workers' Education in the United States. New York: Workers' Education Bureau, 1921, 119-122.
An examination of the different methodological approaches which can be used in workers' classes.

138. _____. "The Psychology of the Learning Process for Workers." Conference of Teachers in Workers' Education. Katonah, N. Y.: Brookwood, 1925, 16-20.
An outline on the psychology of the learning process in workers' classes.

139. Fincke, William M. "Literature and Economics." The Affiliated Schools Scrapbook. I (June, 1936), 10-12.
An examination of the advantages of teaching economics to workers who have industrial experiences from which to draw examples.

140. _____. "Recreation and the Youth Movement." Mass Education for Workers. Second Annual Conference of Teachers in Workers Education. Katonah, N. Y.: Brookwood, 1925, 83-88.
An explanation of the need for play in the life of children and for recreation in the life of workers.

141. _____. "Written Words." Journal of Adult Education.
VII (April, 1935), 185-187.
An explanation of various experiments in creative
writing done with students attending the Affiliated Schools
for Workers.

142. Freidmann, Ernestine. "Tutorial Method." Conference of
Teachers in Workers' Education. Katonah, N.Y.: Brook-
wood, 1925, 27-29.
A description of the tutorial method used at the Bryn
Mawr Summer School for Women Workers.

143. Frey, John P. "Value of Cultural Education for Workers."
American Teacher. XV (November, 1930), 4-5.
The thesis of this article maintains that since the ma-
ture adult worker cannot fit into the educational mold of
the traditional public school, the teacher must be transformed from an instructor into a guide, philosopher, and
friend.

144. Fuller, Paul W. "Labor Chautauquas." Mass Education for
Workers. Second Annual Conference of Teachers in Workers' Education. Katonah, N.Y.: Brookwood, 1925, 23-
25.
A description of how to organize and run a labor
chautauqua.

145. Gompers, Samuel. "American Labor Movement and Labor Education." Proceedings of the Second National Conference
on Workers' Education in the United States. New York:
Workers' Education Bureau, 1922, 89-93.
A suggestion that workers' education classes for trade
unionists should be taught by trade unionists.

146. Green, William. "Education for Trade Unionists." Journal of
Electrical Workers and Operators. XXV (Sept., 1926),
423, 458.
An explanation of how the working person can educate
himself through his everyday experiences and translate
these into future policies of the union movement.

147. Haber, William G. "Workers' Education and the Workshop."
Justice. (June 17, 1927), 6.
A development of the workshop concept for the teach-
ing of economics in workers' education classes.

148. Hader, John and Eduard C. Lindeman. What Do Workers
Study? New York: Workers' Education Bureau, 1929,
66 p.
An examination of the curricula of various workers'
education programs between 1920 and 1927.

149. Hall, Ladson. "The Recitation Method." Conference of Teach-

ers in Workers' Education.   Katonah, N. Y. :   Brookwood,
1925, 54.
An outline in which the advantages of the recitation
method of teaching for workers' classes is given.

150. Hardman, (Salutsky) J. B.   "Journalism and Workers' Education. "   Proceedings of the Second National Conference on
Workers' Education in the United States.   New York:
Workers' Education Bureau, 1922, 184-186.
A call for the WEB to disseminate information that
workers are really interested in rather than dry, intellectual publications which dampen their curiosity.

151. Harley, Harrison.   "Contributions of Modern Psychology. "
The Promotion and Maintenance of Workers' Education.
Third Annual Conference of Teachers in Workers' Education.   Katonah, N. Y. :   Brookwood, 1926, 92-98.
A discussion of several methods the teacher of a
workers' class can utilize in order to keep the student
interest.

152. Hendley, C. J.   "Method in Correspondence Courses. "   Conference of Teachers in Workers' Education.   Katonah,
N. Y. :   Brookwood, 1925, 54-58.
A report of how correspondence courses can be used
to supply materials and direction to isolated groups of
workers who are in need of help.

153. Hewes, Amy.   "How to Build on the Workers' Experience. "
The Promotion and Maintenance of Workers' Education.
Third Annual Conference of Teachers in Workers' Education.   Katonah, N. Y. :   Brookwood, 1926, 61-64.
An examination of how to draw upon workers' past
experiences in the development of a meaningful educational
program.

154. "How to Teach in Labor Classes. "   Justice.   (December 28,
1933), 10.
A discussion of the value of student participation in
the classroom.

155. Kilpatrick, William.   "Problems of Adult Instruction. "   Pro-
ceedings of the Second National Conference on Workers'
Education in the United States.   New York: Workers'
Education Bureau, 1922, 173-176.
An explanation of the opinion that adult learning should
be connected with some purpose that the worker feels.

156. Kopald, Sylvia.   "The Remaking of the Teacher. "   The Promotion and Maintenance of Workers' Education.   Third Annual Conference of Teachers in Workers' Education.   Katonah, N. Y. :   Brookwood, 1926, 78-89.
An outline of methods the author found helpful in sus-

taining pupil interest in workers' education classes.

157. "Labor College Curricula." Survey. XLIV (April 17, 1920),
114.
A listing of courses offered in various workers' education programs.

158. Lasser, Florence. "A Drama Project." The Affiliated
Schools Scrapbook. I (June, 1936), 13-14.
An examination of the educational possibilities of a
class creating and producing its own dramatic production.

159. Lee, Algernon. "Camp Tamiment--Workers' Vacation School."
Workers' Education. I (July-August, 1923), 11-12.
A brief description of the summer session at Camp
Tamiment, an auxiliary of the Rand School of Social Sciences.

160. _____. "Development of System, Application, and Economy
Effort." Conference of Teachers in Workers' Education.
Katonah, N.Y.: Brookwood, 1925, 23-27.
An explanation of the various tools and methods of
study which should be used to teach students in a workers'
class.

161. _____. "Methods of Mass Education." Proceedings of the
First National Conference on Workers' Education in the
United States. New York: Workers' Education Bureau,
1921, 112-116.
This article discusses the many problems of purposes
and methods which developed in the first fifteen years of
the Rand School.

162. Lefkowitz, Abraham. "The Problems of Opening the Field."
The Promotion and Maintenance of Workers' Education.
Third Annual Conference of Teachers in Workers' Education. Katonah, N.Y.: Brookwood, 1926, 5-8.
A suggestion of ways to get the vast mass of workers
to desire education and ways of getting the leaders to support the educational movement and pay for the courses offered.

163. _____. "The Public Schools as a Factor in Mass Education." Mass Education for Workers. Second Annual Conference of Teachers in Workers' Education. Katonah,
N.Y.: Brookwood, 1925, 19-20.
A listing of the various failures of the public school
system.

164. Leslie Mable. "How to Attract Students." Workers' Education. II (February, 1926), 19-20.
A discussion of the methods that can be used in attracting students to workers' classes.

165. Lever, E. J. "Possibilities of Workers' Education." American Federationist. XXXIII (February, 1926), 172-176.
     An outline of the current educational methods being used and suggestions for their implementation in other workers' classes.

166. _____. "Training Labor's Army." Labor Age. XIV (November, 1925), 18-20.
     An emphasis on the need for worker's classes and a description of how classes are organized and taught.

167. Levin, Max. "Education and the Jewish Worker." Proceedings of the Second National Conference on Workers' Education in the United States. New York: Workers' Education Bureau, 1922, 181-183.
     A call for much more educational work to be done at the local level.

168. Lindeman, Eduard C. "The Kind of Education Workers Want." The Locomotive Engineers' Journal. LVII (March, 1923), 197-198.
     The author describes two types of education which he feels workers do not want.

169. _____. "A Proposal for the Training of Teachers." Workers' Education. I (November, 1923), 9-10.
     A proposal for a traveling teacher-training institute which will prepare teachers in various educational methods for use in workers' classes.

170. _____. Workers' Education and the Public Libraries. New York: Workers' Education Bureau, 1926. 17 p.
     A philosophical analysis of adult education and how libraries should play an effective part in such education.

171. Linville, Henry R. "The Scientific Method in Workers' Education." Conference of Teachers in Workers' Education. Katonah, N.Y.: Brookwood, 1925, 35-36.
     A discussion of the use of the scientific method in workers' classes.

172. _____. "What Workers' Education Can Learn from Experimental Schools." The Promotion and Maintenance of Workers' Education. Third Annual Conference of Teachers in Workers Education. Katonah, N.Y.: Brookwood, 1926, 74-77.
     A listing of various methods which workers' schools can adopt from experimental schools in order to keep from "telling" the worker-student all the information he needs.

173. Long, Cedric. "Cooperative Education." Proceedings of the Second National Conference on Workers' Education in the

United States. New York: Workers' Education Bureau, 1922, 80-84.
A discussion and explanation of cooperative education and a cooperative society.

174. MacKaye, Hazel. "Our Experiment in Dramatics at Brookwood." The Promotion and Maintenance of Workers' Education. Third Annual Conference of Teachers in Workers' Education. Katonah, N. Y. : Brookwood, 1926, 37-39.
A discussion of what is meant by labor drama and how it can be applied to a trade union class.

175. _____. "Plays for Workers." Workers' Education. IV (May, 1926), 11-18.
A description of the different plays for workers used at Brookwood College.

176. Mailly, Bertha H. "Physical Recreation in Workers' Education." Mass Education for Workers. Second Annual Conference of Teachers in Workers' Education. Katonah, N. Y. : Brookwood, 1925, 5-7.
An enumeration of those bodily functions which should be the aim in the training of workers in physical education.

177. Martindale, John W. "Workers' Education and Dramatics." Brookwood, Labor's Own School. Katonah, N. Y. : Brookwood, 1936, 44.
An examination of the role and function of the Brookwood Labor Players, a theatrical group, in a labor chautaqua.

178. Miller, Spencer, Jr. "A Regional Teacher Institute." Workers' Education. II (May, 1924), 16-17.
A report of a conference on the methods of teaching in workers' education.

179. _____. "Weekend Conferences in Workers' Education." American Federationist. XXXV (February, 1928), 198-201. Also in Workers' Education. V (February, 1928), 1-4.
A description of the role the weekend conference could have utilized as a new technique in workers' education.

180. _____. "What Subjects Do American Workers Study?" The Journal of Electrical Workers and Operators. XXVI (September, 1928), 456.
A report of the research done by the WEB to discover what courses of study were offered in workers' education classes.

181. Mitchell, Broadus. "Helping Workers to Think." Educational
      Review. LXI (May, 1921), 389-398.
               An examination of the current thoughts on teaching
      methods in workers' education.

182. _____. "How to Start a Workers' Study Class." Interna-
      tional Molders Journal. LXII (May, 1926), 267-273.
               An explanation of the steps to be taken in the estab-
      lishment of a workers' study class.

183. _____. "What Can Workers' Teacher Expect of His Stu-
      dents?" Proceedings of the First National Conference on
      Workers' Education in the United States. New York:
      Workers' Education Bureau, 1921, 125-129.
               An explanation of how much effort a teacher of work-
      ers can expect his students to put into their courses.

184. Mufson, Israel. "A Saturday Discussion Group." Workers'
      Education. VI (October, 1928), 8-11. Also in American
      Federationist. XXXV (October, 1928), 1243-1246.
               A description of the dynamics of a discussion group
      conducted at the Philadelphia Labor College.

185. _____. "What Do I Get Out of It?" Labor Age. XIII
      (April, 1924), 7-8.
               A call for the development of workers' classes in var-
      ious cities. Workers' education conducted in this mode
      would reach more workers than workers' education which
      must be resident in nature.

186. Muste, A. J. "Education and the Unorganized." Labor Age.
      XVII (April, 1928), 8-10.
               A plea for the workers' education movement to devel-
      op extension classes, and take the educational opportunities
      to the workers rather than waiting for the workers to come
      to the classes.

187. _____. "Ritual in Mass Education." Mass Education for
      Workers. Second Annual Conference of Teachers in Work-
      ers' Education. Katonah, N.Y.: Brookwood, 1925, 58-66.
               A discussion of how ritual can best be used in a posi-
      tive way in workers' education. The author mentions the
      use of ceremonies, pageantries, parades, etc. and their
      use at various public labor events.

188. _____. "Summer Institute as a Promotion Measure." The
      Promotion and Maintenance of Workers' Education. Third
      Annual Conference of Teachers in Workers' Education.
      Katonah, N.Y.: Brookwood, 1926, 25-34.
               A discussion of the use of the summer institute as a
      promotional device for workers' education in general.

189. Nearing, Nellie. "The Scientific Method as Applied to the So-

cial Sciences." Conference of Teachers in Workers' Education. Katonah, N.Y.: Brookwood, 1925, 36-40.
A definition and description of the scientific method as it can be applied to the teaching of the social sciences.

190. Ogden, Jess. "Brass Tacks." The Affiliated Schools Scrapbook. I (March, 1936), 5-9.
An explanation of the nuts and bolts of putting on a play for a workers' group.

191. "Outlines of a Broader Workers' Education Appear." The Journal of Electrical Workers and Operators. XXVI (September, 1927), 451.
This article outlines the types of workers' classes needed by electricians. It chides some labor colleges for moving away from the practical and technical training needed to abstract political theories.

192. Overstreet, Harry A. "The Psychology of Mass Education." Mass Education for Workers. Second Annual Conference of Teachers in Workers' Education. Katonah, N.Y.: Brookwood, 1925, 51-54.
An explanation of the two central aims of workers' education which involve the worker's view of history and the belief which all workers must be inculcated with--that labor can do and has done socially constructive work.

193. _____. "The Surmounting of Limited Viewpoints and Special Mechanism Peculiar to Working Class Students. Conference of Teachers in Workers' Education. Katonah, N.Y.: Brookwood, 1925, 29-32.
A description of the limitations of the workers' mental training and hints as to how the instructor in a workers' class should deal with this problem.

194. _____. "The Use of the Discussion Method in Workers' Education." Workers' Education. II (August, 1924), 13-14.
Through a report of a class conducted by the author, he examines how the tool of discussion can be used as a teaching method in workers' classes.

195. Peterson, Ester. "The Medium of Movement." Journal of Adult Education. VII (April, 1935), 182-185.
A report of the experimentation that is being done with dance and physical education in general as a teaching technique in workers' classes held at the Bryn Mawr Summer School for Women Workers.

196. Plunder, Olga Law. Monograph on Methods of Teaching English to Workers. New York: American Labor Education Service, 1931, 14 p.
An examination of a methodology to be used in teaching English to worker-students.

197. Ransdell, Hollace. "Amateur Dramatics in the Labor Move-
     ment." The Affiliated Schools Scrapbook. I (March,
     1936), 2-4.
          An examination of the use of dramatic performances
     as an educational device in workers' education.

198. _____. "The Soap Box Theater." The Crisis. XLII (Ap-
     ril, 1935), 122, 124-125.
          A description of how workers' groups in various sec-
     tions of the country are presenting labor drama with top-
     ics drawn from their job experiences.

199. Robinson, James H. "A Comment on the Teacher Training
     Proposal." Workers' Education. I (November, 1923),
     10-11.
          An examination of a proposal to provide teacher train-
     ing for workers' education specialists.

200. Russell, Phillips. "Visual Education for Workers." Ameri-
     can Teacher. XXIV (December, 1939), 20.
          An examination of the educational significance of the
     graphic arts workshop conducted at the Southern Summer
     School for Workers.

201. Sakmann, Marianne. "Teaching Economics in Workers'
     Classes." The Affiliated Schools Scrapbook. I (June,
     1936), 8-9.
          An explanation of the techniques used in teaching eco-
     nomics to workers.

202. Saposs, David J. "Circuit Riding Among the Miners." The
     Affiliated Schools Scrapbook. I (June, 1936), 32-33.
          A description of the author's experience of circuit rid-
     ing through Illinois mining towns in order to discuss the
     background of the labor movement with local workers' edu-
     cation classes.

203. _____. "The Labor Chautauqua and Mass Education." Mass
     Education for the Workers. Second Annual Conference of
     Teachers in Workers' Education. Katonah, N. Y. : Brook-
     wood, 1925, 28-31.
          A description of a labor chautauqua held in Hastings,
     Pennsylvania under the auspices of the Education Depart-
     ment of District #2 of the United Mine Workers. A pro-
     gram for the five day event is included.

204. _____. "Labor Chautauquas and Mass Education." Justice.
     August 7, 1925, 10.
          A description of the methods and procedures of organ-
     izing a labor chautauqua as an education event for workers.

205. _____. "Research and Education Are Inseparable." The
     Journal of Electrical Workers and Operators. XXV (Sep-

tember, 1926), 429, 470.
    An article which calls for applied and pure research in the labor movement linked to workers' education. A definition of both types of research and how they apply to the labor movement is included.

206. Scharrenberg, Paul.   "Why Workers' Education." American Teacher. XV (May, 1931), 17-18.
    An analysis of a typical curriculum in workers' education which includes a discussion of how and why each course area is taught.

207. Sheffield, Alfred D.   "Education for Crew Mindedness Through Discussion." Conference of Teachers in Workers' Education. Katonah, N.Y.: Brookwood, 1925, 66-68.
    A statement concerning how organized discussion can be helpful as a teaching method of controversial subjects in workers' classes.

208. _____. "Getting Good Discussion in the Union Meeting." American Federationist. XXXIV (April, 1927), 414-418.
    An analysis of the techniques for leading group discussion.

209. _____. "Public Discussion." Proceedings of the Second National Conference on Workers' Education. New York: Workers' Education Bureau, 1922, 186-189.
    An examination of the role of public discussion as a means for extending democracy.

210. Shepherd, Susan D.   "The Mass Recitation." The Affiliated Schools Scrapbook. I (March, 1936), 10-14.
    A suggestion for the use of a mass voice to provide dramatically increased meaning.

211. Shoemaker, Alice.   "A Method Made to Order." Journal of Adult Education. VI (January, 1934), 55-58.
    A descriptive examination of the teaching methods used in workers' classes at the University of Wisconsin Summer School for Workers in Industry.

212. Smith, Hilda W.   "Workers' Classes Need Library Aid." American Library Association Bulletin. XXIX (Fall, 1935), 81-83.
    With the federal government involved in workers' education through the Federal Emergency Relief Administration, the number of workers in need of reading materials will increase. Circulating libraries can meet the increased need by stocking materials of specific interest to workers.

213. Snyder, George.   "Correspondence Education." Proceedings of the Second National Conference on Workers' Education in

the United States. New York: Workers' Education Bureau, 1922, 157-158.
A statement of the advantages of correspondence
courses specifically geared for workers.

214. Starr, Mark. "Economics in Workers' Education." The Affiliated Schools Scrapbook. I (June, 1936), 1.
An examination of the aims and the methods of teaching economics to workers.

215. Stillman, Charles. "Labor Education and the Teacher." Pro-
ceedings of the Second National Conference on Workers'
Education in the United States. New York: Workers'
Education Bureau, 1922, 116-121.
A discussion of the differing role of the teacher in
the public school and the workers' education classroom.

216. Stites, Sara. "The Teaching of Economics." Proceedings of
the Second National Conference on Workers' Education in
the United States. New York: Workers' Education Bureau, 1922, 170-173.
In addition to explaining the method of developing a
course outline, the article states that a teacher of workers
should understand their point of view.

217. Stoddard, William L. "What Workers' Want to Know." Industrial Management. LXI (March, 1921), 208-210.
The article cites the objectives and teaching methods
of a labor college.

218. Strakey, Joseph. "The Discussion Group on Social and Economic Questions." The Affiliated Schools Scrapbook. I
(June, 1936), 2-4.
An examination of the role of a discussion leader in
a current events class on social and economic issues.

219. Talbot, Winthrop. "The Visual Method of Adult Education."
Proceedings of the Second National Conference on Workers'
Education in the United States. New York: Workers'
Education Bureau, 1922, 176-181.
Discusses the value of visual aids as a teaching de-
vice for those students who can not read.

220. Ten Years of Workers' Education: A Survey. Eighth Annual
Conference of Teachers in Workers' Education. Katonah,
N.Y.: Brookwood, 1931, 108 pp.
A lengthy examination of methods for teaching and recruiting workers to educational classes. In addition, the
work examines textbooks and teaching materials available
for workers' classes.

221. Tippett, Tom. "The Traveling Teacher in Mass Education."
Mass Education for Workers. The Second Annual Confer-

ence of Teachers in Workers' Education. Katonah, N. Y. :
Brookwood, 1925, 33-44.

A report of an experiment in workers' education done
under the auspices of the United Mine Workers in which
ten sparsely settled communities in Pennsylvania were selected as the locale for workers' education meetings.

222. _____ and Paul Fuller. "How to Sustain Interest." The
Promotion and Maintenance of Workers' Education. The
Third Annual Conference of Teachers in Workers' Educa-
tion. Katonah, N. Y. : Brookwood, 1926, 44-47.

A teacher of miners suggests the problems and some
solutions for sustaining interest in workers' education
among workers.

223. Tompkins, Miriam D. "The Library and Workers' Education."
Mass Education for Workers. The Second Annual Confer-
ence for Teachers in Workers' Education. Katonah, N. Y. :
Brookwood, 1925, 11-17.

A description of the plans the Milwaukee Public Library and other libraries have made to meet the increasing problem of materials in adult workers' education.

224. _____. "The Library and Workers' Education." American
Federationist. XXXIV (April, 1927), 445-448.

An elaboration of the positive points for a union membership which becomes involved with the local library. By
establishing reading and discussion groups, the union leadership can encourage workers to use the library.

225. Tugwell, R. G. "Place of Economics in Workers' Education."
Workers' Education. IV (February, 1927), 3-8.

An examination of the method of teaching economics directly related to the lives of the worker-students rather
than classical economics.

226. Vogt, Paul. "Workers' Education Program Broadens into New
Fields." Workers' Education. XII (July, 1935), 8-12.

A listing of new courses being offered in workers' education, especially in the western half of the country.

227. Ware, Carolyn. "Women Workers Tackle Economics." Adult
Education Bulletin. II (October, 1937), 20-24.

A descriptive analysis of an economics class conducted
at the Southern Summer School for Workers in Industry.

228. Wolfson, Theresa. "Materials, Textbooks, Syllabi." Conference of Teachers in Workers' Education. Katonah, N. Y. :
Brookwood, 1925, 50-53.

A discussion of the procurement of materials, the rig-
idness of textbooks, and the use of the outline as a teaching technique in workers' classes.

229. _____. "The Problem of Perpetuating Interest." The
Promotion and Maintenance of Workers' Education. The
Third Annual Conference of Teachers in Workers' Education. Katonah, N.Y.: Brookwood, 1926, 8-16.
An examination of the two-fold problem of stimulating
the workers' interests in education and retaining their interest in specific workers' classes.

230. _____. "Union Health Education." Proceedings of the Second National Conference on Workers' Education in the
United States. New York: Workers' Education Bureau,
1922, 164-167.
A call for health education for workers.

231. _____. "Women's Auxiliary as a Field of Mass Education." Mass Education for Workers. The Second Annual
Conference of Teachers in Workers' Education. Katonah,
N.Y.: Brookwood, 1925, 69-74.
A call for educating the women's auxiliaries of local
unions in the same way that the male union member is
educated.

232. "Workers' Education and Training." Monthly Labor Review.
XXI (October, 1925), 169-171.
A summary of the proceedings of the second annual
conference of teachers in workers' education held at
Brookwood Labor College, February 20-22, 1925.

INDIVIDUAL ORGANIZATIONS

Workers' Education Bureau of America (WEB)

233. "Address by Spencer Miller, Jr." International Molders Journal. LXIV (February, 1928), 79-86. Also in Report of
the Proceedings of the Forty-seventh Annual Convention of
the American Federation of Labor. Los Angeles, California, October 3-14, 1927, 215-221.
A report of the activities of the WEB to the American
Federation of Labor's convention in Los Angeles, California in 1927.

234. Beard, Charles. "An American Adventure in Workers' Education." Workers' Education. XIII (October, 1936), 15-20.
An historical examination of the first fifteen years of
the WEB.

235. Bradley, Phillips. "Workers' Education--Whither Bound?"
Social Forces. III (May, 1925), 734-737.
An examination of the constitutional changes undertaken
by the WEB and the effect that this will have on the funding and the voting power structure of the Bureau.

236. Brunson, H. L. "Looking over the Field." Labor Age. XIII (April, 1924), 5-6.
A brief summary of the various workers' education groups throughout the country which are under the umbrella of the WEB.

237. _____. "The WEB in the Field." Workers' Education. I (November, 1923), 11-12.
A brief examination of the work of the field secretary of the WEB.

238. _____. "Workers' Education in the South." Workers' Education. II (May, 1924), 18-20.
A report of two Southern state federations of labor resolutions concerning affiliation with the WEB.

239. Chappell, Eve. "Scholar and Worker." Journal of Adult Education. VI (June, 1934), 263-267.
A report of a series of discussion institutes sponsored by the WEB. The topic of each institute centered on an analytical study of labor under the National Industrial Recovery Act.

240. Cohn, Fannia. "The New Year and Workers' Education." Justice. June 2, 1925, 8+.
An exhortation to the AFL to support the WEB with finances from its education fund.

241. _____. "The Workers' Education Bureau--An Arm of The Labor Movement." Workers' Education. XIII (October, 1936), 26-30
An historical examination of the founding of the workers' education movement in general and more specifically the Workers' Education Bureau.

242. Cole, G. D. H. "Workers' Education in America." The Highway. XV (March, 1923), 83.
An examination of the differences between the British Workers' Education Association and the American WEB.

243. Cosgrove, Lloyd M. "What the Workers' Education Bureau Stands For." Workers' Education. II (February, 1925), 17-18.
Examines the methods used by the WEB in carrying out its philosophy of educating workers.

244. Dean, Arthur. "The Workers' Education Bureau." Industrial Education Magazine. XXV (October, 1923), 91-92.
A highly critical analysis of the early conventions of the WEB. The author further examines the implications of the proposed AFL takeover of the WEB.

245. Epstein, Abraham. "Adult Working Class Education in the

United States." Monthly Labor Review. XII (June, 1921), 185-194.
An analysis of a questionnaire sent to all labor schools. This study provided information which eventually resulted in the organization of the WEB. Also included is the first constitution of the WEB.

246. _____. "The Organization of the Workers' Education Bureau." Workers' Education. XIII (October, 1936), 24-26.
An examination of the early organization of the WEB.

247. "Fifteenth Anniversary of the WEB." Journal of Adult Education. IX (January, 1937), 104.
A report of the fifteenth anniversary program of the Workers' Education Bureau.

248. "Fifth National Convention of the WEB. Monthly Labor Review. XXV (August, 1927), 76-77.
A summary of the activities of the biennial convention of the WEB held in Boston, April 22-24, 1927.

249. Fuller, Paul W. "Workers' Education Bureau." American Federationist. XXXIV (November, 1927), 1374-1376.
An examination of how a union on strike can strengthen its cause through educational classes.

250. Gleason, Arthur H. "Workers' Education Bureau." Survey. XLVI (April 9, 1921), 42.
A description of the initial meeting which organized the WEB.

251. _____. "Workers' Education in the United States, A Review." New Republic. XXXIV (March 28, 1923), 143.
A report of the second national conference of the WEB.

252. Gompers, Samuel. "Workers' Education." American Federationist. XXX (May, 1923), 385.
A text of the address delivered by the president of the AFL to the 1923 convention of the WEB.

253. Green, William. "AF of L Policies and Philosophy Defended." International Molders Journal. LXV (May, 1929), 257-262.
An address delivered by the president of the AFL to the 1929 convention of the WEB. In the address, Green re-emphasizes his general opposition to Brookwood Labor College.

254. _____. "Labor and Education." Workers' Education, III (August, 1925), 7-8.
A call for the WEB to assume the responsibility for compiling histories and records of trade union experiences which will preserve them for future workers to learn from.

255. Greenwood, Arthur. "The WEB of America." The Highway.

XIV (January, 1922), 53.
A description by a Britisher of what the WEB is doing for workers in America.

256. Kopald, Steve. "The Convention of the WEB." Justice. (May
8, 1925), 8-11.
A report of the important events of the 1925 convention
of the WEB.

257. Maurer, James. "President's Message to WEB Convention upon His Retirement." Labor Age. XVIII (May, 1929), 3-
5.
In the wake of the AFL-Brookwood controversy, the
long-time president of the WEB resigned due to the reactionary policies which the WEB followed in that controversy.

258. Miller, Spencer, Jr. "Address." Report of the Proceedings
of the Forty-sixth Annual Convention of the American Federation of Labor. Detroit, Michigan, October 4-14,
1926. 173-177.
An examination of the status of workers' education in
general and the WEB in particular.

259. _____. "Address." Report of the Proceedings of the Fifti-
eth Annual Convention of the American Federation of Labor. Boston, Massachusetts, October 6-17, 1930.
299-302.
A descriptive report of the educational activities of
the WEB for the preceeding year.

260. _____. "Address to the AFL Convention." International
Molders Journal. LXIV (February, 1928), 79-86.
A report of the activities of the WEB presented to the
AFL Convention in 1927.

261. _____. "Address to the AFL Convention, Toronto, Ontario." International Molders Journal. LXV (November,
1929), 654-658. Also in Report of the Proceedings of the
Forty-ninth Annual Convention of the American Federation
of Labor. Toronto, Ontario, Canada, October 7-18,
1929. 127-130.
A report of the activities of the WEB during the year
1929 presented to the AFL convention.

262. _____. "AF of L and Workers' Education Bureau Make
Plans for Great Effort." International Molders Journal.
LIX (March, 1923), 145-146.
A discussion of the plans for a close working relation-
ship between the AFL and the WEB in order to develop a
program of adult workers' education.

263. _____. "The Constitutional Changes at the Philadelphia

Convention." American Federationist. XXXII (June, 1925), 462-464.

An examination of the constitutional changes made by the WEB at the 1925 convention.

264. _____. "Fifteen Years of the Workers' Education Bureau of America." Brookwood Labor's Own School. Katonah, N.Y.: Brookwood, 1936, 31-33.

A description of the fifteen year history of the WEB, with some references to the split between Brookwood and the WEB in 1929.

265. _____. "Fifth National Convention of the WEB of America." American Federationist. XXXIV (April, 1927), 409-411.

A review of what will be the main topics of discussion at the upcoming convention of the WEB.

266. _____. "The Fifth National Convention--Workers' Education Bureau." American Federationist. XXXIV (August, 1927), 946-950.

A review of the proceedings of the fifth biennial convention of the WEB.

267. _____. "The First Year of the Workers' Education Bureau." Proceedings of the Second National Conference on Workers' Education in the United States. New York: Workers' Education Bureau, 1922, 66-78.

A report of the activities of the WEB in the first year of operation.

268. _____. "Labor Institutes." Journal of Adult Education. VI (October, 1934), 510-513.

A discussion of the WEB's establishment of various institutes to discuss the National Industrial Recovery Act and its implications for labor.

269. _____. "The New Deal and Workers' Education." Report of the Proceedings of the Fifty-fourth Annual Convention of the American Federation of Labor. San Francisco, California, October 1-12, 1934. 231-236.

A report of the educational activities of the WEB for the preceding year.

270. _____. "The Next Fifteen Years--A Forecast." Workers' Education. XIII (October, 1936), 35-39.

After a short discussion of the history of the WEB, the author examines and attempts to predict new trends in workers' education and their effect on the bureau.

271. _____. "The Revised Constitution of the Workers' Education Bureau." Workers' Education. III (May, 1925), 10-11.

An examination of the provisions for representation and voting in the new WEB constitution.

272. _____. "The Sixth National Convention, Workers' Education Bureau." Workers' Education. VI (June, 1929), 4-11. Also in American Federationist. XXXVI (June, 1929), 728-735 and International Molders Journal. LXV (July, 1929), 385-389.
A significant description by the secretary of the WEB of the sixth biennial convention of the bureau. The author spends much time on the number of controversies which disrupted the convention.

273. _____. "The Supreme Issue and the Education of Labor." Report of the Proceedings of the Fifty-fifth Annual Convention of the American Federation of Labor. Atlantic City, New Jersey, October 7-19, 1935. 309-315.
A report of the educational activities of the WEB and its close connection with the AFL.

274. _____. "Technocracy: A New Challenge to Labor and Education." International Molders Journal. LXIX (January, 1933), 24-30.
An address before the 1932 convention of the AFL outlining the work of the WEB over the previous year.

275. _____. "Trends of Workers' Education in the United States." The Locomotive Engineers Journal. LVII (March, 1923), 174+.
An examination of the services offered by the WEB which stressed that workers' education is closely linked to the American labor movement.

276. _____. "Workers' Education." Survey. XLVIII (May 6, XLVIII (May 6, 1922), 221-222.
A report of the second conference on workers' education in the United States held in New York City, April 22-23, 1922.

277. _____. "Workers' Education." International Molders Journal. LIX (December, 1923), 675-680. Also in Report of the Proceedings of the Forty-third Annual Convention of the American Federation of Labor. Portland, Oregon, October 1-12, 1923. 158-162.
An examination of what education is and why there is a need for workers' education in the United States.

278. _____. "Workers' Education, Its Achievements and Its Future." American Federationist. XXIX (December, 1922), 881-887. Also in International Molders Journal. LIX (January, 1923), 4-7.
A description of the history, organization and objectives of the WEB.

279. _____. "Workers' Education and Industrial Progress."
Report of the Proceedings of the Forty-fifth Annual Convention of the American Federation of Labor. Atlantic
City, New Jersey, October 5-16, 1925, 157-161.
    A report of the joint rules of the AFL and the WEB
in the field of workers' education, and an examination of
the accomplishments of the movement.

280. _____. "Workers' Education and the Machine Job." Report
of the Proceedings of the Forty-eighth Annual Convention
of the American Federation of Labor. New Orleans,
Louisiana, November 19-28, 1928, 181-186.
    A report of the activities of the WEB with a discus-
sion of the role of workers' education in a technologically
oriented society.

281. _____. "Workers' Education and the Recovery Program."
Report of the Proceedings of the Fifty-third Annual Convention of the American Federation of Labor. Washington,
D. C., October 2-13, 1933, 261-266.
    A report of the role of the WEB in outlining educa-
tional programs for economic recovery.

282. _____. Workers' Education and World Peace. 2nd ed.
New York: Workers' Education Bureau, 1924, 20 pp.
    A report on the activities of the WEB submitted to the
1924 AFL Convention. Included is a summary of the
growth in affiliation of various AFL locals with the bureau.

283. _____. "The World Crisis and Workers' Education."
Report of the Proceedings of the Fifty-first Annual Convention of the American Federation of Labor. Vancouver,
British Columbia, Canada, October 5-15, 1931, 226-233.
    A report of the WEB and a discussion of the role of
workers' education during the depression.

284. Mufson, Israel. "WEB Convention 1927, Boston." Survey.
LVIII (June 15, 1927), 326-327.
    A criticism of the fifth national convention of the WEB
by one whose philosophy of workers' education differed
with the philosophy of the leadership of the WEB.

285. Muste, A. J. "Rubber Stamp Education." Labor Age.
XVIII (May, 1929), 5-6.
    A highly critical article concerning the autocratic poli-
cies of the WEB which signal the end of academic freedom in workers' education.

286. _____. "Workers' Education Bureau Surrenders to Reac-
tion." Labor Age. XVIII (March, 1929), 5-8.
    A criticism of the WEB in which the author analyzes
the bureau's inaction and the probable reasons for its
eventual demise.

287. _____. "Workers' Education in the United States." Nation.
CXIX (October 1, 1924), 333-335.
    An analysis of the admissions policy of the WEB with
    special attention given to the denial and subsequent admis-
    sion of the workers' education program of the University
    of California.

288. "The Object of Workers' Education." New Republic. XXXIV
(April 25, 1923), 229-230.
    A two-pronged attack against the American Fund for
    Public Service (Garland Fund) for not contributing to the
    WEB and against Samuel Gompers for his controversial at-
    tack against the Garland Fund.

289. "Report on the Workers' Education Bureau, 1929-1930."
Monthly Labor Review. XXXII (March, 1931), 116-117.
    A review of the activities of the WEB for the years
    1929-1930.

290. "Report on the Workers' Education Bureau, 1931-1932."
Monthly Labor Review. XXXVI (February, 1932), 328-329.
    A review of the activities of the WEB for 1931-1932.

291. "The Research Department of the Workers' Education Bureau."
Workers' Education. IV (November, 1926), 39-41.
    A description of the first three research projects un-
    dertaken by the research department of the WEB.

292. Saposs, David J. "Which Way Workers' Education?" Survey.
LXII (May 15, 1929), 250-251.
    A critical report of the 1929 WEB convention which fo-
    cuses on a constitutional change which redistributed voting
    power to the AFL.

293. "A Successful WEB Convention." Justice. (April 27, 1927),
6.
    An analysis and description of the fifth convention of
    the WEB held in the public library, Boston, Mass., April
    22-24, 1927.

294. Thomas, Norman. "On Workers' Education." New Republic.
XXXIV (May 9, 1923), 296-297.
    A letter to the editor explaining the reasons why the
    American Fund for Public Service (Garland Fund) did not
    contribute to the WEB.

295. Thorne, Florence and Luther C. Steward. "Convention of
Workers' Education Bureau." Federal Employee. XII
(June, 1927), 5, 29-30.
    The report of the AFL delegates to the 1927 WEB con-
    vention held in Boston.

296. Vogt, Paul L. "Workers' Education in the Mid-West." Work-

ers' Education. XII (June, 1934), 9-12.

A discussion of the programs being offered by the
WEB in the midwest. The major topic of the program is
the National Industrial Recovery Act.

297. Winsor, Max. "Three Letters on Workers' Education."
American Labor Monthly. I (June, 1923), 84-90.

A series of letters written by the education director
of the Amalgamated Clothing Workers of America, explaining why that union and the WEB do not have a close working relationship.

298. "WEB Anniversary Conference." Adult Education Journal. V
(July 1, 1946), 140-141.

An activity report of the WEB conference.

299. "WEB." Adult Education Journal. II (October, 1943), 168.

An activity report of the WEB.

300. "Workers' Education Bureau." Journal of Adult Education.
XIII (October, 1941), 450.

An activity report of the WEB.

301. "Workers' Education Bureau." Journal of Adult Education.
VI (February, 1934), 97-98.

An activity report of the WEB.

302. "Workers' Education Bureau of America." American Labor
Yearbook. V, New York: Rand School of Social Science,
1924, 213-218.

An activity report of the WEB.

303. "Workers' Education Bureau of America." American Labor
Yearbook. VI. New York: Rand School of Social Science,
1925, 206-208.

An activity report of the programs conducted by the
WEB from its inception in 1921. Additionally, the report
discusses the role of the field secretary and the progress
the WEB has made in the field of workers' education.

304. "Workers' Education Bureau of America." American Labor
Yearbook. VII. New York: Rand School of Social Science, 1926, 305-306.

A record of the reorganization of the WEB complete
with a list of the members of the executive committee for
1925-1926.

305. "Workers' Education Bureau of America." American Labor
Yearbook. VIII. New York: Rand School of Social Science, 1927, 160-161.

An account of the increased educational activity of the
WEB as a result of the increased financial support by the
AFL.

306. "Workers' Education Bureau." American Labor Yearbook.   X
     New York: Rand School of Social Science, 1929, 211-212.
         A report of the fifth convention of the bureau with an
     examination of new teaching activities. Also included in
     the report is a criticism of the WEB by the progressive
     wing of the workers' education movement.

307. "Workers' Education Bureau." American Labor Yearbook.
     XI   New York: Rand School of Social Science, 1930, 181-
     184.
         A report of the membership, finances, and new lead-
     ership as well as the year's activities.

308. "Workers' Education Bureau." American Labor Yearbook.
     XII New York: Rand School of Social Science, 1931, 220-
     222.
         An activity report of the programs sponsored by the
     WEB.

309. "Workers' Education Bureau." American Labor Yearbook.
     XIII New York: Rand School of Social Science, 1932, 165-
     167.
         An activity report of the WEB stressing the new edu-
     cational work of sponsoring labor institutes on university
     campuses.

310. "The WEB of America." School and Society. XXI (May 2,
     1925), 527-528.
         A short description of the fourth national convention
     held in Philadelphia, April 17-19, 1925.

311. "Workers' Education Bureau of America." School Life.   VI
     (June 15, 1921), 14.
         A description of the newly-formed coordination agency
     for the educational programs conducted by trade unions in
     the United States.

312. "WEB Convention." Journal of Adult Education.   I (June,
     1929), 321-322.
         A description of the 1929 WEB convention and the de-
     bate over the Brookwood issue.

313. Workers' Education Bureau Makes Report." The Journal of
     Electrical Workers and Operators.   XXXIII (February,
     1934), 62.
         A report of how the WEB carried on in spite of the
     depression aided by the Carnegie Corporation.

314. "Workers' Education in the United States." Justice. (Febru-
     ary 16, 1923), 8.
         A discussion of the second national conference on
     workers' education in the United States conducted under
     the auspices of the WEB.

315. Workers' Education Yearbook, 1924. (New York: Workers'
     Education Bureau, 1924), 199 pp.
          A complete report of the proceedings of the third na-
     tional conference on workers' education in the United
     States. Also included is a complete directory of WEB
     members.

316. Wright, Chester M. "Education from a Railroad Bias."
     American Federationist. XXX (April, 1923), 327.
          A response to the attack of the Railway Review on the
     WEB.

Long Term Resident Labor Schools

317. Adams, Frank. "Highlander Folk Schools: Getting Informa-
     tion Going Back and Teaching It." Harvard Educational
     Review. XLII (November, 1972), 497-520.
          An historical examination of the Highlander Folk School
     in Tennessee.

317a. _____. Unearthing Seeds of Fire, The Idea of Highlander.
      Winston-Salem, N.C.: Blair Pub. Co., 1975, 255 pp.
          An historical study of the Highlander Folk School.

318. "The AFL tries Boss Rule." Survey. LX (September 15,
     1928), 585.
          An outline of the "boss rule" tactics employed by the
     AFL when it withdrew its support from Brookwood Labor
     College.

319. "Arkansas Legislature Shows Good Sense." Christian Century.
     LII (April 17, 1935), 501-502.
          An announcement that the Arkansas legislature had de-
     feated a bill designed to close Commonwealth College.

320. Atkinson, Glen. "In Knowing Itself Lies Labor's Hope." Rail-
     way Clerk. XXVII (December, 1928), 580-581.
          An examination of the role of workers' education and
     how Brookwood meets the criteria of that role.

321. "Attack on Commonwealth College Renewed." American Teach-
     er. XXI (January, 1937), 28-29.
          A description of another attack by the Arkansas legis-
     lature upon the college as well as a short history of the
     controversy.

322. "Back Brookwood." World Tomorrow. XV (December 14,
     1932), 558.
          A request for financial backing of Brookwood Labor
     College.

323. Baldwin, Roger N. "Brookwood and the Garland Fund." Brook-

wood, Labor's Own Story.   Katonah, N.Y.: Brookwood,
1936, 39, 41.
  An examination of the financial relationship between
the American Fund for Public Service (Garland Fund) and
Brookwood Labor College.

324. Bennett, Toscan. "The First Resident Workers' College in the
   United States." Locomotive Engineers Journal. LVII
   (March, 1923), 184-186.
    A brief sketch of the history, curriculum, student
  body, and ultimate goals of Brookwood Labor College.

325. "Brickbats and Bouquets for Brookwood." American Teacher.
   XIII (January, 1929), 7-10.
    A series of letters written in support of Brookwood
  Labor College in the midst of its controversy with the
  AFL.   The only brickbat comes from the pages of the
  Daily Worker which denies that Brookwood is communistic.

326. "Brookwood." American Labor Yearbook. VII. New York:
   Rand School of Social Science, 1926, 307-308.
    An activity report of the labor college including a de-
  scription of the student body, curriculum, and the reorganization of the school.

327. "Brookwood." American Labor Yearbook. VIII. New York:
   Rand School of Social Science, 1927, 161-162.
    An activity report of the 1926-1927 school year at the
  college.

328. "Brookwood." American Labor Yearbook. X. New York:
   Rand School of Social Science, 1929, 212-213.
    An activity report of the 1927-1928 school year at the
  college.

329. "Brookwood." American Labor Yearbook. XI. New York:
   Rand School of Social Science, 1930, 184-186.
    An activity report of the 1929-1930 school year at
  Brookwood Labor College.

330. "Brookwood." American Labor Yearbook. XII. New York:
   Rand School of Social Science, 1931, 223-224.
    An activity report of the tenth anniversary year at the
  college.

331. "Brookwood." American Labor Yearbook. XIII. New York:
   Rand School of Social Science, 1932, 167-168.
    An activity report of the 1931-1932 school year at the
  college.

332. "Brookwood Asks Hearing on AF of L Charge." American
   Teacher. XIII (September, 1928), 8.
    A statement from Brookwood asking the AFL to grant

the college a hearing on the charges brought against the school.

333. "Brookwood Carries On." Labor Age. XVII (November, 1928), 3.

An editorial which sharply criticizes the executive board of the AFL for withdrawing its support of Brookwood.

334. "Brookwood Closed." Journal of Adult Education. X (January, 1938), 96-97.

An announcement of the closing of Brookwood Labor College.

335. "Brookwood Condemned Without a Hearing." Railway Clerk. XXVII (December, 1928), 578-586.

A report of the activities of the 1928 AFL Convention and its condemnation of Brookwood Labor College.

336. "Brookwood Labor College." Journal of Adult Education. V (April, 1933), 202.

An activity report on the status of the college.

337. "Brookwood Labor College." New Republic. LVI (August 22, 1928), 2.

A brief editorial comment lamenting the action of the AFL executive board in withdrawing support for Brookwood.

338. "Brookwood Labor College." New Republic. LVI (September 26, 1928), 136.

A listing of several unions which did not follow in the steps of the AFL in the repudiation of Brookwood.

339. "Brookwood Labor College." New Republic. LVI (November 14, 1928), 338.

An article which attacks the AFL for its position that all affiliates withdraw financial support from Brookwood.

340. "Brookwood Labor College." New Republic. LVII (February 6, 1929), 309.

An attack on the AFL for its position concerning Brookwood.

341. "Brookwood Labor College." New Republic. LXXIV (March 22, 1933), 143.

An announcement of the resignation of A. J. Muste from the directorship of Brookwood Labor College. The article examines to some extent the controversy which led to Muste's departure.

342. "Brookwood Labor College." School and Society. XXII (November 7, 1925) , 585.

A short description of the college as it began its fifth year.

343. "Brookwood Labor College and the American Federation of Labor." School and Society. XXIX (January 19, 1929), 92-93.
A scathing indictment of the AFL for the method it used in condemning Brookwood.

344. "Brookwood Labor College Is Incorporated." Justice. (July 10, 1925), 10.
A brief historical sketch of the college and an analysis of its links with the labor movement.

345. Brookwood Labor College--Twelfth Anniversary Review. Katonah, N. Y. : Brookwood Fellowship Bazaar, 1933, 10 pp.
A pamphlet written on the twelfth anniversary of the college, included in the pamphlet is an historical sketch of the school, an examination of faculty, students, and graduates, plus a general discussion of workers' education.

346. "Brookwood Schism." World Tomorrow. XVI (March 22, 1933), 270.
An editorial on the resignation of A. J. Muste and Tom Tippett because of their close association with the Conference of Progressive Labor Action.

347. "Brookwood's Seventh Scholastic Year." Monthly Labor Review. XXVI (March, 1928), 111-112.
A short summary of the activities of Brookwood's academic year for 1927-1928.

348. "Brookwood Shown Up as AFL Ends Convention." American Labor World. XXIX (December, 1928), 14.
A report of the 1928 AFL Convention and the negative attitude of that convention to the question of continued support of Brookwood Labor College.

349. "Brookwood Teaches No Special Doctrine says A. J. Muste." Justice. (September 7, 1928), 6.
A defense of Brookwood drawn from Muste's response to the charges against the school levelled by the executive council of the AFL.

350. "The Brookwood Trade Union Summer School." School and Society. XIX (June 21, 1924), 727.
A list of the teachers and curriculum for the summer school for trade unionists conducted by Brookwood.

351. "Brookwood, Undaunted, Continues Its Work." Labor Age. XVIII (January, 1929), 23.
An article describing the continuation of Brookwood despite the fact that the AFL convention withdrew its endorsement of the school.

352. "Brookwood Workers' College." American Labor Yearbook.
     V. New York: Rand School of Social Science, 1924, 219-
     221.
          A description of the origin, institutional organization,
     finances, curriculum, and student body at Brookwood Col-
     lege.

353. "Brookwood Workers' College." American Labor Yearbook.
     VI. New York: Rand School of Social Science, 1926, 208-
     209.
          An activity report of the college for the 1925-1926
     school year.

354. "Brookwood Workers' College." School and Society. XVIII
     (October 20, 1923), 462.
          A short description of the first two years at Brook-
     wood.

355. Brougham, H. B. "Brookwood: A Workers' College." World
     Tomorrow. VI (May, 1921), 153.
          A discussion of the need for an independent workers'
     college in the midst of a public school system which is
     anti-union.

356. _____. "New Brookwood." Proceedings of the First Na-
     tional Conference on Workers' Education in the United
     States. New York: Workers' Education Bureau, 1921, 51-
     53.
          A brief description of Brookwood Labor College.

357. Calhoun, Arthur. "Brookwood Conference on Workers' Educa-
     tion." Workers' Education. I (February, 1924), 9-10.
     Also in Justice. (March 28, 1924), 3.
          A report of the conference on workers' education.

358. _____. "Mr. Calhoun and Brookwood." New Republic. LX
     (August 21, 1929), 20.
          Arthur Calhoun, recently discharged from the faculty
     of Brookwood College, cites the reasons for his dismissal.

359. "Code of Fair Standards for the Education Industry." Ameri-
     can Teacher. XVIII (October, 1933), 9-10.
          A proposed code of fair standards written for the edu-
     cation industry by the Commonwealth College faculty.

360. Cohen, Harry. "Commonwealth College--Something Real."
     Railway Clerk. XXVII (June, 1928), 284-292.
          A description of the residential school for workers.

361. Cohn, Fannia. "Brookwood's Strength: Relating Facts to
     Ideas." Brookwood, Labor's Own School. Katonah, N. Y. :
     Brookwood, 1936, 9-10, 89.
          After an analysis of the problems which confronted the

labor movement after World War I, how resident labor colleges and workers' education dealt with the problems is examined.

362. "Commonwealth College." American Labor Yearbook. VII. New York: Rand School of Social Science, 1926, 318.
    A description of the aims, courses, and students of Commonwealth College located in Mena, Arkansas.

363. "Commonwealth." American Labor Yearbook. VIII. New York: Rand School of Social Science, 1927, 162.
    A description of the aims, courses, and students of Commonwealth College located in Mena, Arkansas.

364. "Commonwealth." American Labor Yearbook. X. New York: Rand School of Social Science, 1929, 214-215.
    An activity report of the 1928-1929 school year at Commonwealth College.

365. "Commonwealth College." American Labor Yearbook. XI. New York: Rand School of Social Science, 1930, 187-188.
    A description of students, curriculum, and the organization of Commonwealth College.

366. "Commonwealth College." American Labor Yearbook. XII. New York: Rand School of Social Science, 1931, 226-227.
    An activity report of the 1930-1931 school year at Commonwealth College.

367. "Commonwealth College." American Labor Yearbook. XIII. New York: Rand School of Social Science, 1932, 170-172.
    A report of the staff, students, policy, courses, and finances of the Commonwealth College for the 1931-1932 school year.

368. "Commonwealth College Closes." Journal of Adult Education. XII. (June, 1940), 323.
    An announcement of the closing of Commonwealth College.

369. "Commonwealth College Makes a New Start." Christian Century. LIV (August 25, 1937), 1037-1038.
    An announcement of the change in administration of the college made with the hope that the school would return to its original objective of educating the labor movement.

370. Cook, Cara. "Annual Conference of Teachers in Workers' Education." American Teacher. XV (May, 1931), 20-21.
    A description of the eighth annual conference of teachers in workers' education sponsored by Brookwood and AFT Local 189.

371. _____. "Brookwood Auxiliary Institute." Railway Clerk.

XXVII (September, 1928), 431.

A description of the educational experience of the women's auxiliary held at Brookwood.

372. _____. "Brookwood--Labor's Harvard." Railway Clerk. XXVII (August, 1928), 373-374.

A description of the purpose of the college with a statement of what is expected of the student body.

373. _____. "Brookwood Railroad Institute." Justice. (September 4, 1925), 10.

A description of the first Railroad Institute held at Brookwood in 1925.

374. _____. "Brookwood, Stuff that Counts." Labor Age. XVI (September, 1927), 5-7.

An explanation of the various topics discussed at an institute held at Brookwood by the United Textile Workers of America.

375. _____. "Labor's Better Half Goes to College." Justice. (September 16, 1927), 6.

A description of an institute conducted at Brookwood for the Women's Auxiliary.

376. Corraza, A. M. "This Workers' Education--Does It Take?" The Journal of Electrical Workers and Operators. XXV (September, 1926), 426.

A member of the IBEW tells of his experiences in workers' education at Brookwood.

377. "Correspondence." New Republic, LIX (August 7, 1929), 315.

Two opposing letters written concerning the dismissal of Arthur Calhoun from the Brookwood faculty.

378. Coy, Harold. "A New Experiment in Education for Workers." Monthly Labor Review. XX (June, 1925), 10-11.

A description of the workers' education experiment at Commonwealth College.

379. Cunningham, William. "Commonwealth College--An Educational Mutant." World Tomorrow. XII (December, 1929), 503-505.

A discussion of the beginning of a new experimental workers' education project. The article carefully examines the aims, curriculum, administration and student body of the college.

380. _____. "Commonwealth College, Learning and Earning." Bulletin of the American Association of University Professors. XV (February, 1929), 157-159.

An article which contrasts Commonwealth from traditional American colleges.

381. Deverall, Richard. "Commonwealth College." Commonweal.
XXX (April 28, 1939), 9-11.
A description of the author's stay at a "Marxist institution" and of the programs and classes offered by the
Arkansas college. The author's main point is that Catholic workers should establish a similar institution to combat the "Communists" and serve the church.

382. Dewey, John. "Freedom in Workers' Education." American
Teacher. XIII (January, 1929), 1-4. Also in Railway
Clerk. XXVII (December, 1928), 579, 595.
A call for the preservation of academic freedom in
the case of the AFL vs. Brookwood Labor College.

383. _____. "Labor Politics and Labor Education." New Republic. LVII (January 8, 1929), 211-213. Also in School
and Society. XXIX (January 19, 1929), 92-93.
A defense of Brookwood College in the midst of the
attack of the AFL upon the labor school.

384. "Education--With a Difference." The Locomotive Engineers'
Journal. LIX (June, 1925), 424+.
A description of the summer Railroad Labor Institute
conducted at Brookwood.

385. Fincke, William. "How Brookwood Began." Brookwood, Labor's Own School. Katonah, N.Y.: Brookwood, 1936, 14-
16.
Reminiscences by the son of William and Helen Finck
of how his parents were inspired to establish Brookwood
in 1921.

386. "First Labor School in the East." American Labor World.
XXV (August, 1924), 17.
A description of the special summer institute held at
Brookwood for the first time in 1924.

387. Flexner, Jean Atherton. "Brookwood." New Republic. XLIII
(August 5, 1925), 287-289.
A description of the philosophy, student body, curricu-
lum, and future prospects of Brookwood College.

388. "A Good School Under Fire." New Republic. CII (December,
9, 1940), 776.
This article briefly describes the Highlander Folk
School in Monteagle, Tennessee by highlighting the school's
purposes as well as the sponsors of the school. The article was written to bring to the public's attention the vi-
cious campaign going on in Tennessee by newspapers as
well as non-union firms to discredit the school and its
work.

389. Goodhue, F. M. "Seacroft, An Independent Workers' Educa-

tion Community." <u>American Teacher</u>. XX (November, 1935), 5.

A discussion of the aspirations of a small group headed by Dr. William Zeuch, the founder and first director of Commonwealth College, who plans to establish an independent, cooperative workers' educational community.

390. Green, William. "Labor's Answer to Its Critics, Brookwood Defenders. <u>American Labor World</u>. XXX (February, 1929), 5-7.

A defense of the AFL's position to disaffiliate Brookwood Labor College.

391. Hall, Covington. "A College Education for All." <u>Locomotive Engineers Journal</u>. LIX (October, 1925), 735, 786.

A description of the philosophy and plans of Commonwealth College in Arkansas where workers could obtain a college education through self-maintenance.

392. _____. "Something New Underneath the Sun." <u>Labor Age</u>. XV (January, 1926), 19-21.

A description of the life and philosophy of Commonwealth College.

393. Hamilton, Walton H. "The Educational Policy of a Labor College." <u>Social Forces</u>. II (January, 1924), 204-208.

An examination of the function, character, and aims of instruction which should be applied in the establishment of a labor college like Brookwood.

394. Hawes, Elizabeth D. "The Highlander Folk School." <u>Brookwood, Labor's Own School</u>. Katonah, N. Y.: Brookwood, 1936, 40-41.

A description of the educational work of the Highlander Folk School.

395. "The Highlander Folk School." <u>Journal of Adult Education</u>. V (February, 1933), 111.

An activity report of the Highlander Folk School.

396. "Highlander Folk School." <u>Journal of Adult Education</u>. VI (February, 1934), 99.

An activity report of the Highlander Folk School.

397. "Highlander Folk School." <u>Adult Education Journal</u>. V (April, 1946), 102.

A report of the educational activity of the school.

398. "Highlander Folk School. <u>Adult Education Journal</u>. V (July, 1946), 141.

A report of the educational activity of the school.

399. "Highlander Folk School Activities." <u>Adult Education Journal</u>.

VII (July, 1948), 148.
   A report of the educational activities of the school.

400. "Highlander Gets Grant." Adult Education Journal. VI
     (April, 1947), 93.
        An announcement that the school was receiving finan-
     cial assistance.

401. Horton, Myles. "The Highlander Folk School." The Social
     Frontier. II (January, 1936), 117-118.
        A description of the school and its attempts to work
     with organized labor to assist industrial workers in the
     south.

402. "In the Labor Schools." Survey. LXIX (February, 1933),
     80-81.
        A short description of the work of Brookwood and
     Commonwealth Colleges.

403. Jewel, B. M. "The Railroad Institute of 1925." American
     Federationist. XXXII (October, 1925), 935-938.
        An account of railroad workers attending a labor in-
     stitute at Brookwood in the summer of 1925.

404. Kleug, Grace B. "Education for Trade Union Wives." Amer-
     ican Federationist. XXXV (February, 1928), 202-204.
        An analysis of the week-long institute of the women's
     auxiliary of the International Association of Machinists
     conducted at Brookwood.

404a. Koch, Charlotte and Raymond. Educational Commune, The
      Story of Commonwealth College. New York: Schocken
      Books, 1972, 211 pp.
         An historical study of Commonwealth College located
      in Mena, Arkansas.

405. Koch, Lucien and Myles Horton. "Two New Labor Colleges
     in the South." Progressive Education. XI (April, 1934),
     301-302.
        A descriptive analysis of two labor colleges in the
     south, Commonwealth College and Highlander Folk School.

406. Lawrence, Mary. "Labor Education in the South." Ammuni-
     tion. II (December, 1944), 14-16.
        An examination of the educational program of High-
     lander Folk School.

407. Lefkowitz, Abraham. "Shall Brookwood and Academic Free-
     dom Die?" American Teacher. XIII (October, 1928),
     25-26.
        An article strongly supporting Brookwood in its con-
     troversy with the AFL.

408. Linville, Henry R. "Brookwood or Company Union Education--
Which?" Railway Clerk. XXVII (December, 1928), 580.
A critical examination of the actions of the executive
council of the AFL in its unsubstantiated attack on Brookwood.

409. Martindale, John W. "Carrying Brookwood to the Workers."
Brookwood, Labor's Own School. Katonah, N.Y.: Brookwood, 1936, 24.
An examination of the role of the extension department
of Brookwood.

410. Maurer, James H. "Why Labor Schools and Colleges." Life
and Labor. XI (October, 1921), 227-230.
A prediction that labor schools and colleges will continue to increase in number because of the anti-labor educational programs offered in public schools.

411. Morris, James O. Conflict Within the AFL. Ithaca, N.Y.:
Cornell, 1958. Chs. IV, V.
An historical examination of the conflict between the
AFL and Brookwood Labor College. Also examined is the
role of the WEB in this controversy.

412. Morris, R. L. "Experiment in Southern Education." Southwestern Social Science Quarterly. XXIX (December, 1948),
193-205.
An historical examination of Commonwealth College,
organized in 1923 to promote education for workers on a
self-supporting basis.

413. Moskowitz, Charlotte. "Commonwealth College and the Southern Workers." Brookwood, Labor's Own School. Katonah,
N.Y.: Brookwood, 1936, 19.
An examination of the role of Commonwealth in the
education of southern workers.

414. Mufson, Israel. "Brookwood College." The Journal of Electrical Workers and Operators. XXIV (October, 1925),
786-788.
A description of the educational process which occurred at a study session at Brookwood College.

415. _____. "Workers' Education Collides with New Unionism."
Railway Clerk. XXVII (November, 1928), 566-567.
In the midst of the AFL's censure of Brookwood, the
author examines the role of workers' education in light of
the fundamental purpose of the labor movement.

416. Muste, A. J. "Back Up, Labor Education!" Labor Age.
XVII (July, 1928), 5-6.
A sharp answer to the critics of labor colleges who
state that workers' education and the labor schools, in par-

ticular, are unpatriotic, unAmerican, atheistic and radical.

417.   _____. "Brookwood Labor Institute." American Federationist. XXXII (October, 1925), 939-942.
An account of the one-week Railroad Workers' summer institute held at Brookwood.

418.   _____. "The Brookwood Point of View." Workers' Education. I (July-August, 1923), 5-6.
A brief article on the Brookwood viewpoint which the resident labor school strives to impart to its students.

419.   _____. "Brookwood Today." Justice. (July 20, 1923), 8.
A brief description of the college and the methods it uses to relate to workers' needs.

420.   _____. "Brookwood Workers College." Proceedings of the Second National Conference on Workers' Education in the United States. New York: Workers' Education Bureau, 1922, 27-31.
A descriptive report of the beginnings and activities of Brookwood Labor College.

421.   _____. "Freedom in Labor Education." American Teacher. XII (September, 1927), 12+.
The author praises the AFL stand for academic freedom and its denunciation of dictatorship in education, and the labor movement's fight against reactionary, repressive educational laws.

422.   _____. "From Dawn to Dusk at Katonah." Labor Age. XIV (October, 1925), 1-3.
An account of how one day might be spent at the Railroad Labor Institute at Brookwood. The purpose of the article is to show how trade unionists spend their time attending a summer school.

423.   _____. "Labor Vacation and Summer Schooling." Survey. LIV (September 15, 1925), 633-635.
An activity report of the 1925 summer session carried on by Brookwood. Included is a list of the various groups which used the college for a summer school and the teachers utilized in such teaching.

424.   _____. "The One Day Conference on Workers' Education." Workers' Education. II (August, 1924), 24-28. Also in Justice. (August 22, 1924), 10.
A report of a one day conference held at Brookwood for teachers in workers' education.

425.   _____. "Railroad Labor Institute at Brookwood College." Workers' Education. III (August, 1925), 24-26.
A description of the events which took place at the

first Railroad Labor Institute held at Brookwood.

426.   _____.   "Shall Workers' Education Perish?"   Labor Age.
        XVIII (January, 1929), 5-6.
            A critical attack on the 1928 AFL convention in New
        Orleans and the backward stance which the AFL executive
        board took concerning Brookwood.

427.   _____.   "Sketches of an Autobiography." In Nat Hentoff,
        ed., The Essays of A. J. Muste. New York: Simon and
        Schuster, 1970, 84-154.
            In parts eleven through nineteen of his autobiography,
        Muste recounts his personal recollections of workers edu-
        cation in general and his work at Brookwood Labor Col-
        lege specifically.

428.   _____.   "What Price Labor Education?" Labor Age. XVII
        (September, 1928), 15-16.
            After giving a pessimistic overview of the state of
        American labor, the author launches into an explanation of
        two ingredients needed for workers' education, opinion and
        freedom.

429.   _____.   "What Will Brookwood Do New?" American Teach-
        er. XIII (January, 1929), 15-17.
            The author cites the distinguished record of the school
        and explains its plans for the future.

430. Nilsson, Harry. "The Grads Come Through." Brookwood,
        Labor's Own School. Katonah, N.Y.: Brookwood, 1936,
        27-28.
            An analysis of Brookwood from the standpoint of one
        who has graduated from the school.

431. Norton, Helen G. "Brookwood's Summer Institute, 1927."
        Survey. LIX (October 15, 1927), 95-96.
            An examination of the role of women in the labor
        movement, and the role Brookwood is attempting to play in
        their education.

432.   _____.   "Brookwood in the First Decade." Labor Age. XX
        (May, 1931), 18-19, 29.
            An historical examination of the first ten years in the
        history of Brookwood Labor College.

433.   _____.   "Brookwood--Where Students Work." Justice.
        (June 15, 1922), 6.
            A short description of Brookwood College written by
        one of its instructors. Emphasis is placed on the partici-
        pation of students in the life of the school.

434.   _____.   "Brookwood--Where the Students Work." Railway
        Clerk. XXVII (July, 1928), 322.

A description of the cooperative nature of the living arrangements at Brookwood Labor College.

435. _____. "Drama at Brookwood." Labor Age. XV (May, 1926), 18-19.
An explanation of the new interest in labor drama at Brookwood Labor College.

436. _____. "Independent Workers' Classes Flourish." Labor Age. XIX (March, 1930), 18.
A report on the Washington's Birthday Conference for Teachers in Workers' Education held at Brookwood.

437. _____. "Young Labor Speaks Up." Survey. LX (June 15, 1928), 346.
An examination of a Labor Youth Conference conducted by the Brookwood Labor College.

438. O'Connor, Harvey. "Railroaders at Brookwood." The Locomotive Engineers Journal. LX (September, 1926), 656+.
A description of the two-week Railroaders Institute held at the Labor College.

439. Oliver, Eli. "Labor's First Resident College." Life and Labor. XI (October, 1921), 250-252.
A discussion of the opening of Brookwood and an analysis of the differences between workers' education and the traditional educational opportunities available in public schools.

440. Peterson, Ralph. "Utopian Afternoon: Post Mortem on Commonwealth College." Labor Today. II (April, 1942), 17-20.
A description of the closing of the college in 1940 by a former member of the faculty.

441. Preston, Evelyn. "Brookwood Carries On." Brookwood, Labor's Own School. Katonah, N.Y.: Brookwood, 1936, 50-51.
An examination of the philosophical development of the college tracing it through the split with the AFL and the replacement of A. J. Muste with Tucker Smith as director.

442. "Resident Labor College at Katonah, New York." School and Society. XIII (April 9, 1921), 436-437.
A report of a preliminary conference which discussed the founding of Brookwood.

443. "Resident Schools." Journal of Adult Education. III (June, 1931), 342-343.
An activity report of various resident labor colleges in the United States.

444. Robinson, James W. "The Expulsion of Brookwood Labor
     College from the Workers' Education Bureau." Labour
     History. (Canberra). XV (November, 1968), 64-69.
          An examination of the expulsion of Brookwood Labor
     College from the Workers' Education Bureau.

445. Simpkins, Rose. "Brookwood College Meets Katonah." Jus-
     tice. (January 27, 1928), 5, 7.
          A discussion of the activities of the Brookwood stu-
     dents who produced a labor play in the town of Katonah to
     raise money for striking miners.

446. Smith, Tucker. "Brookwood--No Longer an Experiment."
     Brookwood, Labor's Own School. Katonah, N.Y.: Brook-
     wood, 1936, 7-8, 88.
          A short historical examination of the development of
     Brookwood Labor College.

447. _____. "Workers Prepare for Power." Progressive Edu-
     cation. XI (April, 1934), 303-306.
          A presentation of the philosophical tenets upon which
     Brookwood Labor College operates.

448. "Students on Strike." Nation. CXXXVI (January 4, 1933),
     19-20.
          Three separate letters presenting all sides of a stu-
     dent strike at Commonwealth College.

449. "Three Summer Trade Union Institutes." Monthly Labor Re-
     view. XXIII (October, 1926), 119-120.
          A discussion of the inauguration of summer institutes
     on the campus of Brookwood Labor College. The three
     institutes include the Railway Employees, the Textile
     Workers, and the Electrical Workers.

450. Tippett, Tom. "Agencies in the Field." What Next in Work-
     ers' Education? Seventh Annual Conference of Teachers
     in Workers' Education. Katonah, N.Y.: Brookwood,
     1930, 34.
          An activity report of the role of the Brookwood Exten-
     sion Department in the south.

451. "Training of Labor Leaders in the United States." Internation-
     al Labor Review. VIII (July, 1923), 138-139.
          A report on the establishment of Brookwood Labor Col-
     lege and a discussion of the training school of the National
     Womens' Trade Union League in Chicago.

452. "Tucker Smith Heads Brookwood." World Tomorrow. XVI
     (July, 1935), 441.
          An editorial statement on Tucker Smith's acceptance
     of the position as director of Brookwood.

453. Wakefield, Dan. "The Seize at Highlander." Nation.
     CLXXXIX (November 7, 1959), 323-325.
          A description of an attempted closing of Highlander
     Folk School because of its stand for integration and social
     justice.

454. Ward, Harry L. "The Responsibility of Union Teachers in
     the Labor Movement." American Teacher. XIII (January,
     1929), 4-6.
          An address delivered at a meeting of AFT Local 5 in
     New York in which the author attacks the actions of the
     AFL in the controversy with Brookwood.

455. "What Brookwood Means." Nation. CXXVII (September 12,
     1928), 241.
          A statement of Brookwood's position in its controversy
     with Matthew Woll and the AFL.

456. "Where Brookwood Stands Now." World Tomorrow. XII
     (March, 1929), 139-140.
          A short statement by the Board of Directors of Brook-
     wood in response to the action taken by the AFL against
     the college.

457. "Whither Brookwood." Labor Age. XXII (February-March,
     1933), 14-17.
          An editorial which examines the split on the faculty of
     Brookwood between the Saposs-Kennedy group and the Tip-
     pett-Muste group.

458. "Who Is This A. J. Muste?" World Tomorrow. XII (June,
     1929), 250-254.
          A biographical sketch of A. J. Muste, including con-
     siderable information on his work at Brookwood.

459. "Workmen's College." School and Society. XIV (August 20,
     1921), 95-96.
          After a criticism of Ruskin College in England, the
     article surveys workers' colleges and their type of in-
     struction in America.

460. "Workers' College at Katonah, New York." Monthly Labor
     Review. XIV (May, 1922), 230.
          A short description of the beginning of Brookwood
     Labor College.

461. "Workers' Education." The Locomotive Engineers Journal.
     LXII (July, 1928), 506.
          Two short articles which examine Brookwood and the
     summer institutes held there for labor groups and wom-
     en's auxiliaries.

462. Zeuch, William E. "Commonwealth: A Workers' School in

a Social Laboratory." Workers' Education. IV (November, 1926), 16-20.
An examination of the educational objectives and administration of Commonwealth College.

463. Zihlman, Frederick. "Development of Education in the Labor Movement." Railway Maintenance of Way Employee. XXXVII (February, 1928), 5-7.
A descriptive examination of Brookwood Labor College is set forth by a Congressman from Maryland.

Organized Labor

464. "Amalgamated Clothing Workers." American Labor Yearbook. VII. New York: Rand School of Social Science, 1926, 310.
An explanation and description of the publications put out by the Amalgamated Clothing Workers of America as part of its educational campaign.

465. "AF of L and Workers' Education." Journal of Adult Education. V (February, 1933), 112.
A short discussion of the activities of various state federations of labor in the conducting of labor institutes for the summer of 1932.

466. Beard, Charles. "The Potency of Labor Education." American Federationist. XXIX (July, 1922), 500-502. Also in International Molders Journal. LX (December, 1924), 745-746.
An essay discussing the strength and potential of the labor movement and the resulting importance of labor education.

467. Blanshard, Paul "The Future of Workers' Education." American Labor Monthly. II (December, 1923), 33-38.
An examination of the role the AF of L should be playing in the expansion of workers' education through the central trades and labor councils.

468. Budish, Jacob M. and George Soule. The New Unionism in the Clothing Industry. New York: Harcourt Brace and Howe, 1920.
Chapter eight is descriptive of the educational work of the labor organizations in the needle trades.

469. Carman, Harry I. "The ILGWU and Workers' Education." Workers' Education. III (February, 1926), 1-13.
An historical and philosophical examination of the International Ladies' Garment Workers' Union's activities in workers' education.

470. Cohn, Fannia M. "Action Based on Knowledge Is Power."
Workers' Education. XIII (July, 1936), 27-29.
A discussion of the role of the International Ladies'
Garment Workers' Union's education department in prepar-
ing workers with knowledge which can be transformed into
power.

471. _____. "An American Workers' University." The Highway. XIII (March, 1921), 101-102 and (May, 1921), 125-
126.
An historical examination of the development of the
Garment Workers' education department.

472. _____. "The Contribution of Workers' Education to the Labor Movement." Justice. (September 11, 1925), 10.
Workers' education must train workers for a collective experience so that workers and unions become more
aware of their input in industrial society.

473. _____. "Education and Union Progress." Justice. (April
22, 1927), 6.
The author links the development of the union to the
intellectual capabilities of its members. As a result she
makes a strong case for continuing and expanding the Garment Workers' education department.

474. _____. "The Educational Work of the International Ladies
Garment Workers' Union." Proceedings of the Second National Conference on Workers' Education in the United
States. New York: Workers' Education Bureau, 1922,
52-66.
A report of the activities of the education department
of the Garment Workers' Union.

475. _____. "Educational Work of Garment Union Gives Workers
Broader Outlook on World About Them." International
Molders Journal. LXII (September, 1926), 533.
A short analysis of the activities of the Garment
Workers' education department.

476. _____. "The Educational Work of the International Ladies'
Garment Workers' Union." American Labor Yearbook.
III, 1922, 204-206.
A brief history of the educational endeavors of the International Ladies' Garment Workers' Union and a description of how it tried to reach more of its locals with
various educational opportunities through offering classes
in the public school buildings located in New York City.

477. _____. "Facing the Future." Workers' Education. XII
(January, 1935), 6-14.
A listing of the goals of the education department of
the International Ladies' Garment Workers' Union.

478. _____. "First Woman's Auxiliary Institute." American
Federationist. XXXV (January, 1928), 58-63.
A discussion of the importance of women's auxiliaries
to the home life of a union family and the role of workers'
education in sustaining a viable women's auxiliary.

479. _____. "ILGWU. Education Department." Proceedings
of the First National Conference on Workers' Education
in the United States. New York: Workers' Education
Bureau, 1921, 39-49.
An historical and descriptive report of the education
department of the International Ladies Garment Workers'
Union.

480. _____. "A New Era for Labor Education." American Federationist. XLI (February, 1934), 157-160.
An examination of the expanding role played by education in the activities of a trade union.

481. _____. "Reflections on the Eighth Anniversary of Our Educational Work." Justice. (November 27, 1925), 6.
A description of the first eight years of the educational program of the International Ladies' Garment Workers'
Union.

482. _____. "Review of our Education Activity for 1925-1926."
Justice. (June 18, 1926), 6.
A review of the educational activities of the Garment
Workers for the years 1925-1926.

483. _____. "Strike Leaders in a Gymnasium." Life and Labor. XI (March, 1921), 72-73.
An examination of the importance of workers' education in the daily activities of the trade union.

484. _____. "Ten Years of Educational Department." Justice.
(April 15, 1927), 6.
An examination of the difficulties faced by the Garment
Workers' Union education department in its first ten years
of operation.

485. _____. "Training Leaders for Labor." Justice. (June 24,
1927), 6.
A discussion of the need for an intelligent, informed
and articulate labor leadership to enhance the interest of
the workers.

486. _____. "Twelve Years Educational Activities--ILGWU."
American Federationist. XXXVI (January, 1929), 105-111.
Also in Workers' Education. VI (January, 1929), 8-14.
An examination of the role of a trade union education
department in the midst of a depression.

487. _____. "What Workers' Education Really Is." Life and
Labor. XI (October, 1921), 230-234.
      A description of the educational objectives of the edu-
cation department of the Garment Workers' Union.

488. _____. "Why Workers' Education Should Be Under Trade
Unions." Justice. (August 31, 1923), 8.
      An examination of why workers' education should be
under the auspices of trade unions rather than university
and college extension programs.

489. _____. "Workers' Education Aims at Power." Justice.
(November 18, 1927), 6 and (November 25, 1927), 6.
      A comparison of the development of workers' educa-
tion with the development of the labor movement.

490. _____. "Workers' Education--Its Importance." Justice.
(December 19, 1924), 10.
      A discussion of the importance of workers' education
in the training of union people to carry on the labor movement.

491. _____. "Workers' Education and Internationalism." Justice. (July 11, 1924), 10.
      Since the need for the labor movement is internation-
al, workers' solidarity and workers' education programs
through Unions can assist in reaching this goal.

492. _____. "Workers' Education and Labor Leadership."
Workers' Education. XII (July, 1935), 17-19.
      A statement issued by the Garment Workers' Union
education department on the importance of workers' education.

493. _____. "The Workers' University of the ILGWU." Life
and Labor. X (March, 1920), 73-77.
      An activity report on the education department of the
International Ladies' Garment Workers' Union. Included
is the historical development of the department, its curriculum, and its teachers.

494. "Content of Our Courses." Justice. (August 3, 1923), 10
and (August 10, 1923), 10.
      A report to the Workers' Education Bureau suggesting
the types of courses the Garment Workers' Union feels
should be taught in a workers' education program.

495. Cook, Cara. "Labor Congress Sputters." Labor Age. XVII
(December, 1929), 7-9.
      A sharp ridicule of the New England Labor Congress
because of the workers' education program it started. The
article ends with a criticism of the current brand of labor
education.

496. Craig, Leonard. "Pennsylvania." What Next in Workers'
     Education?" Seventh Annual Conference of Teachers in
     Workers' Education. Katonah, N. Y. : Brookwood, 1930,
     21-24.
         A critical examination of the regressive role being
     played by the Pennsylvania State Federation of Labor with
     its curtailment of its department of workers' education.

497. _____. "Workers' Education in Pennsylvania." American
     Federationist. XXXV (September, 1928), 1122-1123. Al-
     so in Workers' Education. V (September, 1928), 14-15.
         An activity report of the work of the department of
     workers' education of the Pennsylvania State Federation of
     Labor, especially the two labor colleges at Shenandoah
     and Wilkes-Barre.

498. _____. "Workers' Education in Pennsylvania." The Place
     of Workers' Education in the Labor Movement. Fifth An-
     nual Conference of Teachers in Workers' Education. Ka-
     tonah, N. Y. : Brookwood, 1928, 54-59.
         An activity report of the work of the department of
     Workers' Education of the Pennsylvania State Federation of
     Labor.

499. "Denver Unemployment Conference." Workers' Education. VI
     (December, 1928), 12-14.
         An analysis of an educational conference sponsored by
     the Colorado State Federation of Labor, the Denver Cen-
     tral Labor Union and the Denver Labor College. Through
     a short analysis of the conference content, the article sug-
     gests some of the topics which the Denver Labor College
     will focus on in the coming year.

500. Douglas, P. H. "Searching after Truth with Labor." Life and
     Labor. XI (October, 1921), 236.
         An examination of how local unions and central labor
     bodies can set up their own schools.

501. "The Education of Adult Workers." School and Society. XIX
     (February 9, 1924), 154-155.
         The text of the recommendation regarding adult work-
     ers' education submitted to the executive council of the
     AFL by the committee on education.

502. "Educational Department of the International Ladies Garment
     Workers' Union." American Labor Yearbook. XIII.
     New York: Rand School of Social Science, 1932, 175-176.
         An activity report of the education department of the
     Garment Workers for 1931.

503. "The Educational Season of the International, 1922-1923."
     Justice. (April 13, 1923), 10.
         A commentary praising the Garment Workers' education-
     al program.

504. "Educational Work of Other National Unions." American Labor
      Yearbook. VI. New York: Rand School of Social Science,
      1925, 212-213.
            A brief listing of the educational activities of the United
      Mine Workers, International Fur Workers, Amalgamated
      Clothing Workers, and the Womens' Trade Union League.

505. Epstein, Abraham. "Educational Department of the Pennsyl-
      vania State Federation of Labor." Proceedings of the
      First National Conference on Workers' Education in the
      United States. New York: Workers' Education Bureau,
      1921, 30-33.
            An activity report of the education department.

506. Fichandler, Alexander. "Labor Education." Survey. XLV
      (January 8, 1921), 542-543.
            This article cites examples of the Garment Workers'
      various educational programs for its rank and file workers.

507. Frey, John P. "The Relation of Workers' Education to the
      Labor Movement." The Place of Workers' Education in
      the Labor Movement. Fifth Annual Conference of Teachers
      in Workers' Education. Katonah, N. Y. : Brookwood,
      1928, 60.
            A short paragraph by a trade union official on the role
      of workers' education vis à vis the labor movement.

508. Friedland, Louis S. "Workers University of the ILGWU."
      School and Society. XI (March 20, 1920), 348-350.
            An article which develops the philosophical tenets of
      the educational department of the Garment Workers.

509. Fuller, Paul W. "Miners' Educational Work." American Fed-
      erationist. XXX (March, 1926), 324-326.
            A description of the workers' education movement
      among the United Mine Workers in central Pennsylvania.

510. _____. "Workers' Education in the Mining Industry."
      Workers' Education. II (November, 1924), 23-25. Also
      in Justice. (May 29, 1926), 10.
            An account of the organization of workers' education
      groups in mining districts by the organizer.

511. _____. "Workers' Education in Passaic." Workers' Edu-
      cation, V (November, 1927), 6-8.
            An examination of the educational work done under the
      auspices of the WEB for the United Textile Workers.

512. Gilbert, Joseph and J. B. S. Hardman. "The Labor Press and
      Workers' Education." What Next in Workers' Education?
      Seventh Annual Conference of Teachers in Workers' Educa-
      tion. Katonah, N. Y : Brookwood, 1930, 60-64.
            A discussion of the role of the labor press as a work-
      ers' educational method.

513. Gluck, Elsie. "Educational Work of Local 25 ILGWU." *Pro-ceedings of the First National Conference on Workers' Education in the United States.* New York: Workers' Education Bureau, 1921, 49-51.

A description of the local union's educational endeavors.

514. Golden, Clinton S. "The Gaining of Union Support." *The Promotion and Maintenance of Workers' Education.* Third Annual Conference of Teachers in Workers' Education. Katonah, N. Y.: Brookwood, 1926, 17-21.

An examination of problems encountered in attempting to interest trade union officials in a workers' education program.

515. _____. "The Workers Educate Themselves." *Labor Age.* XI (April, 1922), 1-2.

A description of the awakening of organized labor to the need for education as a result of one union's success in an organizing drive because of the use of workers' education.

516. Haessler, Carl. "AFL Convention Highlights." *Labor Age.* XVIII (January, 1929), 3-4.

A description of the contradictory proceedings of the American Federation of Labor convention in New Orleans in November 1928. Special attention is given to the Brookwood controversy.

517. Hardman, J. B. (Salutsky). "Labor Educational Programs and Activities of the Amalgamated Clothing Workers of America." *Proceedings of the First National Conference on Workers Education in the United States.* New York: Workers' Education Bureau, 1921, 54-60.

A descriptive report of the activities of the ACWA national education department.

518. Hendley, C. J. "Study Class in Electrical Workers' Union." *American Federationist.* XXXIV (April, 1927), 459-462.

A descriptive analysis of some workers' education classes conducted by Local 3 of the International Brotherhood of Electrical Workers.

519. Hogue, Richard W. "Workers' Education." *Life and Labor.* XIII (October, 1924), 3-4.

A discussion of the activities and workers' education plans of the Pennsylvania Federation of Labor.

520. _____. "Workers Education in Pennsylvania." *Workers' Education.* I (November, 1923), 12-13.

A report of the activities of the first Department of Workers' Education of the Pennsylvania State Federation of Labor.

521. "International Ladies Garment Workers' Educational Depart-
        ment." American Labor Yearbook. V. New York:
        Rand School of Social Science, 1924, 221-225.
        A description of the development and aims in workers'
        education which were pioneered by the Garment Workers.

522. "International Ladies Garment Workers' Union." American
        Labor Yearbook. VI. New York: Rand School of Social
        Science, 1925, 210-212.
        A list of the educational activities sponsored by the
        union.

523. "International Ladies Garment Workers' Union." American
        Labor Yearbook. VII. New York: Rand School of Social
        Science, 1926, 308-309.
        A report of the education department of the Garment
        Workers.

524. "International Ladies Garment Workers' Union." American
        Labor Yearbook. VIII. New York: Rand School of So-
        cial Science, 1927, 164.
        A list of the activities of the educational department
        during the 1926-1927 year.

525. Kallen, Horace M. "The Nub of Workers Education." Survey.
        LIV (July 15, 1925), 449-451.
        A call by the author to eradicate differences between
        national unions through labor education.

526. Kerchen, John L. "Mutual Aid of AFT and Workers' Educa-
        tion." American Teacher. XI (June, 1927), 11.
        After examining the inability of the workers' education
        movement and the AFT to live up to expectations, the
        author cites reasons for his optimism that both, working
        together can reach new heights.

527. Kleug, Grace B. "Educating Workers' Wives." American
        Federationist. XXXIV (April, 1927), 431-435.
        A description of the Women's Auxiliary of the Interna-
        tional Association of Machinists and its educational work.

528. _____. "Education for Trade Union Wives." American
        Federationist. XXXV (February, 1928), 202-204. Also
        in Workers' Education. V (February, 1928), 5-7.
        An account of the educational work of the women's
        auxiliary of the International Association of Machinists in-
        cluding a week-long institute at Brookwood.

529. Kopold, Sylvia. "A Course in Economics and the Labor
        Movement." Justice. (August 31, 1923), 10.
        A course outline of a class in economics.

530. Laidler, Harry W. "A Workers' Chautauqua." Labor Age.

XIV (January, 1925), 5-7.

A description of a labor chautauqua sponsored by the United Mine Workers in western Pennsylvania.

531. Lindeman, Eduard, C. "The Relation of Workers' Education to the Labor Movement." The Place of Workers' Education in the Labor Movement. Fifth Annual Conference of Teachers in Workers' Education. Katonah, N.Y.: Brookwood, 1928. 63-74.

An attempt to answer the question, "Should the workers' education movement be swallowed by an organism called 'labor'?"

532. Linton, Edwin E. "Michigan Labor's Efforts at Workers' Education." American Federationist. XXXIV (April, 1927), 462-464.

A discussion of the founding of the educational movement in the Michigan Federation of Labor.

533. McDougle, Ivan E. "Workers' Education in Baltimore." Workers' Education. III (February, 1926), 14-17.

A criticism of the apathy of union labor in Baltimore and the adverse effect that this is having on the workers' education activities in that city.

534. McMahon, Thomas F. "Textile Workers' Institute." American Federationist. XXXIII (September, 1926), 1100-1102.

An analysis of the activities of the Textile Workers Institute held at Brookwood.

535. Miller, Spencer, Jr. "The Atlantic City Convention and Workers' Education." Workers' Education. III (November, 1925), 1-6. Also in American Federationist. XXXII (December, 1925), 1159-1163.

A discussion of the activities of the AFL convention regarding workers' education.

536. _____. "The Detroit Convention and Workers' Education." Workers' Education. IV (November, 1926), 8-12.

An account of the 1926 convention of the AFL with respect to the approval of the work of the Workers' Education Bureau.

537. _____. "State Federations of Labor and Workers' Education." American Federationist. XXXIII (October, 1926), 1187-1190.

A report on how the individual state federations of labor have taken more active leadership in the promotion of workers' education.

538. _____. "Workers' Education and the Los Angeles Convention." Workers' Education. V (November, 1927), 1-6. Also in American Federationist. XXXIV (November, 1927),

1369-1373.
An account of the 1927 AFL convention with special
reference to the topic of workers' education.

539. _____ . "Workers' Education at the New Orleans Convention." Workers' Education. VI (January, 1929), 1-7.
Also in American Federationist. XXXVI (January, 1929),
98-104.
The author cites the developments in workers' education over the previous years to the national AFL Convention.

540. "More Training Classes." Life and Labor. V (February,
1915), 44-45.
A discussion of a new experiment in workers' education in the United States: the workingman's college. It
was a joint effort between the Garment Workers and the
Rand School of Social Science.

541. Mufson, Israel. "Local Union 98 Operates Large Class in
Shop Work." The Journal of Electrical Workers and Op-
erators. XXVI (May, 1927), 231-276.
A description of a class of electrical workers in a
Philadelphia Labor College class.

542. Muste, A. J. "The Teachers' Union and Workers' Education."
Workers' Education. III (August, 1925), 13-16.
A description of how organized AFT teachers have
made a contribution to the workers' education movement
and how that movement has affected their profession.

543. "New Haven Trades Council." American Labor Yearbook.
XIII. New York: Rand School of Social Science, 1932,
177.
A report of the classes started by the Machinists Union under the auspices of the New Haven Trade Council.

544. "The Next Educational Season." Justice. (October 21, 1927),
6; (October 28, 1927), 6; (November 4, 1927), 6; (November 11, 1927), 6.
Four installments explaining the educational activities
of the Garment Workers for the coming year.

545. "Our Educational Policy." Justice. (June, 15, 1923), 10.
The statement on educational policy which the Gar-
ment Workers education department submitted to the
Workers' Education Bureau.

546. Payntz, Juliet S. "The Unity Movement--The Soul of the Union." Life and Labor. VII (June, 1917), 96-98.
An examination of the educational and recreational
benefits of the "Unity House" concept.

547. Preston, Evelyn. "Workers' Education in Distric Number Two United Mine Workers of America." Workers' Education. IV (May, 1926), 20-22.

A description of a miner's school in central Pennsylvania.

548. "Railway Brotherhood Studies War Debt." Journal of Adult Education. V (June, 1933), 327-328.

A description of a worker's education institute for firemen and engineers held at Brookwood.

549. Reed, Charles. "Educational Work in Salem, Mass." Justice. (September 24, 1926), 6.

An examination of the workers' educational activities conducted in Salem during 1925.

550. _____. "Workers' Education in Salem." American Federationist. XXXIV (April, 1927), 484.

A report of the activities in workers' education conducted by the Salem Central Labor Union.

551. Ross, William. "The Railroad Labor Conference." Workers' Education. VI (March, 1929), 1-2. Also in American Federationist. XXXVI (March, 1929), 326.

A description of the Railroad Labor Conference held at Johns Hopkins University in January, 1929.

552. Schwartz, Joseph. "Philadelphia Activities." What Next in Workers' Education? Seventh Annual Conference of Teachers in Workers' Education. Katonah, N. Y.: Brookwood, 1930, 19-20.

A dismal report of Philadelphia Labor College's attempt to interest organized labor in workers' education classes.

553. Sheffield, Alfred D. "Study Groups Under Union Direction." The Place of Workers' Education in the Labor Movement. Fifth Annual Conference of Teachers in Workers' Education. Katonah, N. Y.: Brookwood, 1928, 61-63.

An examination of the questions of 'control' of the workers' education movement by the labor movement.

554. Starr, Mark. "Education, the Eye Opener." Brookwood, Labor's Own School. Katonah, N. Y.: Brookwood, 1936, 17-18.

A description of how the garment workers support Brookwood and its philosophy, and how the labor college has, in turn, aided the union.

555. "State and Local Activity." American Labor Yearbook. VI. New York: Rand School of Social Science, 1925, 213-214.

A brief listing of the workers' education activities carried on by the state and local federations of labor.

556. Tippett, Tom. "Taylorsville, Illinois." Justice. (July 17, 1925), 10.
     An account of the educational activities of one Mine Workers' district in Illinois.

557. _____. "Will Workers Study?" New Republic. LIV (February 22, 1928), 46-47.
     An examination of the educational achievements of the Mine Workers in Sub District 5.

558. _____. "Workers' Education Among Illinois Miners." American Federationist, XXXIII (September, 1926), 1055-1059.
     An account of the educational work carried on in Sub District 5 of the United Mine Workers.

559. Trowbridge, Lydia. "Education--An Adventure." Justice. (October 17, 1924), 4.
     A discussion of the need and value of workers' education and how the unions have taken hold of it.

560. Troxell, John. "Workers' Education in Union Halls." Survey. LX (June 1, 1928), 281-282, 311-312.
     A description of the educational work of the Department of Workers' Education of the Pennsylvania Federation of Labor from 1923-1928.

561. "Two Years Work of the Educational Department." Justice. (April 18, 1924), 10.
     A detailed two year history of the character and activities of the Garment Workers education department.

562. "United Mine Workers." American Labor Yearbook. VII. New York: Rand School of Social Science, 1926, 309-310.
     A report of the educational work done in Clearfield, Pennsylvania in the soft coal region by the United Mine Workers.

563. United Mine Workers. American Labor Yearbook. VIII. New York: Rand School of Social Science, 1927, 164-165.
     A description of the educational activities of the United Mine Workers in Illinois and Pennsylvania during 1926-1927.

564. Weinzweig, Max. "Amalgamated Clothing Workers' Classes." Proceedings of the Second National Conference on Workers' Education in the United States. New York: Workers' Education Bureau, 1922, 37-45.
     A report of the activities of the union's education department.

565. Wolfson, Theresa. "Education During a Strike." Survey. XLVIII (August 15, 1922), 626.

A brief description of the health education program
undertaken by the Garment Workers in 1921. The purpose
of the educational endeavor was to uphold the workers
morale during the strike.

566. _____. "Schools the Miners Keep." Survey. LVI (June 1,
1926), 308-310, 332.
A description of the educational program established
by Sub-District 5 of the United Mine Workers.

567. _____. "Tom Tippett and the School He Keeps." American Labor World. XXVII (July, 1926), 10-13.
A description of a labor school for sub-District 5 of
the UMWA and the man who runs the educational program.

568. "Workers' Education: An Appeal to Trade Unionists." Justice. (July 3, 1925), 10; (July 10, 1925), 10.
An editorial urging trade unionists to be interested in
workers' education and denoting the difference between
such education and propaganda.

569. "Workers' Education and Training: Research Work of a Milwaukee Workers' School." Monthly Labor Review. XXIV
(April, 1927), 711-712.
A report of a class of eighteen building trade union
members in the Milwaukee Workers' College.

Affiliated Schools for Workers in Industry

570. "Academic Complications at Bryn Mawr College." School and
Society. XLI (June 8, 1935), 778.
A short examination of the controversy which led to
the Summer School for Women Workers in Industry leaving
the Bryn Mawr campus.

571. "Address by M. Carey Thomas." Bryn Mawr Alumnae Bulletin. II (October, 1922), 7-11.
An address given by the former president of the college to the incoming women workers attending the Bryn
Mawr Summer School. The speech outlines the historical
development of the school as well as the reasons why the
educational program was needed.

572. "The Affiliated Schools." Journal of Adult Education. IX
(October, 1937), 466-467.
An activity report of the educational programs conduct-
ed by the Affiliated Schools.

573. "Affiliated Schools for Workers." Journal of Adult Education.
V (October, 1933), 453.
An activity report of the schools.

574. "Affiliated Schools for Workers." Journal of Adult Education. VI (February, 1934), 98-99.
    An activity report of the schools.

575. "Affiliated Schools for Workers." Journal of Adult Education. VII (June, 1935), 337.
    An activity report of the schools.

576. "Affiliated Summer Schools." American Labor Yearbook. XII. New York: Rand School of Social Science, 1931, 231-232.
    A report of the activities of the joint committee which represented the three affiliated summer schools.

577. "Affiliated Summer Schools for Women Workers in Industry." American Labor Yearbook. XIII. New York: Rand School of Social Science, 1932, 181-182.
    A report of the scope of the work undertaken by the Affiliated Schools' joint committee and the education department.

578. "The Art Workshop." Journal of Adult Education. IV (October, 1932), 463.
    An activity report of the art workshop in New York City.

579. "The Art Workshop, New York." Journal of Adult Education. III (October, 1931), 484-485.
    An activity report of the art workshop.

580. "At Bryn Mawr College." School and Society. XLI (June 8, 1935), 778-779.
    A statement by an investigating committee of alumnae of Bryn Mawr, explaining the real reasons for the summer school's omission from the campus for the 1935 summer.

581. Bancroft, Gertrude and Bettina Linn. "An Open Letter on Workers' Education." Bryn Mawr Alumnae Bulletin. XV (May, 1935), 5-8.
    An open letter concerning the removal of the Summer School for Women Workers from the campus. The letter calls for the return of the summer school and the return of workers' education to the college's pioneering curriculum.

582. "Barnard Summer School." Journal of Adult Education. I (February, 1929), 89-90.
    A short descriptive examination of the Barnard Summer School for Women Workers in Industry during the 1928 summer session.

583. "Barnard Summer School." American Labor Yearbook. XII. New York: Rand School of Social Science, 1931, 234.

A brief summary of how Barnard's non-resident summer school differed from Bryn Mawr's.

584. "Barnard Summer School." American Labor Yearbook. XIII.
New York: Rand School of Social Science, 1932, 183.
A report of the curtailment of the 1931 summer school
due to the difficulty in raising scholarships.

585. "Barnard Summer School for Industrial Workers." School and
Society. XXV (June 11, 1927), 687.
An announcement of the first Barnard Summer School
for Women Workers in Industry.

586. "Barnard Summer School." Journal of Adult Education. II
(October, 1930), 470.
An activity report of Barnard Summer School.

587. Bonner, Marion. "Behind the Southern Textile Strikes." The
Nation. CXIX (October 2, 1929), 351-352.
An article which examines the role played by the
Southern Summer School in strike situations, in particular
and more generally what the school is doing to fight
against economic slavery in the south.

588. Bruere, Robert W. "Will It Happen?" Survey. LII (June 15,
1924), 358.
An announcement and explanation of the Florence Sims
Scholarships at Wisconsin for working women.

589. "Bryn Mawr Summer School." Journal of Adult Education. I
(February, 1929), 88-89.
A short descriptive examination of the Summer School
for Women Workers in Industry during the 1928 season.

590. "Bryn Mawr Summer School." Journal of Adult Education. I
(October, 1929), 456.
A report of the activities of the Bryn Mawr Summer
School for Women Workers in Industry.

591. "The Bryn Mawr Summer School of 1931." Journal of Adult
Education. III (October, 1931), 476-477.
An activity report of the Bryn Mawr Summer School
for Women Workers in Industry.

592. "Bryn Mawr Summer School College Weekend." Journal of
Adult Education. V (June, 1933), 326.
A description of the recruitment endeavors of the Summer School through the use of weekend conferences which
serve as an orientation program.

593. "Bryn Mawr Summer School." New Republic. LXXXIII (June
12, 1935), 115.
A critical statement against Bryn Mawr College for

its decision to remove the Summer School for Women
Workers in Industry from the campus.

594. "Bryn Mawr Summer School." Journal of Adult Education.
VIII (April, 1936), 211.
An activity report of the summer school.

595. "Bryn Mawr." Journal of Adult Education. X (October,
1938), 460.
An activity report of the summer school.

596. "Bryn Mawr." Journal of Adult Education. XI (April, 1939),
216.
A report of the summer school's leaving the Bryn
Mawr campus and moving to Hudson Shore.

597. "Bryn Mawr Summer School." American Labor Yearbook.
XII. New York: Rand School of Social Science, 1931,
232-233.
A description of the student body, purposes, methods
of instruction and curriculum of the 1930 summer school.

598. "Bryn Mawr Summer School." American Labor Yearbook.
XIII. New York: Rand School of Social Science, 1932,
183.
A report of the activities of the 1931 summer school.

599. "Bryn Mawr Summer School." Survey. LXXI (August, 1935),
239-240.
An explanation of the reasons why the 1935 session of
the Bryn Mawr Summer School was not held on the Bryn
Mawr campus.

600. "Bryn Mawr Summer School for Women Workers." School and
Society. XXI (May 9, 1925), 555.
An activity report of the summer school.

601. "Bryn Mawr Summer School for Women Workers." School and
Society. XXII (September 19, 1925), 360-361.
An activity report of the summer school.

602. "Bryn Mawr School for Women Workers in Industry." School
and Society. XLI (June 22, 1935), 828-829.
A castigation of Bryn Mawr for its policy of removing
the summer school for women workers from its campus.

603. "Bryn Mawr School for Working Women." New Republic.
XXVI (May 18, 1921), 337-338.
A brief preliminary account of the Bryn Mawr Summer
School describing organization, curriculum, and finances.

604. Carter, Jean. "The Affiliated Schools for Workers." Journal
of Adult Education. VII (June, 1935), 463-465.

A report of the activities of the various member summer schools of the Affiliated Schools for Workers. Included was a report of the Bryn Mawr School the year it was not held at Bryn Mawr.

605.   _____. "Bryn Mawr Summer School." Journal of Adult Education. VIII (October, 1936), 500-501.
An activity report of the summer school.

606.   _____. "The Bryn Mawr Summer School." The Affiliated Schools Scrapbook. I (March, 1937), 4-7.
A description of the summer school with special attention given to the 1936 school.

607.   _____. "Experimenting in Workers' Education." Progressive Education. IX (May, 1932), 372-374.
A discussion of the Bryn Mawr Summer School which emphasizes the grouping of the students and teaching procedures in class.

608.   _____. "For Office Workers." Journal of Adult Education. VIII (January, 1936), 79-82.
A descriptive analysis of the student body and curriculum of the Summer School for Office Workers.

609.   _____. "From Bryn Mawr to Hudson Shore." Bryn Mawr Alumnae Bulletin. XIX (March, 1939), 13-14.
An article describing the move of the Bryn Mawr Summer School for Women Workers in Industry to its new home known as the Hudson Shore Labor School. The advantages of this move for providing wider services for women workers are noted.

610.   _____. "Office Workers Seek Solutions." American Teacher. XX (October, 1935), 14-15.
A description of the third Summer School for Office Workers.

611.   _____. "Schools for Workers Survive." Nation. CXL (May 22, 1935), 602.
A short letter which announces that the summer schools are alive and well even though they have had a series of setbacks.

612.   _____. "Workers' Education in 1934." Woman's Press. XXVIII (June, 1934), 295.
A discussion of the plans for the upcoming 1934 summer schools.

613.   _____ and Eleanor Coit. "The Affiliated Schools Establish Experimental Projects." Journal of Adult Education. VI (October, 1934), 506-509.
With the assistance of federal funds the schools were

able to establish several experimental projects. Most of
the extra work was in the form of record keeping, teacher
training, and schools for the unemployed.

614. Chadwick-Collins, Caroline. "The Bryn Mawr Summer
School, 1922." Bryn Mawr Alumnae Bulletin. II (June,
1922), 19-20.
A report of the plans for the 1922 Summer School for
Women Workers in Industry at Bryn Mawr.

615. Coit, Eleanor. "The Affiliated Schools for Workers." Brookwood, Labor's Own School. Katonah, N.Y.: Brookwood,
1936, 25-26.
A description of the work of the Affiliated Schools.

616. _____. "The Affiliated Schools for Workers." Progressive
Education. XI (April-May, 1934), 247-250.
An examination of the dual role of the Affiliated
Schools as a resource center to member schools and as
an agency for conducting workers' education classes
throughout the country.

617. _____. "After the Summer Schools: Some Fruits of Workers' Education." Journal of the American Association of
University Women. XXVII (January, 1934), 97-99.
An account of some of the activities undertaken by
graduates of the resident worker summer schools when
they returned to their own communities.

618. _____. "Education Department, Affiliated Summer
Schools." What Next in Workers' Education? Seventh
Annual Conference of Teachers in Workers' Education,
Katonah, N.Y.: Brookwood, 1930, 17-19.
An analysis of the reasons for beginning an education
department for the Affiliated Summer Schools and a short
synopsis of its activities.

619. _____. "Office Workers School." Journal of Adult Education. VII (October, 1936), 503-504.
An activity report of the Office Workers' summer
school.

620. _____. "Six Little Schools at Bryn Mawr." American
Teacher. XV (February, 1931), 18-22.
An analysis of an experiment at Bryn Mawr Summer
School in which the one hundred and one students were di-
vided into six different study groups according to their
academic ability.

621. _____. "Summer School Experiences of 1929." Woman's
Press. XXIII (December, 1929), 842-844.
A discussion of the experiences of the four summer
schools connected with the Affiliated Schools: Bryn Mawr,

Barnard, Wisconsin, and the Southern Summer School.

622. _____. "Summer Schools in the Winter Time." American
Federationist. XL (June, 1933), 586-589.
An examination of the ripple effect of the summer
school experience for worker-students. The author discusses the educational work done by graduates of the
schools when they return to their local communities.

623. _____. "Workers' Education and the Community." American Teacher. XVII (December, 1932), 6-7.
A report of how several former students from the
Bryn Mawr Summer School have used their experience
gained at the school upon their return to places of employment and local unions.

624. _____ and Andria Hourwich. "The Affiliated Schools for
Workers." World Association for Adult Education Bulletin. VIII (February, 1937), 1-13.
An examination of the coordinating efforts of the Affiliated Schools in relationship to the four schools connected with it.

625. _____ and _____. "Workers' Education and the Affiliated Schools." American Federationist. XLIV (March,
1937), 270-275.
An examination of the curriculum of the various summer schools associated with the Affiliated Schools.

626. "College Extension." American Labor Yearbook. X. New
York: Rand School of Social Science, 1929, 221-222.
A general descriptive examination of the summer work
done by Bryn Mawr, Barnard, and the Southern Summer
School.

627. Cook, Cara. "Bryn Mawr Turns Out Better Trade Unionist."
The Locomotive Engineers Journal. LIX (November,
1925), 829.
A description of the Bryn Mawr Summer School for
Working Women in its fifth year of operation.

628. Cummings, Frances. "Summer School for Office Workers."
Independent Women. XIII (May, 1934), 152.
An announcement of the second summer school for Of-
fice Workers to be held at Oberlin College.

629. Davenport, Frederick M. "The Educational Movement Among
American Workers." Outlook. CXXXI (June 28, 1922),
375-378.
After a scathing criticism of universal public education in America, the author lauds the attempts of American workers to organize various education enterprises to
meet their educational needs. The most outstanding ex-

ample cited is the Bryn Mawr Summer School.

630. Deardorff, Neva. "Bryn Mawr Summer School." Proceedings of the Second National Conference on Workers' Education in the United States. New York: Workers Education Bureau, 1922, 78-79.

A report of the activities of the Bryn Mawr Summer School in its first year of operation.

631. "Depression and a Workers' School." Survey. LXVI (September 15, 1931), 558.

An announcement of the closing of the Vineyard School because of the inability to raise funds during the depression.

632. Duffy, John F., Jr. "The Pacific Coast School for Workers." Railway Clerk. XXXVII (October, 1938), 433-434, 452-453.

A description of the educational activities and curriculum of one of the Affiliated Schools for Workers conducted on the West Coast.

633. Education that Changes Lives. (New York: Affiliated Schools for Workers, Inc.) n.d., n.p.

An examination of the five schools connected with the Affiliated Schools, Bryn Mawr, Barnard, Wisconsin, Vineyard Shore and the Southern Summer School.

634. "The Experiment of the Summer School." Bryn Mawr Alumnae Bulletin. V (October, 1925), 12-15.

A description of the summer school which explains why every year the school is different with a new faculty and new students.

634a. "For White Collar Workers." Journal of Adult Education. XI (October, 1939), 459-460.

An activity report of the Summer School for White Collar Workers.

635. Fox, Genevieve M. "Workers' Education at Bryn Mawr." New Republic. XXXI (August 16, 1922), 327-328.

A description of the second year of the Bryn Mawr Summer School with special attention given to the types of students and the problems which the faculty of the school encountered with such diverse students.

636. Friedmann, Ernestine. "Barnard Summer School." What Next in Workers' Education? Seventh Annual Conference of Teachers in Workers' Education. Katonah, N.Y.: Brookwood, 1930, 17.

An activity report of the Barnard Summer School for Women Workers in Industry.

637. _____. "The Barnard Summer School for Women Workers in Industry." American Federationist. XXXIV (November, 1927), 1376-1380. Also in Workers' Education. V (November, 1927), 8-12.

    The director of the non-residential summer school at Barnard details the activity of the school program for 1927.

638. _____. "Our City Has Its Own Summer School for Workers." American Federationist. XXXVII (November, 1930), 1395-1396. Also in Workers' Education. VIII (December, 1930), 15-16.

    A short overview of the fourth annual summer school held at Barnard College.

639. _____. "Some Unique Features of the 1928 Barnard Summer School." American Federationist. XXXV (December, 1928), 1503-1505. Also in Workers' Education. VI (December, 1928), 9-11.

    An examination of the attempts at the Barnard School to experiment with several different educational techniques in order to provide the diverse student body with an optimum educational experience.

640. _____. "The Summer School for Women Workers at Bryn Mawr " The Smith Alumnae Quarterly. XIII (February, 1922), 136-140.

    A detailed description of the first summer school for women workers held at Bryn Mawr. The article examines the organization and philosophy of the school.

641. "From Factory to Campus." Survey. LVIII (May 15, 1927), 211-212.

    An examination of the decision of a young woman worker to go to college after graduating from Bryn Mawr Summer School for Women Workers in Industry.

642. Funk, Bertha. "My Eight Weeks at Bryn Mawr." Life and Labor. XI (October, 1921), 247-250.

    A student describes her experiences at the first Bryn Mawr Summer School for Women Workers in Industry.

643. "The Future of the Summer School." Bryn Mawr Alumnae Bulletin. I (November, 1921), 17-18.

    A report of the meetings of the joint administrative council of the Bryn Mawr Summer School and its deliberations on the future prospects of the school.

644. "Girls Look at Their Jobs." Survey. LXIX (March 15, 1933), 119.

    A description of the curriculum, finances and general purposes of the Vineyard Shore School.

645. Goldmark, Josephine. "Report of the Summer School Commit-

tee." Bryn Mawr Alumnae Bulletin. V (April, 1925), 14.
A report of the activities of the college alumnae committee in the successful functioning of the Bryn Mawr Summer School for Women Workers in Industry.

646. Gosling, Laura F. "A Wisconsin Adventure." Survey. LIII
(February 15, 1925), 596-597.
A brief description of the first Wisconsin Summer
School for Women Workers in Industry. The author com-
pares and contrasts Wisconsin's experience with Bryn
Mawr's.

647. Grafton, Samuel. "The Red Scare: A Case History." Nation. CXL (April, 1935), 476-478.
An examination of an attack upon the Affiliated School
and specifically on one of its affiliates for being communist dominated.

648. Griffiths, Mary. "We Teach in Workers' Schools." Woman's
Press. XXXIX (February, 1935), 82-83.
A discussion by an experienced teacher of the meth-
ods used in the resident summer schools for workers.

649. Guynn, Helen. "The Summer School as Seen by a Student."
Bryn Mawr Alumnae Bulletin. I (October, 1921), 10-11.
An examination by a student attending the summer
school of the role Bryn Mawr can play in the workers'
education movement.

650. Haber, William. "Industrial Workers at Wisconsin University." American Federationist. XXXVIII (March, 1931),
332-336. Also in Workers' Education. IX (March, 1931),
1-5.
An historical examination of the Wisconsin Summer
School for Workers in Industry.

651. Hengeveld, Hannah. "What Do They Get Out of It?" Survey.
LVIII (July 15, 1927), 414.
A first-hand account of what the Wisconsin Summer
School meant in the development of a young worker.

652. Herr, Mary E. "Sowing Syntax on Fertile Ground." Bryn
Mawr Alumnae Bulletin. II (October, 1922), 15-16.
A description of a class in English composition and
the expectations that the students had to learn how to
write.

653. Herstein, Lillian. "The Significance of the Southern Summer
School for Women Workers in the Workers' Education
Movement." American Teacher. XV (January, 1931),
19-22.
A discussion of the Southern School and its significance
to the South and to the entire workers' education movement.

654. Hewes, Amy. "Bryn Mawr Summer School." American Federationist. XXXII (August, 1925), 654-658.
A description of the program, students, and accomplishments of the Bryn Mawr Summer School.

655. _____. "New Wine in Old Bottles." Survey. XLVII (December 3, 1921), 372-373.
A description of the psychology of the Bryn Mawr Summer School student body and their classroom experiences.

656. _____. "The Savings of Women Workers." American Federationist. XXXIV (January, 1927), 72-77.
A study of the Bryn Mawr Summer School student body of 1926 to determine their savings capacity.

657. _____. "Women Wage Earners and the N. R. A." American Federationist. XLII (February, 1935), 155-164.
A presentation of a workers' study project conducted by a class at Bryn Mawr Summer School. The class analyzed the effect of the N. R. A. on their own hours and wages.

658. _____. "Women Workers in the Third Year of the Depression." Women's Bureau Bulletin #103. Washington, D. C.: U. S. Department of Labor, 1933, 13 pp. Also in condensed form in Monthly Labor Review. XXXVII (August, 1933), 303-305.
An examination of the employment status of one hundred and nine women who attended the Bryn Mawr Summer School in 1932.

659. Hill, Helen D. "The Bryn Mawr Summer School Survey." Workers' Education. IV (November, 1926), 41-42.
A proposed study to examine the background of the student body of the Summer School and to determine what activities they undertake as graduates of the school.

660. _____. The Effect of the Bryn Mawr Summer School as Measured in the Activities of Its Students. New York: American Association for Adult Education, 1929. 133 pp.
An analysis of the graduates of the Bryn Mawr Summer School to determine the effects of the school on its student body.

661. _____. "Why Is the Summer School." Bryn Mawr Alumnae Bulletin. IV (June, 1924), 5-7.
A discussion of why the summer school exists and where it fits into the workers' education movement.

662. _____ (Miller), et al. "Open Letters About the Summer School." Bryn Mawr Alumnae Bulletin. XV (May, 1935), 4.
A call by alumnae to set forth the facts concerning

why the Summer School for Women Workers' association
with Bryn Mawr College was being dissolved.

663. Hill, Marie P. "The Affiliated Schools for Workers." Smith
     Alumnae Quarterly. XXVI (February, 1935), 141-143.
          An examination of the role of Eleanor Coit, director
     of the Affiliated Schools for Workers.

664. Hourwich, Andria, Taylor. "Back in Her Home Town: The
     Bryn Mawr Summer School Student in Her Community."
     Woman's Press. XXVII (August, 1932), 484-485.
          A brief examination of a student's activities in her
     hometown after graduating from the Bryn Mawr Summer
     School.

665. "Hudson Shore Labor School." Journal of Adult Education.
     XI (October, 1939), 457-458.
          A description of the transplanting of the Bryn Mawr
     Summer School to West Park, New York and the renam-
     ing of the school "The Hudson Shore Labor School." Also
     discussed were policy matters concerning the all female
     student body.

666. Humphrey, Haroldine. "The Play Spirit in Acting." Bryn
     Mawr Alumnae Bulletin. II (October, 1922), 16-17.
          An examination of the role of drama at the Bryn
     Mawr Summer School.

667. "Institute for Office Workers." Journal of Adult Education.
     V (June, 1933), 328.
          A description of a new summer school offered through
     the Affiliated Schools. Although the school was planned
     to be like the Bryn Mawr Summer School, the Institute for
     Office Workers was somewhat curtailed by the lack of
     funds.

668. Jenson, Elsie. "A School for Women Workers in Industry in
     the South." School and Society. XXXVI (October 8,
     1932), 473-475.
          An account of the author's experiences at the South-
     ern Summer School. Detailed information concerning
     classes at the school is presented.

669. Kaiser, Clara A. "Learning to Make History." Social Work
     Today. V (May, 1938), 17-19.
          A brief account of the Summer School for Office
     Workers.

670. Kingsbury, Susan. "Workers at School." Survey. LIII
     (February 15, 1925), 600-603.
          An examination of the Bryn Mawr Summer School's
     effect on former students after they returned to their
     hometowns.

671. Kohn, Lucille. "Schools for Workers." School Life. XIX
     (May, 1934), 190-191.
          A discussion of the role of the Affiliated Schools in
     workers' education under the New Deal.

672. Leonard (McClaren), Louise. "New Summer School for Wom-
     en Workers." American Federationist. XXXIV (Decem-
     ber, 1927), 1487-1490. Also in Workers' Education. V
     (December, 1927), 9-12.
          A discussion of the administration of the first summer
     school for women workers in the South held at Sweet Briar
     Cliff College in Virginia during the summer of 1927.

673. _____. "A School in the Old South." Labor Age. XVII
     (December, 1928), 22-23.
          A description and explanation of the summer school
     for women workers in the South after its second year of
     operation.

674. _____. "The South Begins Workers' Education." American
     Federationist. XXXV (November, 1928), 1381-1389. Also
     in Workers' Education. IV (November, 1928), 1-6.
          An examination of the Southern Summer School for the
     first two years of its operation.

675. _____. "Southern Summer School." Journal of Adult Edu-
     cation. IV (October, 1932), 452-454.
          A description of the Southern Summer School for 1932
     and an analysis of the possible benefits derived from the
     classes.

676. _____. "Southern Summer School." Journal of Adult Edu-
     cation. VIII (October, 1936), 502-503.
          An activity report of the tenth annual summer school
     with a description of the curriculum and student body.

677. _____. "Southern Summer School for Women Workers in
     Industry." The Place of Workers' Education in the Labor
     Movement. Fifth Annual Conference of Teachers in Work-
     ers' Education. Katonah, N.Y.: Brookwood, 1928, 53-
     54.

678. _____. "South's Problems Faced at Workers' Own School."
     Journal of Electrical Workers and Operators. XXVIII (May,
     1929), 233, 277.
          A general description of the type of workers' education
     conducted by the Southern Summer School for Women Work-
     ers in Industry.

679. _____. "Summer Schools for Workers in Industry." Pro-
     gressive Education. IX (November, 1932), 503-507.
          A description of the four summer schools connected
     with the Affiliated Schools.

680. _____. "Workers' Education in the South." American
       Teacher. XIII (November, 1928), 8-10.
       A discussion of the students, curriculum, teachers,
       and administration of the Southern Summer School.

681. _____. "Workers' Education in the South." Vassar Quar-
       terly. XX (May, 1935), 100-105.
       An examination of the role of the Southern Summer
       School.

682. _____. "A Workers' School and Organized Labor." Amer-
       ican Teacher. XIV (December, 1929), 10-13.
       A description of the aims, curriculum and student
       body of the Southern Summer School.

683. Lockwood, Helen D. "The Bryn Mawr Summer School for
       Women Workers." Vassar Quarterly. VI (November,
       1921), 319-325.
       An examination of the Bryn Mawr Summer School with
       special attention given to the philosophy behind this experi-
       ment and some of the general outcomes of the first sum-
       mer session.

684. Lumpkin, Grace. "For the South's New Workers." Social
       Work Today. V (May, 1938), 18-20.
       A descriptive narrative of the Southern Summer School
       for women workers.

685. MacDonald, Lois. "A New School in the Old South." Survey.
       LIX (October 15, 1927), 96-97.
       A statistical description of the student body of the
       first Southern Summer School.

686. _____. "Southern Labor Looks at Itself." Survey. LXI
       (December 15, 1928), 358-360.
       A brief discussion of the significance of the Southern
       Summer School.

687. _____. "Southern Summer School for Women Workers."
       What Next in Workers' Education? Seventh Annual Confer-
       ence of Teachers in Workers' Education. Katonah, N.Y.:
       Brookwood, 1930, 35-39.
       An activity report of the Southern Summer School.

688. _____ and Louise (McLaren) Leonard. "The Southern Sum-
       mer School." The Affiliated Schools Scrapbook. I (March,
       1937), 8-11.
       An examination of the special educational needs of
       Southern workers and how the summer school attempts to
       meet those needs.

689. Miller, Spencer, Jr. "Summer Schools for Workers." Amer-
       ican Federationist. XXXII (July, 1925), 569-571.

A discussion of several topics the author would like
to see considered in the 1925 summer sessions.

690. _____. "Workers' Summer School--1927." American Federationist. XXXIV (October, 1927), 1211-1217. Also in
Workers Education. V (October, 1927), 1-6.
A discussion of the various summer schools conducted
during 1927. In addition to the Affiliated Schools, the author cites Brookwood, Denver, and a Labor Chautauqua
held in Passaic, New Jersey.

691. Mitchell, Broadus. "The Working Women's Classes at Bryn
Mawr College." Educational Review. LXVIII (October,
1924), 126-128.
A report of the achievements and programs of the
Bryn Mawr Summer School in its fourth year of operation.

692. "A New Plan of Organization of the Summer School." Bryn
Mawr Alumnae Bulletin. VI (April, 1926), 6-7.
A description of the plan for administrative reorgani-
zation of the Bryn Mawr Summer School for Women Workers.

693. "Occidental College Summer School for Workers." School and
Society. XXXIX (May 19, 1934), 642.
A description of a summer school for workers jointly
sponsored by the California Association of Adult Education,
the Extension Division of the University of California, the
California State Federation of Labor, and the YWCA in
Los Angeles.

694. "Occidental School for Workers." Journal of Adult Education.
V (June, 1933), 326-327.
A descriptive report of a western summer school for
workers.

695. Otley, Elizabeth Lewis. "Impressions of the Summer School."
Bryn Mawr Alumnae Bulletin. III (October, 1923), 17-18.
A former student at Bryn Mawr College evaluates the
Summer School for Women Workers in Industry.

696. Palmer, Gladys. Industrial Experience of Women Workers at the
Summer Schools, 1928-1930. U.S. Women's Bureau Bulletin
#89. Washington, D.C.: U.S. Department of Labor, 1931, 62 p.
A study of the background experience of the students at
the Bryn Mawr Summer School. The purpose of the study is
to assist the teachers to better understand the educational
needs of the students.

697. Pancoast, Elinor. "Social Education in an Adult Summer School."
Social Education. II (November, 1938), 536-640.
An examination of the Summer School for Workers as an
experiment in education. Topics considered in the article include teaching methods, recreation, and curriculum.

698. _____. "Summer School for Office Workers." American Federationist. XLIII (October, 1936), 1052-1055.
A discussion of how this summer school can interest an unorganized group of workers in the labor movement.

699. Park, Marion Edwards. "President Park Replies." Bryn Mawr Alumnae Bulletin, XV (May, 1935), 5.
A letter to the alumnae of Bryn Mawr College alluding to the misunderstanding between the college and the summer school, and indicating that conferences between the two parties were to be held in order to find a "common basis of agreement for a future relationship."

700. _____. "The Relation of the College to the Bryn Mawr Summer School." Bryn Mawr Alumnae Bulletin. XV (April, 1935), 13-14.
A statement explaining why the Board of Directors of the Bryn Mawr College suggested that the Summer School for Women Workers not be held on the campus in 1935.

701. _____. "Summer School." Bryn Mawr Alumnae Bulletin. XVI (November, 1936), 11-13.
A report of the 1936 Bryn Mawr Summer School for Women Workers by the president of Bryn Mawr College.

702. Pell, Orlie. "Summer School for Office Workers--Why?" Journal of Electrical Workers and Operators. XXXV (April, 1936), 179-180.
An examination of the reasons why white collar workers who usually have a minimum of a high school education still need to be students of workers' education.

703. _____. "A Workers' School for the Office Worker." American Federationist. XLII (June, 1935), 622-624.
A description of the workers' education program held for Office Workers at Oberlin College.

704. Perlman, Selig and Ernest E. Schwarztrauber. "Wisconsin Summer School for Workers in Industry." American Federationist. XL (March, 1933), 272-278. Also in International Molders Journal. LXIX (April, 1933), 200-204.
An historical examination of the Wisconsin Summer School.

705. "Recommendations of Bryn Mawr Students." Woman's Press, XVIII (October, 1924), 727-728.
A list of recommendations composed at the Bryn Mawr Summer School by the women from the YWCA. These recommendations transmitted to the local industrial departments of the YWCA would aid women who would be going to Bryn Mawr the following summer.

706. "Removal of the Summer School for Women Workers in Indus-

try from Bryn Mawr College." New Republic. LXXXIII
(June 12, 1935), 115.
An examination of the underlying reasons why the
Bryn Mawr Summer School would not be holding its classes
on the Bryn Mawr campus.

707. "The Reorganized Summer School Returns to the Campus."
Bryn Mawr Alumnae Bulletin. XVI (February, 1936), 6-
7.
A report of the return of the Summer School for Wom-
en Workers to the Bryn Mawr campus after a one year's
absence.

708. Saunders, Louise Brownell. "Four Weeks' Experience in the
Bryn Mawr Summer School for Labor." Bryn Mawr Alumnae Bulletin. I (November, 1921), 13-16.
A description of the Summer School from the point of
view of the English teachers at the school. The article
examines the difficulties encountered in teaching workers
who had industrial experience on one hand and who had
difficulty in reading on the other.

709. Saxton, Martha P. "Spencer Miller, Jr. on the Summer
School." Bryn Mawr Alumnae Bulletin. III (February,
1923), 5-8.
A report of an interview with Spencer Miller, Jr.,
Secretary of the WEB on the value of the Bryn Mawr Sum-
mer School.

710. Schneider, Florence H. Patterns of Workers' Education:
The Study of the Bryn Mawr Summer School. Washington,
D.C.: American Council on Public Affairs, 1941, 158 pp.
A documented examination of the development of the
Bryn Mawr Summer School.

711. "School for Office Workers." Journal of Adult Education.
VII (January, 1935), 100.
An activity report of the Summer School for Office
Workers.

712. "The School for Workers in Industry at the University of Wisconsin." School and Society. XL (November 17, 1934),
653-654.
A short examination of the 1933-1934 academic year
at the School for Workers.

713. "Schools for Women Workers in Industry." Bryn Mawr
Alumnae Bulletin. IX (December, 1929), 2-10.
A discussion of the beginning of the Bryn Mawr Summer School and the growing need for worker-graduates of
the school to have a place to further their education. As
a result, the Vineyard Shore School developed. This article describes the location and education program of
Vineyard Shore.

714. Schwarztrauber, Ernest E. "A Workers' Summer School."
American Teacher. XV (November, 1930), 11-15.
An appraisal of the activities of the Workers' Summer
School at the University of Wisconsin.

715. Shoemaker, Alice. "The Early Years of the School for Workers." School for Workers: Thirty-Fifth Anniversary Papers. Madison: University of Wisconsin School for Workers, 1960, 32-35.
An historical examination of the founders of the Wisconsin Summer School for Women Workers.

716. _____. "Wellesley in Wisconsin." Wellesley Magazine.
XIX (April, 1935), 301-303.
A description of the Wisconsin School for Workers and
the role Wellesley played in the education of its director,
Alice Shoemaker.

717. _____. "The Wisconsin School." The Affiliated Schools
Scrapbook. I (March, 1937), 12-15.
A description of the curriculum, goals and student
body of the Wisconsin School for Workers.

718. _____. "The Wisconsin School for Workers in Industry."
Workers' Education. XIV (January, 1937), 29-31.
A description of both the summer school and the Insti-
tute program held at Wisconsin for industrial workers.

719. _____. "The Wisconsin Summer School and the Labor
Movement." American Federationist. XL (October,
1933), 1086-1089.
An analysis of the question, Is labor education of practical use or is it another of the sidelines that have dis-
tracted the labor movement from its main business throughout its history? Based on the experiences of the Wisconsin Summer School for Workers in Industry.

720. _____. "Wisconsin Summer School for Workers in Industry." Journal of Adult Education. IV (October, 1932),
451-452.
An activity report of the Wisconsin Summer School.

721. _____. "Wisconsin University Workers' School." American Federationist. XXXVI (November, 1929), 1380-1383.
Also in Workers' Education. VII (October, 1929), 1196-
1199.
A description of the operation, aims, teaching methods, recreational opportunities, and student body of the
Wisconsin Summer School.

722. _____. "Wisconsin Workers' School." Journal of Adult
Education. VIII (October, 1936), 502.
An activity report of the Wisconsin Summer School.

723. Smith, Ethel M. "Women Workers at the Bryn Mawr Summer School." Railway Clerk. XXVIII (August, 1929), 364-394.

    A report of the activities of the Bryn Mawr Summer School and a description of the student body.

724. Smith, Hilda W. "The Bryn Mawr Summer School of 1923." Workers' Education. I (July-August, 1923), 9-11.

    A descriptive report of the curriculum and student body of the Bryn Mawr Summer School.

725. _____. "The Bryn Mawr Summer School of 1927." American Federationist. XXXIV (October, 1927), 1217-1224. Also in Workers' Education. V (October, 1927), 6-12.

    A progress report of the activities of the Bryn Mawr Summer School in 1927.

726. _____. "The Bryn Mawr Summer School of 1928." American Federationist. XXXV (October, 1928), 1498-1500. Also in Workers' Education. VI (December, 1928), 4-6.

    An activity report of the Bryn Mawr Summer School of 1928.

727. _____. "The Bryn Mawr Summer School of 1929." American Federationist. XXXVI (September, 1929), 1107-1110. Also in Workers' Education. VI (September, 1929), 6-8.

    An activity report of the Bryn Mawr Summer School for 1929.

728. _____. "Bryn Mawr Summer School." School and Society. XXXIV (October 31, 1931), 588-589.

    An activity report of the Bryn Mawr Summer School for 1931.

729. _____. "The Bryn Mawr Summer School. Journal of Adult Education. IV (October, 1932), 449-451.

    An activity report of the Bryn Mawr Summer School for 1932.

730. _____. "Bryn Mawr Summer School and Vineyard Shore." What Next in Workers' Education? Seventh Annual Conference of Teachers in Workers' Education. Katonah, N.Y.: Brookwood, 1930, 16-17.

    An activity report of the Bryn Mawr Summer School and the year round resident school at Vineyard Shore.

731. _____. "Bryn Mawr and the Workers' Education Movement." Bryn Mawr Alumnae Bulletin. XXVIII (April, 1948), 13-16.

    An historical account of how Bryn Mawr, as the first college to open its doors to workers during the summer for study, spawned other resident summer schools and Workers' education programs throughout the country.

732.   _____. "Chapter 13 of the Bryn Mawr Story." Journal of
Adult Education. V (October, 1933), 425-427.
A report of the 1933 session of the Bryn Mawr Sum-
mer School.

733.   _____. "Contributions to Workers' Education Made by President Parks." Supplement to Bryn Mawr Alumnae Bulletin. XXII (July, 1942), 12-13.
An article describing Miss Marion Park's active role
in the Bryn Mawr Summer School for Women Workers while
she was president of the college.

734.   _____. "Eager Feet." Journal of Adult Education. II
(October, 1930), 439-443.
On the tenth anniversary of the Bryn Mawr Summer
School, the author describes its program and achievements
over the previous decade.

735.   _____. "A Free Lance Venture in Workers' Education."
The Place of Workers' Education in the Labor Movement.
Fifth Annual Conference of Teachers in Workers' Educa-
tion.   Katonah, N. Y.: Brookwood, 1928, 48-53.
An activity report of the Bryn Mawr Summer School.

736.   _____. "New Plans for Bryn Mawr Summer School for
Women Workers in Industry." Workers' Education. IV
(August, 1926), 38-39.
An announcement of the new policy to let former stu-
dents of the summer school sit on the board of directors
of the Bryn Mawr Summer School.

737.   _____. "Old Trails for New Explorers: An Experiment
in Workers Education." Survey. LXI (March, 1929), 802-
804.
An examination of an attempt to institute winter study
classes for workers in New York City.   These classes
were jointly sponsored by the Women's Trade Union
League, Bryn Mawr Summer School, Barnard Summer
School, Metropolitan Museum of Art and Columbia University Extension Division.

738.   _____. "Schools for Women Workers in Industry." In
Dorothy Rowden, ed.   Handbook of Adult Education in the
United States.   New York: American Association for Adult
Education, 1934, 306-308.
A short description of the various summer schools
for women workers in industry.

739.   _____. "Schools for Women Workers in Industry." Journal of the American Association of University Women.
XXIII (April, 1930), 115-121.
An examination of the history of the Bryn Mawr summer school.

740. _____ . "The Summer School of 1922." Bryn Mawr Alumnae Bulletin. II (October, 1922), 11-15.
A report of the progress of the school including a comparison of 1922's problems and their solutions with those of the previous year. Also included is an analysis of the student body with a description of their daily life.

741. _____ . "The Summer School of 1923." Bryn Mawr Alumnae Bulletin. III (October, 1923), 5-11.
A detailed description of the activities of the 1923 Bryn Mawr Summer School.

742. _____ . "The Summer School of 1924." Bryn Mawr Alumnae Bulletin. IV (October, 1924), 9-11.
A report of the activities of the Bryn Mawr Summer School for the year 1924.

743. _____ . "The Summer School of 1926." Bryn Mawr Alumnae Bulletin. VI (November, 1926), 5-10.
A description of the activities of the 1926 summer school with special reference to the student body, especially to the Black women who attended the school. Faculty and curriculum are also mentioned.

744. _____ . "The Summer School of 1928: An Experiment in Correlation." Bryn Mawr Alumnae Bulletin. VIII (November, 1928), 4-8.
A descriptive study of the 1928 summer school including an examination of foreign worker-students coming to the school and the difficulty of recruiting students when employment is uncertain. Also included is a discussion of curriculum and the beginning of the Affiliated Schools.

745. _____ . "Summer School for Women Workers in Industry." Woman's Press. XVI (November, 1922), 533-534.
A short description of the Bryn Mawr Summer School.

746. _____ . "Summer School for Workers--1932." Bryn Mawr Alumnae Bulletin. XII (July, 1932), 9-11.
A description of the activities proposed for the Bryn Mawr Summer School of 1932. Also discussed are the other schools, including Office Workers, Southern, Wisconsin, and Barnard.

747. _____ . "Summer Session for Women Workers." Journal of Adult Education. I (October, 1929), 465-466.
A discussion of the problems confronting the planners of the Bryn Mawr Summer School for Women Workers in Industry. Also mentioned is the expansion of that summer school concept.

748. _____ . "This Year's Summer School." Bryn Mawr Alumnae Bulletin. III (April, 1923), 7-12.
A description of the upcoming 1923 Summer School for

Women Workers in Industry, with special emphasis on the administration and curriculum of the school.

749. _____. "Women Workers at Bryn Mawr." Journal of Adult Education. I (February, 1929), 14-22.
A description of the first few days at the Bryn Mawr Summer School and how the students felt about their experiences at the school and at work.

750. _____. Women Workers at the Bryn Mawr Summer School. New York: Affiliated Schools for Workers and American Association for Adult Education, 1929, 346 pp.
A comprehensive and detailed study of the first seven years of the Bryn Mawr Summer School.

751. _____. "Workers' Morning Classes." What Next in Workers' Education? Seventh Annual Conference of Teachers in Workers' Education. Katonah, N.Y.: Brookwood, 1930, 13-15.
A report of an attempt to offer courses for workers during the morning hours in cooperation with Columbia University Extension Department.

752. Snyder, Eleanor M. Job Histories of Women Workers at the Summer Schools, 1931-1934 and 1938. Women's Bureau Bulletin #174. Washington, D.C.: U.S. Department of Labor, 1939, 25 pp.
An examination of the employment history of students who attended the various summer schools for women workers.

753. "Southern Summer School." Journal of Adult Education. I (February, 1929), 90-91.
A descriptive examination of the 1928 summer school.

754. "Southern Summer School." Journal of Adult Education. I (October, 1929), 456.
An activity report of the Southern Summer School for the 1928 session.

755. "Southern Summer School." Journal of Adult Education. II (October, 1930), 469-470.
A report of the activities of the Southern Summer School for 1930.

756. "Southern Summer School." Journal of Adult Education. III (October, 1931), 478.
An activity report of the Southern Summer School for 1931.

757. "Southern Summer School." Journal of Adult Education. V (October, 1933), 454-455.
An activity report of the Southern Summer School.

758. "Southern Summer School." Journal of Adult Education. VII

(January, 1935), 101.
An activity report of the Southern Summer School.

759. "Southern Summer School." Journal of Adult Education. X
(October, 1938), 460.
An activity report of the Southern Summer School.

760. "Southern Summer School for Women Workers in Industry."
American Labor Yearbook. XII. New York: Rand School
of Social Science, 1931, 236-237.
The purpose and controlling body of the school are
described as are the students, faculty, courses and extension work.

761. "Southern Summer School for Women Workers in Industry."
American Labor Yearbook. XIII. New York: Rand
School of Social Science, 1932, 180-181.
A description of the student body, faculty, curriculum
and extension work of the school.

762. Stewart, E. and H. McKelvey. "As Two Undergraduates See
the Summer School." Bryn Mawr Alumnae Bulletin. VII
(November, 1927), 18.
A description of the summer school students by two
undergraduates who served as tutors for the 1927 summer
school.

763. Strauss, Lillian. "Report of the Alumnae Committee of the
Bryn Mawr Summer School. Bryn Mawr Alumnae Bulletin.
III (March, 1923), 23-24.
A report of the student-recruitment and fund-raising
efforts of the Bryn Mawr Alumnae Committee for the Sum-
mer School.

764. "Summer Courses for Workers at the University of Wisconsin.
School and Society. XXVIII (July 28, 1928), 106.
An examination of the funding, student body and cur-
riculum of the University of Wisconsin Summer School for
Workers.

765. "Summer Institute for Office Workers." Journal of Adult Edu-
cation. V (October, 1933), 453-454.
An activity report of the Office Workers Summer
School.

766. "The Summer School Moves to Its Own Campus." Bryn Mawr
Alumnae Bulletin. XIX (February, 1939), 4-5.
A report of the board of directors of the Bryn Mawr
Summer School for women leasing two houses at West
Park, New York for the purpose of moving the summer
school to that location and renaming it the Hudson Shore
Labor School.

767. "Summer School for Office Workers." Journal of Adult Education. X (October, 1938), 458-459.
    An activity report of the Summer School for Office Workers.

768. "The Summer School for Women Workers at Barnard College." School and Society. XXX (July 27, 1929), 115-116.
    A short description of the opening of the third term of the Barnard Summer School.

769. "Summer School for Women Workers in Industry at Bryn Mawr College." Bryn Mawr Alumnae Bulletin. I (March, 1921), 7-9.
    An examination of the proposed school for women workers in industry to be held at the Bryn Mawr campus in the summers. Closely examined is the proposed administration of the school and its curriculum.

770. "Summer School for Workers at the University of Wisconsin." School and Society. XXXV (April 30, 1932), 589-590.
    An announcement of the 1932 summer session of the Wisconsin Summer School.

771. "Summer Schools for Women Workers." Monthly Labor Review. XXV (October, 1927), 76.
    A short summary of the student body statistics of the summer schools of the Affiliated Schools.

772. "Summer Schools for Women Workers in Industry." American Labor Yearbook. XI. New York: Rand School of Social Science, 1930, 191-193.
    A description of the controlling body of the Affiliated Schools followed by reports on each of the summer schools and Vineyard Shore.

773. "Summer Schools for Working Women." School and Society. XXVI (September 10, 1927), 326-327.
    A description of the attempt made by Bryn Mawr Summer School to recruit foreign students.

774. Symonds, Katherine. "The Students of the Summer School." Bryn Mawr Alumnae Bulletin. VI (May, 1926), 10-13.
    A description of the women worker students of the summer school by an undergraduate college student who acted as a tutor for the school.

775. "Three Labor Summer Schools, 1931." Monthly Labor Review. XXXIII (December, 1931), 139-141. Also in Journal of Adult Education. III (October, 1931), 476-478.
    A descriptive examination of Bryn Mawr, Wisconsin, and Southern Summer Schools.

776. Troxell, John. "Next Summer at Wisconsin." Survey. LV

(March 15, 1926), 693-694.
An appraisal of the first session of the Wisconsin Summer School and a listing of minimum goals for the second session.

777. _____. "Wisconsin's Summer School for Working Women." American Federationist. XXXII (October, 1925), 943-945. Also in Workers' Education. IV (November, 1926), 33-35.
The examination and comparison of the Wisconsin Summer School with the Bryn Mawr Summer School.

778. "The Vineyard Shore School." Journal of Adult Education. II (February, 1930), 93-94.
A report of the activities of the Vineyard Shore School for Women Workers in Industry.

779. "The Vineyard Shore School." Journal of Adult Education. III (October, 1931), 478-479.
An activity report of the Vineyard Shore School.

780. "Vineyard Shore School." American Labor Yearbook. XII. New York: Rand School of Social Science, 1931, 235-236.
A report of the purpose and student body of the Vineyard Schore School.

781. "Vineyard Shore School." American Labor Yearbook. XIII. New York: Rand School of Social Science, 1932. 184.
A description of the shortened school year because of financial problems.

782. "Western Summer School for Industrial Workers." Journal of Adult Education. VI (October, 1934), 467.
A report of the curriculum of activities offered to workers and unemployed adult education teachers at the summer school for workers held at Occidental College, Los Angeles, California.

783. "Western Summer School." Journal of Adult Education. VII (October, 1935), 465.
A brief report of the third session of a summer school held at the University of California, Berkeley.

784. "Western Summer School for Workers." Journal of Adult Education. VIII (June, 1936), 284.
A discussion of the make-up of the supervisory committee which plans and administers the workers summer school held on the Berkeley campus.

785. Williamson, Margaret. "White Collars at Oberlin." Woman's Press. XXVIII (January, 1934), 30.
A description of the first summer school for Office Workers held at Oberlin College.

786. [No entry.]

787. "Wisconsin School for Workers." Journal of Adult Education.
     V (October, 1933), 455.
          An activity report of the Wisconsin School for Work-
     ers for the year 1933.

788. "Wisconsin School for Workers." Journal of Adult Education.
     VII (January, 1935), 101.
          An activity report of the Wisconsin School for Workers
     for the year 1934.

789. "Wisconsin School for Workers." Journal of Adult Education.
     X (October, 1938), 459-460.
          An activity report of the Wisconsin School for Work-
     ers for the year 1938.

790. "Wisconsin School for Workers." Journal of Adult Education.
     XI (October, 1939), 458-459.
          An activity report of the Wisconsin School for Work-
     ers for the year 1939.

791. "Wisconsin Summer School." Journal of Adult Education. III
     (October, 1931), 477-478.
          An activity report of the Wisconsin Summer School
     for 1931.

792. "Wisconsin Summer School." American Labor Yearbook. XII.
     New York: Rand School of Social Science, 1931, 234-235.
          A brief description of the 1930 Wisconsin Summer
     School and the special projects the students worked on.

793. "Wisconsin Summer School. American Labor Yearbook. XIII.
     New York: Rand School of Social Science, 1932, 183-184.
          An activity report of the 1931 Wisconsin Summer
     School.

794. "Wisconsin Summer School for Workers." Journal of Adult
     Education. V (June, 1933), 327.
          An activity report of the Wisconsin Summer School.

795. "Women Workers at School." Survey. LXIII (October 13,
     1929), 92-93.
          A very brief account of the activities of the Southern
     Summer School and the Bryn Mawr Summer School.

796. "Women Workers of South Study Mill Problems." The Journal
     of Electrical Workers and Operators. XXVII (June, 1928),
     292.
          An announcement of the upcoming Southern Summer
     School for Working Women to be held at Carolina New
     College, Burnsville, North Carolina. The article de-
     scribes courses offered, plus how this type of workers'

education can help the anti-unionism in the south.

797. "Workers' Education Movement in the South." Monthly Labor
     Review. XXVII (December, 1928), 156-157.
          A summary of the activities of the Southern Summer
     School.

798. "Workers' Education Moves West: First Summer School for
     Workers on Pacific Coast." Survey. LXIX (December,
     1933), 418.
          An examination of the first session of the Pacific
     Coast school and the history of how it developed from
     YWCA industrial clubs.

799. "Workers' Education Under NIRA: Wisconsin Summer School."
     Survey. LXIX (November, 1933), 386.
          A short analysis of Alice Shoemaker's article on the
     Wisconsin Summer School and the labor movement which
     appeared in the October, 1933 issue of the American Fed-
     erationist.

800. "Workers' School at Wisconsin University." Journal of Adult
     Education. II (October, 1930), 468-469.
          An activity report of the Wisconsin Summer School.

Universities

801. Aggers, Eugene E. "The Labor Institute at Rutgers." Amer-
     ican Federationist. XXXVIII (August, 1931), 936-942.
     Also in Monthly Labor Review. XXXIII (October, 1931),
     71-72.
          An examination of the development of the first labor
     institute held on the Rutgers campus in June 1931.   The
     institute was jointly sponsored by the Workers' Education
     Bureau, Rutgers University Extension Division and the
     New Jersey State Federation of Labor.

802. Commons, John R. "Workers' Education and the Universi-
     ties." American Federationist. XXXIV (April, 1927),
     424-426. Also in American Labor World. XXVIII (May,
     1927), 26.
          A suggestion that workers need resident college work
     to supplement their evening study classes.   To meet this
     need the author calls for state universities to provide la-
     bor courses similar to the short sessions they provide for
     farmers.

803. Crystal, George. "Life as Observed." American Federation-
     ist. XXXIX (February, 1932), 190-195.
          An examination of university and union personnel meet-
     ing together at the first Rutgers Labor Institute.

804. Daniels, Roger. "Workers' Education and the University of California, 1921-1941." Labor History. IV (Winter, 1963), 32-50.
    An historical examination of the development of the workers' education program at the University of California.

805. Dwyer, Richard E. "Union University Cooperation: The Education of Organized Labor at the University." Journal of General Education. XXVIII (Summer, 1976), 145-158.
    Through an examination of the Rutgers Labor Institute, the author develops the historical foundation for union-university cooperation.

806. Egbert, J. C. "University Extension for Organized Labor." Proceedings of the Seventh Annual Conference of the National University Extension Association at Lexington, Ky., April 20-22, 1922. 53-60.
    A consideration of the extension opportunities which could be available for organized labor.

807. Eubank, Earle E. "Trade Union and University." Survey. LIV (July 15, 1925), 451-452, 461.
    A description of the two-year-old program at the University of Cincinnati in which extension courses were offered to workers. The program was planned and administered with the joint cooperation between the university and the central labor council.

808. Gray, Wil Lou. "Adventuring in Adult Education." American Federationist. XXXVII (December, 1930), 1518-1522.
    An examination of one southern state which opened its state college during the summer to workers.

809. Hill, Robert T. "Workers' Education." School and Society. XV (February 25, 1922), 225-228.
    A report of a conference of university and college personnel and trade union officials concerning educational experiments for workers in New York State.

810. _____. "Workers' Education in New York." Proceedings of the Eighth Annual Conference of the National Extension Association, at St. Louis, Missouri, April 19-23, 1923. Boston: Wright & Potter, 1923, 51-54.
    A discussion of some of the problems found in university extension work in the field of workers' education in Syracuse, New York.

811. Kerchen, John L. "California Experiment in Workers' Education." American Federationist. XXXIII (August, 1926), 989-993.
    An examination of the cooperation between the extension division of the University of California and the California State Federation of Labor in the establishment of a

Committee on Workers' Education.

812. _____. "The California Plan." American Teacher. XV
(May, 1931), 18-19.
     A short description of the union-university cooperation
effort which helped establish the workers' education program at the University of California.

813. _____. "California Plan Expanded on Pacific Coast."
Journal of Adult Education. VI (October, 1934), 521-525.
     An activity report of the workers' education program
of the University of California.

814. _____. "Grants-in-Aid for State Support of Workers' Education in California." Workers' Education. XIV (April,
1937), 10-11.
     An examination of the development of state funding for
workers' education at the University of California.

815. _____. "Recent Workers' Summer School in California."
American Federationist. XXXVIII (November, 1931), 1377-
1381.
     An overview of the 1930 summer school program of
the University of California.

816. _____. "Workers' Education in California." What Next in
Workers' Education? Seventh Annual Conference of Teachers in Workers' Education. Katonah, N.Y.: Brookwood,
5-7.
     An activity report and short historical summary of the
workers' education department at the University of California.

817. _____. "Workers' Education on the Pacific Coast."
Workers' Education. XI (June, 1934), 2-5.
     An historical examination of workers' education on the
West Coast. Also discussed were the implications of the
NRA and its relationship to workers' education.

818. _____. "Workers' Summer School Experiment in California." American Federationist. XXXV (December,
1938), 1501-1503. Also in Workers' Education. VI (December, 1928), 7-9.
     An examination of the curriculum content of an exper-
imental summer school conducted jointly under the direction of the joint committee on workers' education consisting of representatives of the California State Federation of
Labor and the extension division of the University of California.

819. "Labor Institutes." Journal of Adult Education. V (October,
1933), 452-453.
     An examination of the participants, format and out-

come of the third annual labor institute held at Rutgers University.   Also discussed was the general theme of various labor institutes for 1933.

820. "Labor Institutes." Journal of Adult Education.   VI (April, 1934), 228.
        A discussion of the general aim of various labor institutes held during February 1934.   The general theme of all the institutes was the impact of the National Industrial Recovery Act on Labor.

821. "Lectures for Working Men and Women at the University of Cincinnati." School and Society.   XIX (April 19, 1924), 456.
        A short descriptive article outlining a series of courses offered for workers by the University of Cincinnati in joint cooperation with the central labor body.

822. "Michigan Labor Institute." Journal of Adult Education.   IV (October, 1932), 464.
        An activity report of the labor institute conducted for one week at the University of Michigan campus.   The institute was jointly sponsored by the University of Michigan, the state federation of labor, and the Workers' Education Bureau.

823. Miller, Spencer, Jr.   "Workers' Education in the United States." Proceedings of the National University Extension Association held at New York City on May 7-9, 1930. 141-147.
        After examining the need for university extension's involvement in workers' education based upon union-university cooperation, the author then describes the new developments in the field.

824. _____.   "Workers' Education and University Extension." Proceedings of the Eighth Annual Conference of the National University Extension Association at St. Louis, Missouri, April 19-23, 1923.   Boston: Wright & Potter, 1923, 13-20.
        An examination of the status of workers' education in the United States and the role university extension could play in developing the field.

825. Reber, Louis E.   "Workers' Education Movement in America." Proceedings of the National University Extension Association at Madison, Wisconsin, May 8-10, 1924.   Boston: Wright & Potter, 1924, 131-140.
        An examination of the current activities of workers' education at institutions of higher learning and the difficulties inherent in a cooperative effort between the NUEA and the workers' education movement.

826. "Report of the Committee on Workers' Education. Proceed-
     ings of the National University Extension Association at
     Madison, Wisconsin, May 8-10, 1924. Boston: Wright &
     Potter, 1924, 140-145.
          An examination of the cooperation between the WEB
     and the AFL in the area of the education of workers. Al-
     so discusses the educational methods used in the field.

827. "Report of the Committee on Workers' Education." Proceed-
     ings of the National University Extension Association at
     Charlottesville, Virginia, April 30-May 2, 1925. Boston:
     Wright & Potter, 1925, 42-48.
          An historical examination of workers' education trac-
     ing its development from a stage of predominantly voca-
     tional education to a stage of development which encom-
     passes a much broader range of topics.

828. "Report of the Committee on Workers' Education." Proceed-
     ings of the National University Extension Association at
     Salt Lake City, Utah, June 7-10, 1926. Boston: Wright
     & Potter, 1926, 47-52.
          A report of the growth of workers' education as a vi-
     able educational program. Examines both the size of the
     student body and the teachers in the field.

829. "Report of the Committee on Workers' Education." Proceed-
     ings of the National University Extension Association at
     Chapel Hill, North Carolina, April 25-27, 1927. Boston:
     Wright & Potter, 1927, 179-182.
          A discussion of the aims and objectives of workers'
     education.

830. "Report of the Committee on Workers' Education." Proceed-
     ings of the National University Extension Association at
     Lawrence, Kansas, April 25-27, 1928. Boston: Wright
     & Potter, 1928, 201-204.
          A brief report on the development of Labor Summer
     Schools and Industrial Conferences as new techniques in
     workers' education.

831. "Report of the Committee on Workers' Education." Proceed-
     ings of the National University Extension Association at
     Austin, Texas, May 13-15, 1929. Boston: Wright & Pot-
     ter, 1929, 179-181.
          A brief discussion and description of workers' educa-
     tion program being carried on by extension divisions of
     various universities. Included as reports from the Uni-
     versity of California, University of Wisconsin, University
     of Oklahoma and Rutgers University.

832. "Rutgers Labor Institute." Journal of Adult Education. IV
     (October, 1932), 463-464.
          An activity report of the second week-long labor insti-

tute held at Rutgers University.

833. "Rutgers Labor Institute." Journal of Adult Education. V
(June, 1933), 327.
    An announcement of the third annual labor institute at
Rutgers University.

834. "Unemployment Conference." Journal of Adult Education. III
(October, 1931), 480.
    An activity report of the first labor institute conducted
on the Rutgers University campus.

835. "Workers' Education in Michigan." Monthly Labor Review.
XXV (July, 1927), 77-78.
    An examination of recent developments in workers' ed-
ucation conducted with the assistance of universities.

Local Labor Colleges

836. "Amherst College and Workers' Education Classes." School
and Society. XVI (October 21, 1922), 464-465.
    An announcement of the third consecutive year that the
faculty of the Amherst College would conduct evening
classes for workers. The administration of the school
through a joint union-university committee is explored.

837. Anderson, Gust. "Portland Clears Labor Temple Debt!"
American Federationist. XXXVII (May, 1930), 585-587.
    An examination of the history and function of the Port-
land Labor Temple Association.

838. _____. "Portland Labor Temple." American Federationist. XXXIV (May, 1927), 575-577.
    A report on the Portland Labor Temple and its finan-
cial situation.

839. Beck, Gustav F. "Labor Temple School." American Federationist. XXXV (August, 1928), 996-998. Also in Workers' Education. V (August, 1928), 14-16; American Labor
World. XXIX (September, 1928), 44-45.
    A discussion of the efforts of Drs. Will Durant and
Edmund Chaffee in founding the Labor Temple School.

840. _____. "These My People." Journal of Adult Education.
V (October, 1933), 378-383.
    A discussion of the author's experience at the Labor
Temple School on the lower east side of New York City.

841. Blanshard, Paul. "Rochester Labor College." Proceedings
of the First National Conference on Workers' Education
in the United States. New York: Workers' Education
Bureau, 1921, 17-20.

A description of a labor college in Rochester which is closely associated with the education department of the Amalgamated Clothing Workers of America.

842. _____. "Rochester Labor College." Proceedings of the Second National Conference on Workers' Education in the United States. New York: Workers' Education Bureau, 1922, 19-23.
     An activity report of the labor college in Rochester.

843. "Boston Trade Union College." School and Society. IX (April 12, 1919), 443-444.
     An announcement of the opening session of the Boston Trade Union College organized by the central labor union of that city.

844. Budish, Jacob M. "United Labor Education Committee." Proceedings of the First National Conference on Workers' Education in the United States. New York: Workers' Education Bureau, 1921, 11-15.
     An examination of the functions of the labor committee with proposals for its future functioning.

845. _____. "The Work of the United Labor Education Committee." Proceedings of the Second National Conference on Workers' Education in the United States. New York: Workers' Education Bureau, 1922, 121-128.
     A report of the activities of the New York City United Labor Education Committee.

846. _____. "The United Labor Education Committee." American Labor Yearbook. III. New York: Rand School of Social Science, 1921, 203-204.
     A brief description of the activities conducted by the United Labor Education Committee for union members.

847. Carner, Lucy. "Shorter Hours for Women Workers." Workers' Education. VI (October, 1928), 11-14. Also in American Federationist. XXXV (October, 1928), 1246-1249.
     A description of a conference sponsored by the Philadelphia Labor College.

848. "Chicago Trade Union College." School and Society. X (November 1, 1919), 516.
     A description of the formation of a trade union college under the auspices of the Chicago Federation of Labor and the Chicago Trade Union League.

849. "Colorado Springs Labor College." American Labor Yearbook. XIII. New York: Rand School of Social Science, 1932, 136.
     An activity report of the Colorado Springs Labor School.

850. Cosgrove, Lloyd. "Sacrifice Incurred in Workers' College."
American Federationist. XXXII (August, 1925), 687-689.
A general description of existing workers' colleges and
of the importance of workers' education.

851. Creech, George. "What Came of a Kindergarten?" Labor
Age. XIV (September, 1925), 1-3.
A description of the practical aspects of the forerunner
of the Philadelphia Labor College known as the Kindergarten.

852. Dana, H. W. L. "Boston Labor College." Socialist Review.
VIII (December, 1919), 27.
A short description of the first semester of the Boston
Trade Union College, organized by the Boston Central La-
bor Union.

853. _____. "Boston Trade Union College." American Labor
Yearbook. III. New York: Rand School of Social Science,
1921, 206.
A brief description of the organization and operation of
the labor college.

854. Dent, Mary. "Washington Trade Union College." Proceedings
of the Second National Conference on Workers' Education
in the United States. New York: Workers' Education Bureau, 1922, 15-19.
A report of the activities of the Washington Trade Union College.

855. "Denver Labor College." Journal of Adult Education. VI (February, 1934), 99.
An activity report of the Denver Labor College.

856. "Denver Labor College." American Labor Yearbook. XIII.
New York: Rand School of Social Science, 1932, 176-177.
A description of the 1931 curriculum of the Denver La-
bor College.

857. Director, Aaron. "A Western Experiment in Workers' Education." American Federationist. XXXIV (May, 1927), 538-
540.
A description of the formation and function of the Portland Labor College begun in 1922.

858. Durant, Will. "The Labor Temple School." New Republic.
XXVIII (October 12, 1921), 192.
A letter to the editor announcing the beginning of the
Labor Temple School in New York City. Courses to be
taught are outlined and a listing of the teachers names are
given.

859. "Established Labor Schools Open Doors on New Era." The

Journal of Electrical Workers and Operators.   XXV (September, 1926), 421-423+.

A short editorial on trade union education followed by news notes of activities at various workers' colleges.

860. Flury, Henry. "West Virginia Labor School." Journal of Adult Education. VI (October, 1934), 468.

A description of the purposes, faculty and student body of the school.

861. Foley, Maud. "Boston Trade Union College." Proceedings of the Second National Conference on Workers' Education in the United States. New York: Workers' Education Bureau, 1922, 49-52.

A report of the activities of the Boston Labor College.

862. Fox, Genevieve. "Education By the People and for the People." The Association Monthly. XIV (July, 1920), 325-327.

A description of the opening of new labor colleges in the United States and the programs sponsored by them.

863. Frankfurter, Estelle. "Trade Union College of Boston." Proceedings of the First National Conference on Workers' Education in the United States. New York: Workers' Education Bureau, 1921, 15-17.

An examination of the basic problems confronting the Boston Labor College.

864. Fuller, Paul W. "Educational Campaigns in Augusta." American Federationist. XXXVIII (June, 1931), 702-704. Also in Workers' Education. IX (June, 1931), 28-30.

A description of the labor chautauqua held in Augusta, Georgia.

865. Golden, Clinton. "Workers' Education in Philadelphia." Justice. (October 3, 1924), 10.

This article lists the historical development of the Philadelphia Labor College.

866. Gross, John E. "Colorado Summer School." American Federationist. XXXII (August, 1925), 689-691.

A report of the former labor summer school held at Idaho Springs, Colorado, including a list of speakers and a short summary of what happened.

867. Haber, William G. "Workers' Education and the Workshop." Workers' Education. IV (February, 1927), 45-48. Also in Monthly Labor Review. XXIV (April, 1927), 51-58.

868. Hale, Anna Riley. "Trade Union College of Greater New York." Proceedings of the First National Conference on Workers' Education in the United States. New York:

Workers' Education Bureau, 1921, 20-23.

869. Heinold, George. "Our Workers College." International Mold-
      ers Journal. LXII (October, 1926), 593-594. Also in
      Workers' Education. IV (May, 1926), 8-10.
          A discussion of the establishment of a labor college by
      Kanawha Central Labor Union of Charleston, West Vir-
      ginia.

870. Hoke, George Wilson. "It Can Be Done." Journal of Adult
      Education. VI (January, 1934), 42-46.
          An interview with the founder of the Rochester Athen-
      aeum and Mechanic Institute and his examination of the
      history, purpose and accomplishments of the school.

871. Holwell, Raymond V. "Colorado and Wyoming Education Enter-
      prises." American Federationist. XXXIV (April, 1927),
      442-444.
          An examination of the attempt of the Colorado Labor
      College to engage their worker-students in the educational
      process through the staging of one-act plays.

872. _____. "Workers' Education in Wyoming." American Fed-
      erationist. XXXIII (July, 1926), 862-864.
          A report of the state of workers' education in Wyo-
      ming.

873. _____. "Workers' Summer Schools in Colorado and Wyoming."
      American Federationist. XXXIV (October, 1927), 1223-1226.
      Also in Workers' Education. V (October, 1927), 12-15.
          An activity report of the Colorado Summer School.

874. Kennedy, J. C. "Workers' Education in the Northwest."
      What Next in Workers' Education? Seventh Annual Confer-
      ence of Teachers in Workers' Education. Katonah, N. Y. :
      Brookwood, 1930, 7-9.
          An historical examination of the Portland Labor Tem-
      ple and the Seattle Labor College.

875. "Labor Temple N. Y. C." Journal of Adult Education. III
      (February, 1931), 113.
          An activity report of the Labor Temple School in New
      York City.

876. "Labor Union Colleges." Educational Review. LXI (May,
      1921), 446-449.
          A report of the new movement to establish labor union
      colleges.

877. "Labor Temple School." Journal of Adult Education. IV
      (April, 1932), 205-206.
          An activity report of the New York City Labor Temple
      School.

878. "Labor in Quest of Beauty." Survey. XLII (May 3, 1919),
     199.
          An explanation of the beginning of art, labor and sci-
     ence conferences as a part of the program of the United
     Labor Education Committee.

879. Lackland, George S. "The Rocky Mountain Farmer-Labor
     Summer School." Workers' Education. I (July-August,
     1923), 7-9.
          A description of the week-long summer school held at
     Strontia Springs, Colorado.

880. Lefkowitz, Abraham. "New York Classes." What Next in
     Workers' Education? Seventh Annual Conference of Teach-
     ers in Workers' Education, Katonah, N. Y. : Brookwood,
     1930, 10-11.
          A pessimistic examination of the status of workers'
     education in the city of New York. Considering the num-
     ber just a few short years before, there is a dirth of
     classes at the present time.

881. Lions, Zelda. "Prospect Union Educational Exchange." Na-
     tional Municipal Review. XIX (August, 1930), 538-541.
          A pioneering organization in workers' education, the
     Prospect Union now finds its greater service in serving
     as an advisory bureau to adults seeking to continue their
     education while at work.

882. "Local Activity." American Labor Yearbook. VIII. New
     York: Rand School of Social Science, 1927, 167-168.
          A report of the activities of various workers' educa-
     tion schools including the Boston Trade Union College,
     Labor College of Philadelphia, and Portland Labor Col-
     lege.

883. "Local Activity." American Labor Yearbook. X. New York:
     Rand School of Social Science, 1929, 220.
          An activity report of workers' education in Pennsyl-
     vania in general and at the Labor College of Philadelphia
     in particular.

884. "Local Activity." American Labor Yearbook. XI. New York:
     Rand School of Social Science, 1930, 193-194.
          A description of the educational activities of the Phila-
     delphia and Baltimore Labor Colleges.

885. "Local Activity." American Labor Yearbook. XII. New
     York: Rand School of Social Science, 1931, 238-239.
          A descriptive analysis of the control body and students
     of the Philadelphia and Baltimore Labor College.

886. Machin, Robert E. "Baltimore Labor Begins Education."
     American Federationist. XXXIV (April, 1927), 429-430.

A brief account of the activities of the labor college in its fourth year.

887. May, F. Stacy. "Amherst Classes for Workers." Proceedings of the First National Conference on Workers' Education in the United States. New York: Workers' Education Bureau, 1921, 33-35.
A descriptive report of the Amherst classes for workers.

888. _____. "Amherst Classes for Workers." Proceedings of the Second National Conference on Workers' Education in the United States. New York: Workers' Education Bureau, 1922, 25-27.
An activity report of Amherst College's establishment of workers' classes in Mt. Holyoke and Springfield, Massachusetts.

889. _____. "Workers' Education at Amherst." Survey. XLVI (September 16, 1921), 675-676.
A description of the nature and extent of workers' education conducted by the faculty of Amherst College.

890. McGrath, P. J. "Trade Union College of Pittsburgh." Proceedings of the First National Conference on Workers' Education in the United States. New York: Workers' Education Bureau, 23-25.
A description of the function and problems of the labor college which was established by the Streetcarmen and Molders Unions.

891. Miller, Frieda. "Philadelphia Trade Union College." Proceedings of the Second National Conference on Workers' Education in the United States. New York: Workers' Education Bureau, 1922, 34-37.
An activity report of the Philadelphia Labor College.

892. _____. "Trade Union College of Philadelphia." Proceedings of the First National Conference on Workers' Education in the United States. New York: Workers' Education Bureau, 1921, 28-30.
A report of the founding of the Philadelphia Labor College.

893. Moore, Ernest C. "Workingman's College." School and Society. V (May 26, 1917), 606-608.
A statement of the need for workingmen's colleges and a statement of some experiences in the education of workers.

894. Mufson, Israel. "Education to Meet Workers' Needs." American Federationist. XXXIV (April, 1927), 465-468.
An examination of student participation in the entire

educational process of the Philadelphia Labor College.

895. _____. "Electrical Workers Break New School Paths."
The Journal of Electrical Workers and Operators.   XXVIII
(February, 1928), 68, 110.
A description of a class held at Philadelphia Labor
College for electrician apprentices in order to acquaint the
workers with the techniques of becoming more intelligent
trade unionists.

896. _____. "A Weekend Conference of the Philadelphia Labor
College." Workers' Education.   IV (November, 1926),
28-30.
A discussion of the events which occurred at a conference held by the Philadelphia Labor College.

897. _____. "Why an Unemployment Conference?" American
Federationist.   XXXIV (September, 1927), 1051-1053.
A descriptive analysis of a conference conducted by the
Philadelphia Labor College.

898. Palmer, Frank L.   "Workers' Education in Colorado." Labor
Age.   XVIII (October, 1929), 29.
An activity report of the Colorado Workers' Summer
School.

899. "Planning a Workers' College." International Molders Journal.   LXI (September, 1925), 529-530.   Also in Justice.
(August 14, 1925), 10.
A Workers' Education Bureau release encouraging and
explaining the establishment of a workers' college.

900. Rohan, Thomas F.   "The Holyoke Labor College Classes for
Workers." American Federationist.   XXXV (August,
1928), 994-995.   Also in Workers' Education.   V (August,
1928), 12-13.
A description of the program of the Mt. Holyoke Labor College.

901. Russell, Harry A.   "Workers' Education in New England."
Workers' Education.   XII (July, 1935), 13-14.
A description of the various labor colleges in New
England.

902. Saltus, Freeman M.   "Union Educational Center." American
Federationist.   XXXIII (April, 1926), 601-602.
A description of the Union Labor Temple in Massachu-
setts.

903. Silverman, Harriet.   "Workers' University, Cleveland, Ohio."
Proceedings of the First National Conference on Workers'
Education in the United States.   New York: Workers' Ed-
ucation Bureau, 1921, 36-39.

A descriptive report of a labor college in Cleveland sponsored mainly by the International Ladies Garment Workers' Union.

904. Stoddard, William L. "Boston Trade Union College." Nation. CIX (August 30, 1919), 298-300.
An examination of the beginning of the Boston Trade Union College.

905. Van Voerenewyck, John. "The First Trade Union College." American Federationist. XXXIII (April, 1926), 598-600.
An historical and descriptive study of the Boston Trade Union College.

906. Vogt, Paul L. "Workers' Education in Oklahoma." American Federationist. XXXVI (September, 1929), 1105-1107. Also in Workers' Education. VI (September, 1929), 4-6.
An examination of the development of workers' education classes before the regular union meeting taught with the assistance of the state university.

907. Warne, Colston. "Workers' Education Forges Ahead in Colorado." American Federationist. XXXVIII (December, 1931), 1534-1535.
A short listing of local speakers and subjects taught at the Colorado Labor College.

908. White, Earl. "Passaic Trade Union College." Proceedings of the Second National Conference on Workers' Education in the United States. New York: Workers' Education Bureau, 1922, 31-34.
A report of the activities of the Passaic Labor College.

909. Withington, Anne. "Boston Central Labor Body's Successful Trade Union College." Life and Labor, IX (September, 1919), 239.
A discussion of the establishment and curriculum of the Boston Trade Union College.

910. "Workers' Education." The Locomotive Engineer's Journal. LXII (September, 1928), 667.
An examination of a conference conducted by the Philadelphia Labor College and a discussion of the establishment of labor colleges in many Pennsylvania industrial centers.

911. "Workers' Education in St. Paul." American Teacher. XIV (May, 1930), 20.
A description of a workers' school conducted at the St. Paul Labor Temple. Included in the description is the curriculum of the school, a list of the teachers, and a list of the students.

912. "Workers' Education and Training: Research Work of a Mil-
     waukee Workers' School." Monthly Labor Review. XXIV
     (April, 1927), 711-712.
          A report of a class of eighteen building trade union
     members in the Milwaukee Workers' College and the re-
     search project they undertook.

Young Women's Christian Association (YWCA), Settlements, and
National Women's Trade Union League (NWTUL)

913. "Another Idea for Workers' Education." Life and Labor Bulle-
     tin. II (August, 1924), 2.
          A report of a week-long labor institute held at Brook-
     wood by the NWTUL.

914. Bishop, Dorothy Hubbard. "Earmarks of Workers' Educa-
     tion." The Woman's Press. XXXIII (January, 1939), 20.
          A description of the different types of workers' class-
     es sponsored by the YWCA.

915. Borchardt, Selma. "When Outside Help Is Inside Help in
     Workers' Education." American Teacher. XI (November,
     1926), 8-9.
          An examination of the Industrial Departments of the
     YWCA's attempt at educating working women.

916. Bradley, Phillips. "Learning While You Play: Another Ad-
     venture in Workers' Education." Social Forces. VI (De-
     cember, 1927), 287-290.
          A report of a two week summer school conducted by
     the Industrial Department of the YWCA.

917. Burns, Agnes. "At the League's Training School." Life and
     Labor. VI (March, 1916), 38-40.
          An examination of the goals of the NWTUL "School for
     Active Workers in the Labor Movement."

918. Carner, Lucy P. "An Educational Opportunity for Industrial
     Girls." Social Forces. I (September, 1923), 612-613.
          A discussion of the educational program of the Indus-
     trial Department of the YWCA and its similarities to
     workers' education.

919. _____. "Working Girls Talk It Out." Survey. LVII (Oc-
     tober 15, 1926), 81-82.
          A description of the summer industrial conferences
     conducted by the YWCA.

920. Christman, Elizabeth. "Conventions--A Compliment to Work-
     ers' Education." American Federationist. XXXVI (Aug-
     ust, 1929), 921-925. Also in Workers' Education. VI
     (August, 1929), 1-5.

A summary of the eleventh convention of the NWTUL and its function in the field of workers' education.

921. _____. "Women's Trade Union League of America." Labor Information Bulletin. VII (September, 1940), 10-12.
This article describes the history of the National Women's Trade Union League and the involvement in workers' education that the League had in the year 1939-1940.

922. Coit, Eleanor G. "Fields of Adventure." Survey. LIX (December 15, 1927), 370-371.
An examination of the YWCA's experimentation in the field of workers' education.

923. _____. "The Summer Industrial Conference of the Young Women's Christian Association." Workers' Education. IV (November, 1926), 35-36.
An examination of the methods of study and the educational values of the conference.

924. "Educational Program of Women's Trade Union League." American Labor World. XXIX (October, 1928), 29-30.
A description of the educational program of the New York WTUL; included is a list of courses and a description of each.

925. Elliot, John L. "The Settlements and Workers' Education." Proceedings of the Second National Conference on Workers' Education in the United States. New York: Workers' Education Bureau, 1922, 80.
An examination of the role of the settlement house in the field of workers' education.

926. Ely, Mary L. "Traveling Teacher." Survey. LX (August 15, 1928), 509-510.
A description of the National League of Girls' Clubs establishment of a series of traveling teachers to instruct working women.

927. Gluck, Elsie. "The Educational Work of the New York Women's Trade Union League." Brookwood, Labor's Own School. Katonah, N.Y.: Brookwood, 1936, 46-47.
A description of the educational work of the New York Women's Trade Union League.

928. Henry, Alice. "Educational Work of the NWTUL." Life and Labor. XI (October, 1921), 241-242.
An historical examination of the importance of the Women's Trade Union League's School for Women Organizers in the development of workers' education in the United States.

929. Hill, Helen. "Workers' Education in the South." World To-

morrow. XVII (April 26, 1934), 202-203.
    A report of a worker's education conference held in
Richmond, Virginia, co-sponsored by the Industrial Clubs
of the YWCA and the workers' educational committees of
North Carolina, Virginia, Maryland, and Washington, D.C.

930. Kennedy, Anne Belle. "Something Different in Workers' Edu-
        cation." Journal of Adult Education. II (October, 1930),
        444-447.
            A program report of a ten-day industrial conference
        sponsored by the YWCA.

931. Kohn, Lucille. "Women's Trade Union League." What Next
        in Workers' Education? Seventh Annual Conference of
        Teachers in Workers' Education. Katonah, N.Y.: Brook-
        wood, 1930, 11-13.
            A report of the workers' education activities of the
        WTUL.

932. Kurtagh, Emerie. "Workers' Education and the Settlement."
        Journal of Adult Education. VIII (June, 1936), 330-331.
            An examination of the development of workers' educa-
        tion programs being instituted by various settlements
        throughout the United States.

933. Leslie, Mabel. "An Adventure in Education." American Fed-
        erationist. XXXIV (April, 1927), 436-438.
            An examination of the educational efforts of the New
        York chapter of the WTUL.

934. MacDonald, Lois. "Education by Conference." American Fed-
        erationist. XXXIV (February, 1927), 188-190.
            A description of the summer conferences sponsored by
        the Industrial Department of the YWCA and their contribu-
        tions in the field of workers' education.

935. Muste, A. J. "A Project in Workers' Education." Woman's
        Press. XXII (October, 1928), 688-690.
            A description of the Summit Lake Conference conducted
        by the Industrial Department of the YWCA.

936. "The National Training School." Life and Labor Bulletin. II
        (April, 1924), 3.
            An activity report of the 1923-1924 NWTUL's training
        school.

937. Robins, Margaret Dreier. "Educational Plans of the NWTUL."
        Life and Labor. IV (June, 1914), 164-167.
            An examination of the organization of a training school
        for women organizers by the NWTUL.

938. _____. Need of a National Training School for Women Or-
        ganizers. Chicago: NWTUL, 1913, 15 pp.

A speech delivered to the fourth biennial convention of the NWTUL in which several recommendations for the organization of a training school for women organizers is put forth.

939. _____. "Women in Industry." Survey. XXXI (December 27, 1913), 351.
An examination of the educational proposals of the NWTUL.

940. Schneiderman, Rose. "Education and the Worker-Student." Journal of Adult Education. VIII (June, 1936), 346-347.
A report of the activities of the NWTUL in the field of workers' education.

941. "School for Active Workers in the Labor Movement--Correspondence Courses." Life and Labor. VI (August, 1916), 126.
Outlines of the new correspondence courses offered by the NWTUL.

942. "Schools for Grown Ups." Life and Labor Bulletin. III (May, 1925), 3.
A report of the NWTUL's training school.

943. Smith, Ethel M. "Developing a New Organizing Technique." American Federationist. XXXIII (August, 1926), 928-934.
A discussion of the educational program conducted by the NWTUL at their national convention.

944. Smith, Hilda W. "The New Educational Program of the Women's Trade Union League." Workers' Education. IV (November, 1926), 25-27.
A description of the changes in the educational policy of the NWTUL.

945. "Training School of the National Women's Trade Union League of America." Life and Labor Bulletin. I (February, 1923), 1.
A short statement of the activities and offerings of the training school.

946. "Training School for Women Organizers." Life and Labor. IV (March, 1914), 90.
A description of the students and curriculum of the NWTUL school for women organizers.

947. Wade, Louise C. "The Educational Dimensions of the Early Chicago Settlements." Adult Education. XVII (Spring, 1967), 166-178.
An historical sketch of the development of Hull House and other settlement houses with special attention given to its educational activities, including workers' education.

948. Wallerstein, Bertha. "Workers Who Like to Use Their
      Minds; Summer School of the National League of Girls'
      Clubs." Survey. LV (November 15, 1925), 219.
         A report of the classroom techniques used in the first
      summer school sponsored by the National League of
      Girls' Clubs.

949. "Women's Trade Union League." American Labor Yearbook.
      VII. New York: Rand School of Social Science, 1926,
      313.
         A brief account of the work of the NWTUL.

950. "Women's Trade Union League." American Labor Yearbook.
      VIII. New York: Rand School of Social Science, 1927,
      165.
         A report of the activities of the NWTUL and also the
      educational work of the New York chapter.

951. "Women's Trade Union League." American Labor Yearbook.
      XI. New York: Rand School of Social Science, 1930,
      189-190.
         An announcement of the educational policy which the
      national league is expected to follow in the future.

Radical Political Parties

952. Bohn, William E. "The Rand School of Social Science."
      What Next in Workers' Education? Seventh Annual Confer-
      ence of Teachers in Workers' Education. Katonah, N.Y.:
      Brookwood, 1930.
         An activity report of the work of the Rand School of
      Social Science in the field of workers' education.

952a. Chafee, Zechariah, Jr. Free Speech in the United States.
      Cambridge: Harvard University Press, 1967, 7th print-
      ing. Chpt. VII entitled, "The Rand School Case," 306-
      317.
         An examination of the legal problems encountered by
      the Rand School as a result of the Lusk Committee's in-
      vestigation into education subversive activity from 1919-
      1922.

953. Lee, Algernon. "The Rand School of Social Science." Amer-
      ican Labor Yearbook. III. New York: Rand School of
      Social Science, 1921, 206-208.
         A history of the Rand School and a discussion of the
      activities carried on by the school.

954. _____. "Rand School of Social Science." Proceedings of
      the Second National Conference on Workers' Education in
      the United States. New York: Workers' Education Bur-
      eau, 1922, 45-49.

A report of the workers' education activities of the
school of the Socialist Party.

955. _____. "Socialist Experiences in Workers' Education."
The Place of Workers' Education in the Labor Movement.
Fifth Annual Conference of Teachers in Workers' Educa-
tion. Katonah, N. Y. : Brookwood, 1928.
An historical and philosophical examination of the role
of the Socialist Party in workers' education.

956. Mailly, Bertha H.   "Rand School of Social Science."   Proceedings of the First National Conference on Workers' Education in the United States.   New York: Workers' Education
Bureau, 1921, 25-27.
A description of the function of the Rand School in
workers' education.

957. "New Yorkers' School." American Labor Yearbook.   XIII.
New York: Rand School of Social Science, 1932, 175.
A report of the activities of the New Workers' School
sponsored by the Majority Group of the Communist Party.

958. "Rand School, New York." Journal of Adult Education.   III
(October, 1931).   486.
An activity report of the school of the Socialist Party
in New York City.

959. "Rand School, New York." Journal of Adult Education.   V
(October, 1933), 468-469.
An activity report of the educational work of the Rand
School.

960. "Rand School of Social Science." Journal of Adult Education.
IV (October, 1932), 463.
An activity report of the Rand School.

961. "Rand School of Social Science." American Labor Yearbook.
V.   New York: Rand School of Social Science, 1924, 225-
227.
A description of the purposes and management of the
Rand School.

962. "Rand School of Social Science." American Labor Yearbook.
VI.   New York: Rand School of Social Science, 1925, 209-
210.
An activity report of the Rand School for the year
1924.

963. "Rand School of Social Science." American Labor Yearbook.
VII.   New York: Rand School of Social Science, 1926,
314.
A report of the curriculum, labor research and summer camp (Tamiment) of the Socialist Party.

964. "Rand School of Social Science." American Labor Yearbook.
    VIII.   New York: Rand School of Social Science, 1927,
    163.
       A general report of the activities of the school for the
    year 1926.

965. "Rand School of Social Science." American Labor Yearbook.
    X.   New York: Rand School of Social Science, 1929,
    217-218.
       A description of the educational policy of the Rand
    School and a report of its activities for 1928.

966. "Rand School of Social Science." American Labor Yearbook.
    XI.   New York: Rand School of Social Science, 1930,
    186-187.
       A report of a change in leadership and the length of
    the educational program at the Rand School.

967. "Rand School of Social Science." American Labor Yearbook.
    XII.   New York: Rand School of Social Science, 1931,
    224-225.
       A description of the faculty, students, and curriculum
    of the school in its twenty-fifth year of operation.

968. "Rand School of Social Science." American Labor Yearbook.
    XIII.   New York: Rand School of Social Science, 1932,
    168-170.
       An activity report of the school during the year 1931.

969. "Trade Union Institute of Rand School." Journal of Adult Edu-
    cation. IX (October, 1937), 467.
       An activity report of the trade union education of the
    Rand School.

970. "Work People's College." American Labor Yearbook. VIII.
    New York: Rand School of Social Science, 1927, 162-163.
       An announcement of a five-month course of study of-
    fered at the Work People's College in Duluth, Minnesota.

971. "Work People's College." American Labor Yearbook. X.
    New York: Rand School of Social Science, 1929, 215-216.
       An historical examination of the college.

972. "Work People's College." American Labor Yearbook. XI.
    New York: Rand School of Social Science, 1930, 188-189.
       An activity report of the college, including details on
    finances, administration, curriculum, and students.

973. "Work People's College." American Labor Yearbook. XII.
    New York: Rand School of Social Science, 1931, 228-229.
       A description of the Wobbly control of the school
    and a report of its recent activities.

974. "Work People's College." American Labor Yearbook. XIII.
     New York: Rand School of Social Science, 1932, 172-173.
     An activity report of this Wobbly school.

975. "Workers' School." American Labor Yearbook. VII. New
     York: Rand School of Social Science, 1926, 315-316.
     An activity report of the scope, work courses and ex-
     tension classes of the Workers' School in New York City
     and other cities.

976. "Workers' School." American Labor Yearbook. VIII. New
     York: Rand School of Social Science, 1927, 163-164.
     An activity report of the educational work carried on
     by the Communist Party in New York City.

977. "Workers' School." American Labor Yearbook. X. New
     York: Rand School of Social Science, 1929, 216-217.
     An activity report of the school for the year 1928.

978. "Workers' School." American Labor Yearbook. XI. New
     York: Rand School of Social Science, 1930. 189.
     An activity report and educational policy statement of
     the Workers' School of the Communist Party.

979. "Workers' School." American Labor Yearbook. XII. New
     York: Rand School of Social Science, 1931, 229-230.
     A report of the aim, curriculum and student body of
     the school in 1930.

980. "Workers' School." American Labor Yearbook. XIII. New
     York: Rand School of Social Science, 1932, 173-175.
     A report of the activities of the school for the 1931-
     1932 school year.

Federal Government Support

981. Amidon, Beulah. "Emergency Education." Survey Graphics.
     XXIII (September, 1934), 415-419+.
     A birdseye view of what FERA has done in the area of
     education, partly dealing with the field of workers' educa-
     tion.

982. Bestor, Arthur E. "The ABC of Federal Emergency Educa-
     tion." Journal of Adult Education. VI (April, 1934), 150-
     154.
     A general description of the educational programs con-
     ducted under FERA, including workers' education.

983. Carroll, Mollie Ray. "The Emergency Education Program and
     Labor." Journal of Adult Education. VI (October, 1934),
     493-498.

An examination of the Federal Emergency Education
Program and its possibilities for developing workers'
classes within the general adult education category.

984. Coit, Eleanor. "Government Subsidies for Workers' Education in Denmark and Sweden." Workers' Education. XIV
(January, 1937), 24-28.
An analysis of the methods and consequences of government support for workers' education in Denmark and
Sweden. From this base, the author develops a case for
government's financial support for workers' education in
the United States.

985. _____. "Workers' Education and Government Support."
Journal of Adult Education. VIII (June, 1936), 263-266.
An examination of the implications and problems
raised by the increase in federal support for workers'
education.

986. Danton, Emily Miller. "The Federal Emergency Adult Education Program." In Dorothy Rowden, ed., Handbook of
Adult Education in the U.S. New York: American Association for Adult Education, 1936, 28-53.
A lengthy article devoted to the educational work of
the Federal Emergency Relief Act. In this article a small
section is devoted to FERA's workers' education projects.

987. "Recent Developments in Workers' Education in Various States."
Monthly Labor Review. XL (April, 1935), 948-953.
An examination of recent developments in the field of
workers' education under FERA.

988. "Residential School for Unemployed Women." Journal of Adult
Education. VI (June, 1934), 340.
A discussion of a project of the Federal Emergency
Relief Administration to establish schools for unemployed
women.

989. Rutz, Henry. "Workers' Education in Wisconsin." Brookwood, Labor's Own School. Katonah, N.Y.: Brookwood,
1936, 35-36.
An examination of the increased activity in the state's
workers' education program due to federal funding under
FERA.

990. "Schools for Unemployed Women." Journal of Adult Education.
VII (June, 1935), 337.
A brief description of the development and funding of
twenty-eight schools and camps established for unemployed
women.

991. Smith, Hilda W. "Education Via Relief." Journal of Adult
Education. VI (January, 1934), 118-120.

A discussion of the problems and benefits of the new educational opportunities offered to working adults because of the relief program's use of unemployed teachers.

992. _____. "The Emerging Program of Workers' Education." Journal of Adult Education. VIII (June, 1936), 347.
An evaluation of the field of workers' education since its inclusion in the Emergency Education Program of 1933.

993. _____. "Federal Cooperation in the Education of Workers." Journal of Adult Education. VI (October, 1934), 499-505.
An historical examination of the Federal Emergency Education Program and the role various workers' education groups played in its development.

994. _____. "New Aspects of Workers' Education." Woman's Press. XXVIII (July, 1934), 369-370.
A review of workers' education under the auspices of the federal government after its first year in existence.

995. _____. "New Plans for Adult Education." American Federationist. XLI (March, 1934), 261-267.
A description of workers' education under FERA.

996. _____. "Resident Schools and Camps for Unemployed Women." Journal of Adult Education. VI (October, 1934), 461-462.
A descriptive examination of resident schools and educational camps for unemployed women.

997. _____. "Teacher Training in Workers' Education." Journal of Adult Education. VIII (June, 1936), 384-385.
An examination of teacher training in workers' education under FERA.

998. _____. "Workers' Education and the Federal Government." Progressive Education. XI (April-May, 1934), 239-245.
A brief history of the workers' education program under the auspices of the New Deal and the Works Project Administration.

999. _____. "Workers' Education and the Public Schools." Journal of Adult Education. VII (April, 1935), 241-243.
An examination of the role of workers' education under the Emergency Education Program.

1000. _____. Workers' Education under FERA. Labor Information Bulletin. II (June, 1935), 1-3.
A descriptive study of the operation of the workers' education classes under FERA.

1001. _____. "Workers' Education with Federal Support."

Workers' Education. XIII (October, 1936), 31-34.
    A discussion which enumerates the benefits of federal
support for workers' education.

1002. _____. "Workers' Education in the States." American
    Federationist. XLII (May, 1935), 490-493.
        A report on the progress of workers' education in
    several states under the Federal Emergency Relief Admin-
    istration.

1003. _____ and Barbara Donald. "Workers' Education in the
    States." American Federationist. XLII (August, 1935),
    835-840.
        An examination of the administration and program con-
    tent in workers' education conducted under the Federal
    Emergency Education program.

1004. _____ and _____. "Workers' Education in the States."
    American Federationist. XLII (August, 1935), 1073-1075.
        A report of the increased interest in summer school
    camps across the country. Also included is the support
    the Work Project Administration provides the camps when
    difficulties arise.

1005. _____ and _____. "Workers' Education under the Fed-
    eral Government." Labor Information Bulletin. III (June,
    1936), 7-9. Also in American Library Association Bulle-
    tin, (January, 1936), 9-12.
        A report of the third year of the federal program in
    workers' education which had been transferred from the
    auspices of the Federal Emergency Relief Act to the
    Works Project Administration.

1006. _____ and _____. "Workers' Education under W. P. A."
    American Federationist. XLIII (February, 1936), 198-
    199.
        A discussion of the adult education program under the
    Works Project Administration.

1007. _____ and Nancy Hart. "Workers' Education in the F. E.
    R. A." Opportunity. XIII (January, 1935), 19-20.
        A discussion of the negligent impact of any racial
    problems in the workers' education program under the sup-
    port of the federal government.

1008. "Workers' Education in Puerto Rico." American Federation-
    ist. XLIII (April, 1936), 409-412.
        An examination of the accomplishments of the federal-
    ly funded workers' education project on the island.

1009. "Workers' Education under the W. P. A." Journal of Adult
    Education. IX (October, 1937), 466.
        An activity report of the work of the federally funded
    workers' education program.

GENERAL, HISTORICAL AND DESCRIPTIVE STUDIES

1010. Anderson, Frank V. "Evolution of Workers' Education."
      Educational Review. LXI (May, 1921), 384-388.
          A brief history of the evolution of workers' education
      as a movement in the United States.

1011. Beard, Charles A. "Workers' Education. New Republic.
      XXVIII (November 9, 1921), 327-328.
          A review of the status of workers' education in the
      United States.

1012. Browne, Waldo R. What's What in the Labor Movement.
      New York: Heubsch, 1921, 566-568
          A section entitled, "Working Class Education" contains
      an examination of the organizations engaged in workers'
      education.

1013. Cohn, Fannia. "New Paths in Workers' Education Movement."
      Labor Age. XIV (October, 1925), 15-18. Also in Jus-
      tice. (April 9, 1926), 6; (April 16, 1926), 6; and (May 9,
      1926), 6.
          A panoramic view of the accomplishments of workers'
      education in the United States.

1014. Coit, Eleanor G. "Workers Go to School." The Crisis.
      XLIII (June, 1936), 176, 178.
          A descriptive contrast between workers' education in
      Sweden and in the United States.

1015. "Education for Workers." Survey. XLIII (January 17, 1920),
      437.
          A brief review of the various groups involved in work-
      ers' education in the United States.

1016. "The Education of the Worker Is the Hope of America."
      American Teacher. XI (November, 1926), 10-11.
          A short description of various workers' education en-
      terprises, as well as short statements from William
      Green and Sam Gompers on what they think workers' edu-
      cation will do.

1017. Epstein, Abraham. "After Eight Years: A Review of Work-
      ers' Education." Labor Age. XVIII (March, 1929), 9-11.
          A review of the history of workers' education and a
      lament over the apathy and indifference which surrounds
      the movement.

1018. _____. "What We Can Learn from the History of Workers'
      Education Since the War." The Place of Workers Educa-
      tion in the Labor Movement. Fifth Annual Conference of

Teachers in Workers' Education, Katonah, N.Y.: Brookwood, 1928, 10-11.

A dismal examination of the present state of workers' education in the United States.

1019. Feis, Herbert. "Workers' Educational Movement in the United States." School and Society. XIV (September 10, 1924), 144-149.

An examination of the movement of workers' education in the United States and an analysis of the various agencies involved in the field.

1020. Fox, Genevieve. When Labor Goes to School. New York: Young Women's Christian Association, 1920, 18-30.

After an introductory examination of workers' education in Europe, the author explains the various activities in the movement here in the United States.

1021. Gleason, Arthur H. "Workers' Education." New Republic. XXVI (April 20, 1921), 235-237.

A general consideration of the field of the education of workers in the United States.

1022. _____. Workers' Education: American Experiments, with a Few Foreign Examples. New York: Bureau of Industrial Research, 1921. 87 pp.

A general examination of the various organizations in the field of workers' education in the United States.

1023. Good, H. G. "Workers' Education." Journal of National Education Association. XIII (March, 1924), 91-94.

An examination of the educational work of the Amalgamated Clothing Workers of America, the Boston Trade Union College, and Brookwood.

1024. Hansome, Marius. "Three Schools and a Schoolmaster." Labor Age. XII (July, 1923), 18-20.

A descriptive study of workers' education in Minnesota which focuses on the three workers' colleges in the state.

1025. _____. World Workers' Education Movements. New York: Columbia University Press, 1931. 558 pp.

Interspersed throughout the book is an historical examination of workers' education in the United States.

1026. Hewes, Amy. "Early Experiments in Workers' Education." Adult Education. VI (Summer, 1956), 211-220.

An historical examination of the beginnings of workers' education in the United States.

1027. Hodgen, Margaret T. "Workers' Education." Vassar Quarterly. VI (November, 1920), 25-28.

An examination of the various organizations involved in workers' education in the United States.

1028. _____. Workers' Eduation in England and the United States. New York: E. P. Dutton & Co., 1925.
An enumeration of workers' educational enterprises in the two countries.

1029. Kennedy, J. C. and A. J. Muste. "Next Steps in Workers' Education." What Next in Workers' Education? Seventh Annual Conference of Teachers in Workers' Education, Katonah, N. Y.: Brookwood, 1930, 65-72.
An examination of the predicament of workers' education and suggestions for the role of the movement in the 1930s.

1030. Lindsay, K. "Workers' Education That Works." Survey. L (September 15, 1923), 632-634.
A general survey of the operation of Labor Colleges in the United States.

1031. "Local and State Activity." American Labor Yearbook. V. New York: Rand School of Social Science, 1924, 227-230.
A general description of the activities of the various enterprises involved in workers' education.

1032. Machin, Robert and A. J. Muste. "Labor Schools Round Out Nearly a Decade." The Journal of Electrical Workers and Operators. XXVI (September, 1927), 458.
Short sketches of various labor colleges throughout the United States as the 1927-1928 academic year opened.

1033. Man, Henri de. "Labor's Challenge to Education." New Republic. XXVI (March 2, 1921), 16-18.
A description of the beginning of workers' education in this country and the importance of this for the labor movement.

1034. Miller, Spencer, Jr. "American Beginnings." Labor Age. XI (April, 1922), 6-7.
A very brief history of workers' education which traces the demand for this movement to the first quarter of the nineteenth century.

1035. _____. "A Brief Review of Summer Schools and Labor Institutes." Workers' Education. IV (August, 1926), 34-37.
An account of various organizations' activities in workers' education.

1036. _____. "Five Years of American Workers' Education." American Federationist. XXIII (March, 1926), 336-339.
An examination of the state of workers' education and the details of the development of the new movement.

1037. _____ . "Workers' Education." In Fred S. Hall, ed.,
Social Work Yearbook, 1929. New York: Russell Sage
Foundation, 1930.
A descriptive article outlining the history and present
status of the movement.

1038. _____ . "Workers' Education." Social Work Yearbook.
New York: Russell Sage Foundation, 1933, 550-553.
A general survey of the workers' education movement
in the United States.

1039. _____ . "Workers' Education." In Dorothy Rowden, ed.,
Handbook of Adult Education in the United States. New
York: American Association for Adult Education, 1934,
299-305.
A descriptive analysis of the development of workers'
education in the United States. Included is a short de-
scription of the various organizations engaged in Workers'
Education.

1040. _____ . "Workers' Education." In Dorothy Rowden, ed.,
Handbook of Adult Education in the United States. New
York: American Association for Adult Education, 1936,
336-344.
After a short introduction to the field of workers' education, the author lists and describes the agencies in the
field.

1041. Muste, A. J. "Current Issues in Workers' Education." The
Place of Workers' Education in the Labor Movement.
Fifth Annual Conference of Teachers in Workers' Education. Katonah, N. Y.: Brookwood, 1928, 9-22.
An examination of the present status of workers' education and special attention is given to new experiments
being conducted in the field.

1042. _____ . "Workers' Education in the United States." Religious Education. XXIV (October, 1929), 738-745.
An analysis of the various types of workers' education
programs in the United States. Emphasis is given to the
advantages of workers' education for the union and its leadership.

1043. Nestor, Agnes. "Workers' Education for Women in Industry."
Proceedings of the National Conference of Social Work in
Toronto, Ontario, June 25-July 2, 1924, 345-348.
A brief account of the educational work of various
workers' education organizations, especially for women.

1044. Peffer, Nathaniel. New Schools for Older Students. New
York: Macmillan Co., 1926. Chapter VIII, 203-243.
This chapter entitled "Workers' Education" provides a
descriptive and philosophical examination of the field in the
United States.

1045. Perlman, Selig. "Workers' Education. " Encyclopedia of the Social Sciences. 1937, 484-487.
A discussion of the early history of the movement in both the United States and several foreign countries.

1046. "Recent Developments in Adult Workers' Education in the U.S." Monthly Labor Review. XXIII (July, 1926), 91-100.
A series of short summaries of the various agencies involved in workers' education.

1047. Report of the Executive Committee Workers' Education Bureau of America to the Third Annual Convention in New York City, April 14-15, 1923. New York: Workers' Education Bureau, 1923, 19 pp.
A general examination of the status of workers' education and the functions of the Workers' Education Bureau.

1048. Report of the Executive Committee Workers' Education Bureau of America to the Fourth National Convention in Philadelphia, April 17-19, 1925. New York: Workers' Education Bureau, 1925, 47 pp.
A general report of the status of workers' education.

1049. Report of the Executive Committee Workers' Education Bureau of America to the Fifth National Convention in Boston, April 22-24, 1927. New York: Workers' Education Bureau, 1927, 63 pp.
A general report on the status of the workers' education movement.

1050. Report of the Executive Committee Workers' Education Bureau of America to the Sixth National Convention in Washington, D.C., April 5-7, 1929. New York: Workers' Education Bureau, 162 pp.
A general report of the status of workers' education in the United States. Of specific interest this year was the expulsion of Brookwood from the Workers' Education Bureau.

1051. Schneiderman, Rose. "Women Workers and Education." Proceedings of the Second National Conference on Workers' Education in the United States. New York: Workers' Education Bureau, 1922, 101-104.
A description of those organizations specifically dealing with the education of women workers.

1052. Smith, Hilda W. "Workers' Education as Determining Social Control." Annals, American Academy of Political and Social Science. CLXXXII (November, 1935), 82-92.
An historical examination and description of the workers' education movement.

1053. "State and Local Activity." American Labor Yearbook. VIII.
New York: Rand School of Social Science, 1926, 310-312.
A narrative of various workers' education organiza-
tions, including the Workers' Education Bureau and the
New York City Labor Temple.

1054. "Summer Schools." American Labor Yearbook. VII. New
York: Rand School of Social Science, 1926, 313.
A description of various workers' summer schools held
during the summer of 1925 throughout the United States.

1055. Sweeney, C. P. "Adult Working Class Education in Great
Britain and the United States." Monthly Labor Review.
XI (November, 1920), 137-139.
An examination of the development of workers' educa-
tion in the United States and Great Britain.

1056. Walton, Dorothy. "A Hobo College and Its Kin." Life and
Labor. X (December, 1920), 305-308.
A description of some of the various educational of-
ferings available specifically for workers.

1057. "Workers' Education." Journal of Adult Education. II (June,
1930), 315-316.
An activity report of developments in the field of workers' education.

1058. "Workers' Education." Journal of Adult Education. II (October, 1930), 464-466.
An activity report of developments in the field of workers' education.

1059. "Workers' Education." Journal of Adult Education. VI (June,
1934), 312-315.
An abstract of papers delivered by William Green and
Hilda Smith at the Ninth Annual Meeting of the American
Association of Adult Education.

1060. "Workers' Education." New Republic. XXVIII (October 12,
1921), 173-174.
A brief discussion and description of the various agencies involved in workers' education in the United States.

1061. "Workers' Education Taking Root." The Locomotive Engineers
Journal. LXI (November, 1927), 843.
An historical summary of many of the labor colleges
in the United States.

1062. "Workers' Education in the United States." The Locomotive
Engineers Journal. LVII (March, 1923), 170-172.
An historical examination of the need for adult workers' education in the United States and an overview of the
various agencies involved in the field.

1063. Workers Education in the United States.   Proceedings of the
      Fourth National Convention of the Workers' Education
      Bureau.   New York: Workers' Education Bureau, 1927,
      112 pp.
          Although many of the addresses at this convention
      were concerned with workers' education in foreign coun-
      tries, the reports of the various committees provide an
      insight into the status of the United States movement.

1064. Workers' Education in the United States.   Proceedings of the
      Fifth National Convention of Workers' Education Bureau.
      New York: Workers' Education Bureau, 1929, 136 pp.
          Through committee reports, the status of workers'
      education in the United States is examined.

1065. "Workers' Education in the United States."   American Labor
      Yearbook.   IV.   New York: Rand School of Social Sci-
      ence, 1923, 202-204.
          A listing of the events of 1921 in workers' education
      which made it the first distinctive year for that movement
      in the United States.

1066. "Ye Olde School Bell."   Journal of Electrical Workers and
      Operators.   XXIV (October, 1923), 776-779.
          A short description of a variety of institutions in-
      volved in workers' education.

                          MISCELLANEOUS

1067. Budenz, Louis, F.   "Industrial Unionism vs. Company Union-
      ism "   Labor Age.   XV (October, 1926), 4-7.
          A discussion of the topics of industrial and company
      unions from the standpoint that they are subjects of con-
      cern to workers' education.

1068. Clark, Evans.   "Workers' Education."   Nation.   CXIII (De-
      cember 7, 1921), 670-673.
          A review of three reports on workers' education.

1069. Cohn, Fannia.   "Arthur Gleason."   Workers' Education.   II
      (February, 1925), 5-6.
          A eulogy for Arthur Gleason who was very active in
      sponsoring workers' education within the labor movement.

1070. _____.   "Workers' Education for Workers' Children."
      Labor Age.   XV (January, 1926), 15-18.   Also in Justice.
      (January 15, 1926), 6; (January 22, 1926), 6; (January 29,
      1926), 6.
          A descriptive examination of the need for workers'
      children to understand the role of trade unions in our
      country.

1071. _____. "Company Unions and Workers' Education." Labor Age. XV (October, 1926), 1-3. Also in International
Molders Journal. LXIII (January, 1927), 13-16.
        Outlines the role of workers' education in combatting
the propaganda of company unionism.

1072. "Conference in Washington." Journal of Adult Education.   IX
(January, 1937), 103.
        A discussion of the content of a workers' education
conference which examined "the necessity for ... diverting
our attention from educational institutions to the persons
who are to be educated."

1073. "Federal Conference on Workers' Education." Journal of
Adult Education. VI (April, 1934), 221-222.
        A description of a conference sponsored by the De-
partments of Labor and Education to examine what the
federal government can do with unemployed teachers in
workers' education.

1074. Fitzpatrick, Alfred. "Fifth University, the Greatest of Them
All." American Federationist. XXXVI (February, 1929),
222-230. Also in Workers' Education. VI (February,
1929), 1-9.
        A discussion of the "fifth university"--the proud poor
homes of the workers--and its place in workers' education.

1075. Frey, John P. "Organization and Education." Workers'
Education. III (August, 1925), 10.
        A statement that Labor Day should be a day of educa-
tion through mass meetings where workers can receive
a more thorough understanding of the trade union movement.

1076. Geliebter, P. "Workmen's Circle Education Department."
What Next in Workers' Education? Seventh Annual Confer-
ence of Teachers in Workers' Education. Katonah, N.Y.:
Brookwood, 1930, 26-30.
        An activity report of the Workmen's Circle Education
Department. The majority of the courses were offered in
Yiddish with most of its work done in the industrial cen-
ters of New York, Philadelphia, and Chicago.

1077. Harris, Abraham. "The Southern Negro and Workers' Education." What Next in Workers' Education? Seventh Annual
Conference of Teachers in Workers' Education. Katonah,
N.Y.: Brookwood, 1930, 40-49.
        An indepth examination of the role of the black worker
in the South and his problems vis-a-vis organization and
workers' education.

1078. Kerchen, John L. "What About the Unfinished Education of

Yours?" Workers' Education. III (November, 1925), 10-12.

A plea for workers to continue their education through the workers' education movement.

1079. "Labor Broadcasts." Journal of Adult Education. VIII (January, 1936), 113.

A description of the educational endeavor of the WEB in securing radio time for labor education broadcasts.

1080. "Labor Conference." Journal of Adult Education. I (February, 1929), 99.

A description of a conference sponsored by the Boston Central Labor Union.

1081. Lefkowitz, Abraham. "The Crisis in Labor Education." Labor Age. XVIII (February, 1929), 9-11.

A call to alarm over the declining fortunes of the labor and workers' education movements.

1082. Long, Cedric. "Education in the Consumers' Co-operation Movement." The Place of Workers' Education in the Labor Movement. Fifth Annual Conference of Teachers in Workers' Education. Katonah, N. Y. : Brookwood, 1928.

An examination of the philosophical base of the consumer cooperative movement as a varied form of workers' education.

1083. "Lynchberg Conference for Workers." Journal of Adult Education. V (April, 1933), 202.

A report of a conference on unemployment insurance sponsored by the Affiliated Schools of Workers.

1084. Miller, Spencer, Jr. "Arthur Gleason, Interpreter of Workers' Education." Workers' Education. I (February, 1924), 7-9.

A eulogy to Arthur Gleason in praise of his work and devotion to workers' education.

1085. _____, Clinton Golden, and E. J. Lever. "Who Should Pay for Workers' Education?" Labor Age. XV (June, 1926), 1-6.

Three separate discussions of the financing of workers' education. Special attention is paid to the Garland Fund.

1086. Mitchell, George. "Nature of the Work to Be Undertaken." What Next in Workers' Education? Seventh Annual Conference of Teachers in Workers Education. Katonah, N. Y. : Brookwood, 1930, 39-40.

An examination of the problems involved in conducting workers' education in the south.

1087. Mufson, Israel and Charles L. Reed.   "Who Should Pay for
      Workers' Education?" Labor Age. XV (December, 1926),
      11-12.
            An examination of the reasons why labor alone should
      pay for workers' education.

1088. Myers, Gary C. "Adult Education and Wage Earners."
      American Federationist. XL (January, 1933), 28-32.
            A plea for all workers to take advantage of the educa-
      tional opportunities available to them.

1089. "The Oberhoff Conference." Journal of Adult Education. I
      (February, 1929), 96.
            A description of the paper delivered by Spencer Miller,
      Jr. on workers' education at the Assembly of the Council
      of World Association for Adult Education of Oberhoff,
      Thuringia.

1090. Pangburn, Weaver. "The Workers' Leisure and His Individu-
      ality." American Journal of Sociology. XXVII (January,
      1922), 433-441.
            A discussion of how the worker can take advantage of
      his expanding leisure time and pursue educational oppor-
      tunities.

1091. Smith, Hilda W. "Teachers Wanted." Survey. LVII (Febru-
      ary 15, 1927), 650-651.
            An examination of the need for teachers in the field of
      workers' education and the need for training such teachers.

1092. _____. "Unemployment a Challenge to Workers' Education."
      Journal of the American Association of University Women.
      XXV (April, 1932), 134-139.
            An expression of the need for workers' education and
      an examination of the numerous problems confronting the
      worker-student because of the depression.

1093. Soule, George. "Education in Wage Disputes." Workers' Edu-
      cation. IV (August, 1926), 8-9.
            A discussion of the educational value of the process of
      settling wage disputes.

1094. Tippett, Tom. "Workers' Education and the Negro." Oppor-
      tunity. XIV (July, 1936), 202-204.
            A discussion of the relation between workers' education
      and economic understanding, and the attitudes that develop
      between racial groups.

1095. Troxell, John P. "Democracy in Workers' Education." Amer-
      ican Federationist. XXXIV (April, 1927), 426-428.
            A discussion of the extent to which democracy pervades
      the student body of a workers' education class.

1096. "Voice of Labor." Journal of Adult Education. VIII (April, 1936), 225.
      A description of the educational benefits of radio broadcasts conducted and sponsored by labor.

1097. Ward, Edward J. "Open the Schools." Life and Labor. I (August, 1911), 238-240.
      Urges the use of public school facilities for the purpose of workers' education. Also outlines the scope of the educational endeavor.

1098. "Workers' Education." Journal of Adult Education. I (June, 1929), 314-315.
      A report of the activities in the workers' education section of the annual meeting of the American Association of Adult Education.

1099. "Workers' Education Bulletin." Journal of Adult Education. VI (June, 1934), 341.
      A description of the content of a new bulletin published by the FERA workers' education service.

1100. "Workers School of Municipal Government." Survey. XXVII (February 10, 1912), 1730-1731.
      A descriptive article which focuses on the extension of the Chicago School of Civics and Philanthropy to offer classes for working people designed to make them better citizens.

BIBLIOGRAPHY ON LABOR EDUCATION

PHILOSOPHY AND GOALS

1101. Abbott, William L. "Can Idealism Lift Labor Education Out of Its Outdated Dogma?" Adult Leadership, XI (June, 1962), 37-38.
    Labor education can no longer prepare workers for the status quo since that is already outdated. The labor educator must consider himself a member of labor's clergy and worry about the labor movement's spiritual well-being.

1102. Allen, Russell. "What's Lacking in Labor Education?" IUD Digest. III (Fall, 1958), 109-118 (Synopsis). Also in Management Record. XXI (January, 1959), 22.
    An examination of the quality of labor education.

1103. Brameld, Theodore. "Toward a Philosophy of Workers' Education." Theodore Brameld, ed., Workers' Education in the United States. New York: Harper, 1941, 278-302.
    A discussion of the need for and the elements of a philosophy for labor education.

1104. _____. "Workers' Education--A Neglected Opportunity." Educational Forum. IV (May, 1940), 401-408.
    An examination of the role of the labor educator in changing attitudes of the student-workers.

1105. Byrne, Thomas R. "Training Union Leaders." American Federationist. LXI (January, 1954), 17.
    A call for the goal of labor education to be one of training competent union leaders.

1106. Carlson, Kenneth. "Labor Education in America." Review of Educational Research. XLI (April, 1971), 115-130. ERIC Accession Number EJ 037766.
    A philosophical examination of the goals of labor education with special emphasis on the role of education in the trade union movement.

1107. Carroll, Mollie Ray. "Building Union Organization Through Study." Workers' Education. XIV (April, 1937), 16-18.
    An examination of the changing nature of workers' education with a call for building and preserving the organizational integrity of the trade union movement.

1108. _____. "Workers' Education." Workers' Education. XIV
(July, 1937), 16-20. Also in Proceeding of the National
University Extension Association, 1937, 57-61.
    A report of the discussion between the Workers' Edu-
cation Bureau, Brookwood, and Bryn Mawr and other agencies in the field of workers' education searching for a
plan and philosophy for the continued development of workers' education.

1109. _____ and Spencer Miller, Jr. American Workers' Education. New York: Workers' Education Bureau Press, 1936,
33 pp.
    An examination of the meaning, methods, and policies
of workers' education from the Workers' Education Bureau's point of view.

1110. Cohn, Fannia. "Understanding Basic Problems." American
Federationist. LVI (November, 1949), 34-38.
    A discussion of the basic goal of labor education which
is to prepare young trade unionists to be able to assume
leadership positions within the movement.

1111. _____. Workers' Education and Labor Leadership. New
York: Workers' Education Bureau, 1935. 4 pp.
    A discussion of the importance of leadership to the la-
bor movement and the need for workers' education to be
experienced by many in union leadership.

1112. _____. "Workers' Education and the Social Studies." Social Education. IX (April, 1945), 157-160.
    A short discussion of the need for social literacy in
labor education and the broadening of goals to educate
workers for better citizenship.

1113. _____. Workers' Education in War and Peace. New York:
Workers' Education Press, 1943. 40 pp.
    A statement on the function, scope, and aims of labor
education.

1114. Coit, Eleanor G. "Labor Unions Educate." Progressive Education. XXIII (January, 1946), 99.
    A short discussion of the need for labor education to
help workers educate themselves about social problems in
the post-World War II era.

1115. _____. "Progressive Education at Work." In Theodore
Brameld, ed., Workers' Education in the U.S. New York:
Harper & Row, 1941, 153-180.
    An examination of the changes in the scope and func-
tion of workers' education over the years.

1116. Connors, John D. "Learning Can't Stop." American Federationist. LXIV (September, 1957), 10-11, 30-31.

A discussion of the importance of and necessity for labor education.

1117. _____. Workers' Education and the Atomic Age. New York: Workers' Education Bureau, 1946. 7 pp.

The goal of labor education must be to prepare workers to deal with the world problems of the atomic age.

1118. _____. "Workers' Education What? Why? How?" New York: Workers' Education Bureau, 1947. 18 pp.

An examination of the what, why, and how of labor education.

1119. Cook, Alice H. "New Goals for Labor Education." Adult Leadership. VI (October, 1957), 108-109+.

A progress report of the labor education section of the Adult Education Association and a discussion of its aims, program, and future plans.

1120. Eby, Kermit. "Bread and Stone of Workers' Education." Phi Delta Kappan. XXXVI (February, 1955), 187-190.

A philosophical examination of the responsibility of labor education to prepare workers for a community attachment which will eventually lead to feelings of realistic commitment to brotherhood and world peace.

1121. _____. "Education for Social Well-Being." Labor and Nation. IV (May-June, 1948), 30-31.

This article depicts the aims of labor education as one which "changes and adjusts the environment to serve the needs of the worker."

1122. _____. "For Academic Freedom in Labor Education." Labor and Nation. V (September-October, 1949), 102-103.

Practical education in the long run will lead to labor's undoing. Only through a drastic re-examination of the aims currently espoused by labor education can this movement aid the labor movement.

1123. _____. "General Education for Economic Well-Being." Junior College Journal. XVIII (May, 1948), 504-511.

An examination of the role labor education must assume to make up for the lack of leadership in public education.

1124. Godfredson, Svend. "Workers' Education, It's Place in the Community." Yearbook of Workers' Education, 1926-1943. New York: American Labor Education Service, 1943, 18-19.

An examination of the need of labor education to stress and expand its relationship to the community and allow the needs of the community as well as those of the union to shape the educational program.

1125. Golden, Clinton S. "Workers' Education: The New Job. "
Yearbook of Workers' Education, 1926-1943. New York:
American Labor Education Service, 1943, 9-11.
An examination of the role which labor education must
fulfill among workers who have been neglected by the tra-
ditional education system.

1126. Hanson, (Cook) Alice. "Action and Study: Some Representa-
tive Examples of Workers' Education Programs. " In
Theodore Brameld, ed. , Workers' Education in the U. S.
New York: Harper & Bros. , 1941, 114-152.
An examination of how labor education must seek to be
of assistance to the trade union movement.

1127. Hayes, A. J. "Labor Must Train to Meet Challenge of Changing Times. " Machinist Monthly Journal. LXVI (January,
1954), 2-3+.
A discussion of the role of education in the labor
movement in an address by the president of the IAM to the
graduating class of the Harvard Trade Union Fellowship
Program.

1128. Hillock, Edward J. "Needed--More Labor Education. " American Federationist. LX (January, 1953), 31.
An examination of the pressing needs of the labor
movement which call for a greater commitment to labor
education.

1129. Hochman, Julius. "Workers' Education, Its Job in Public Relations. " Yearbook of Workers' Education, 1926-1943.
New York: American Labor Education Service, 1943, 20-
22.
A call for labor education to educate its membership
for democracy to prevent a repressive period in the post
war era.

1130. Johnson, Alvin. "After School and College. " Survey Graphics. XXVIII (October, 1939), 601-603, 642-643.
The majority of the article deals with adult education,
but a section does examine the philosophical bases of labor
education.

1131. Kallen, Horace M. "The American Worker and His Educa-
tion. " Social Research. XI (February, 1944), 100-111.
A lengthy examination of the "dignity of labor" and the
American dream and the effect of public education on both.
The author also examines the differences between the edu-
cation of workers and workers' education.

1132. Kattsoff, Louis O. "Education for Industrial Peace. " The
Educational Forum. XVII (November, 1952), 101-114.
A lengthy discussion of the pro's and con's of labor
education as well as management education programs. The

author urges that the aims of labor education move away from the pragmatic training for union functions towards an education with social conscience, education for democracy.

1133. _____. "Education or Indoctrination in Workers' Education." The Educational Forum. XV (November, 1950), 51-62.

A critical article of labor education which purportedly has as its only goal that of equipping workers with "tools" for union work. The author insists that the worker must be educated to be a thinking citizen.

1134. _____. "Workers' Education--A Problem in Adult Education." The Educational Forum. XIV (January, 1950), 177-190.

An examination of the need for an informed, educated laboring class as a preservative of the American democratic system.

1135. Lindeman, Eduard C. "Workers' Education, An Instrument for Building the New World." Yearbook of Workers' Education, 1926-1943. New York: American Labor Education Service, 1943, 39-41.

An examination of the need for an educated worker to be able to make intelligent decisions concerning the shape of the post-war world.

1136. Liveright, Alexander A. "A Long Look at Labor Education." Adult Education. IV (February, 1954), 101-108; (March, 1954), 137-145; and (May, 1954), 184-187.

This article and the comments appearing in three separate issues of the journal analyze the problems facing labor education and suggest some solutions which might be attempted.

1137. London, Jack. "Goals for Workers' Education." School for Workers, Thirty-fifth Anniversary Papers. Madison: University of Wisconsin School for Workers, 1960, 84-101.

A definition and discussion of the importance and the goals of labor education. Also included is a model for organizing a labor education program.

1138. McCollum, John. "Labor Education: Education, Training, or Information?" Adult Education. XIII (Autumn, 1962), 42-48.

After defining and comparing education, training, and information, the author questions the validity of defining labor education so precisely that it would fit into any of the three categories.

1139. _____. "Union Leadership Program--University of Chicago." In Freda Goldman, ed., Reorientation in Labor

Education. Chicago: Center for the Study of Liberal Education for Adults, 1962, 75-88. ERIC Accession Number
ED 027445.
    A discussion of the aims and objectives of the Union
Leadership Training Program conducted at the University
of Chicago.

1140. Miller, Glenn W. "Goals and Achievements of Workers' Edu-
      cation." IUD Digest. VI (Winter, 1961), 139-146.
          An examination and comparison of the goals of labor
      education as expressed by the worker-student and the
      goals of the actual programs expressed by the profession-
      al labor educator.

1141. Miller, Harry. "Philosophy and Issues, Labor Education."
      Review of Educational Research. XXIX (June, 1959), 233-
      234.
          Part of a larger article on adult education. This sec-
      tion examines the literature in the field of labor education
      during the decade of the 1950s concentrating on the larger
      issues in the field.

1142. Miller, Spencer, Jr. "Education of Workers for the Post-
      War Period." Public Affairs. VIII (Winter, 1945), 84-87.
          An examination of the new educational needs of work-
      ers in the post-war period.

1143. _____. "Labor Cooperates with Community Agencies."
      Journal of Adult Education. XI (April, 1939), 180-183.
          A discussion of the goals of labor education which
      must be, "an instrument not for the emancipation of the
      working class, but rather for the emancipation of all peo-
      ples from the fetters of ignorance."

1144. _____. "The Supreme Issue and the Education of Labor."
      Workers' Education. XI (October, 1935), 6-9.
          A discussion of the social legislation of the New Deal
      era and its implications for labor education.

1145. _____. "Workers' Education Retrospect and Forecast."
      Workers' Education. XIII (July, 1936), 5-10. Also in
      Journal of Adult Education. VIII (June, 1936), 345-346.
          An examination of recent trends in labor education, in-
      cluding closer cooperation with the labor movement, uni-
      versities, and the federal government.

1146. "The Nature and Purpose of Workers' Education." Journal
      of Adult Education. XI (October, 1940), 502-507.
          A report of the proceedings of the Fifteenth Annual
      Meeting of the American Association for Adult Education.
      The first section recounts the speeches of practitioners
      such as Fannia Cohn from the ILGWU, Mollie Ray Carrol
      from the WEB and Howell Broach for IBEW Local 3. The

second section consists of statements from students in labor education classes explaining the effects the classes had on their lives.

1147. Pragan, Otto. "Meeting Labor's Education Needs." Labor Education Viewpoints. (Fall, 1959), 15-22.
An examination of the needed changes in the field of labor education so that it will become relevant to the labor movement.

1148. Reuter, Ralph R. "Who Says Labor Education's Ineffective?" Adult Leadership. XI (October, 1962), 110-112.
An analysis and praise of labor education with a discussion of how union educational programs are meeting labor's needs better than colleges or universities could.

1149. Rogin, Lawrence. "The Unions and Liberal Education for Labor." In Freda Goldman, ed., Reorientation in Labor Education. Chicago: Center for the Study of Liberal Education for Adults, 1962, 5-10. ERIC Accession Number ED 027445.
A discussion of the goals of labor education in the United States with a statement on the need for union-university cooperation.

1150. Russell, Harry A. "New England Labor Prepares for New Deal." Journal of Adult Education. VI (October, 1934), 526-528.
A discussion of the formulation of revised aims for labor education, so that the aims may be relevant for the needs of the times.

1151. Schwarztrauber, Ernest E. "The Aim of Workers' Education." The Wisconsin Idea in Workers' Education. Madison, Wisconsin: University of Wisconsin School for Workers, 1946, 16-19.
An examination of the aims labor education should be pursuing both in the short and long terms.

1152. _____. "Industrial Relations vs. Workers' Education." The Wisconsin Idea in Workers' Education. Madison: University of Wisconsin School for Workers, 1946, 3-8.
An examination of the differences in goals and aims between labor education and industrial relations.

1153. Sexton, Brendan. "Achieving Excellence in Labor Education." School for Workers Thirty-Fifth Anniversary Papers. Madison: University of Wisconsin School for Workers, 1960, 79-83.
An examination of the ingredients for excellence needed in labor education.

1154. _____. "Letter to the Editor." Adult Education. IV

(September, 1954), 221-224.
    A critical response to the Liveright article entitled
"A Long Look at Labor-Education."

1155. Shapiro, Theodore. "The Challenge of Workers' Education."
    Adult Education. I (February, 1951), 91-94. Comments
    by Irvine Kerrison, Arthur Elder, and Orlie Pell, 95-99.
        The author ties labor education to its radical tradition
    and calls for the development of individualism in the field.
    The commentators feel that the discussion is severely lim-
    ited by linking labor education with radical ideology.

1156. Smith, Hilda W. "The Need for Workers' Education During
    the War." Adult Education Bulletin. VII (December,
    1942), 45-46.
        The author discusses the broad goals of labor educa-
    tion in an attempt to gain acceptance for the idea that
    workers need education during and after the war.

1157. Starr, Mark. "Building and Defending Democracy: The Role
    of Workers' Education." The Educational Forum. XIII
    (March, 1949), 287-292.
        An examination of the expanding role of labor educa-
    tion coupled with a warning that labor education must still
    be to train for trade union service.

1158. _____. "Let's Look at Workers' Education." American
    Federationist. XLIV (August, 1957), 22-25.
        An examination of the goals of labor education by ex-
    ploring what is being offered by various unions and univer-
    sities.

1159. _____. "Operation Trade Union Education." Teacher Col-
    lege Record. LII (November, 1950), 114-123.
        An examination of the goals of labor education by dis-
    cussing the content of a union education program.

1160. _____. "The Role of Workers' Education." The Carpenter.
    LXX (February, 1950), 18-22.
        The author replaces the "3 R's" of education with the
    "3 D's." The "3 D's" which labor education teaches are
    discipline in life, direction in philosophy and dynamics in
    social action.

1161. _____. "Why Union Education? Aims, History and Phi-
    losophy of the Educational work of the ILGWU." American
    Philosophical Society, Proceedings. XCII (1948), 194-202.
        The article examines the history and philosophical bas-
    is of the ILGWU Education Department.

1162. _____. "Workers' Education." American Federationist.
    LIX (February, 1952), 13.
        A short definition of labor education.

1163. _____. "Workers' Education in Overalls." Journal of
Adult Education. XI (January, 1939), 55-58.
A discussion of the role and importance of workers'
education and its need to be recognized and supported.

1164. _____. "Workers' Education, Time to Change." Labor
and The Nation. (September-October, 1949), 102.
An exhortation to revamp the aims of labor education.

1165. Townsend, Willard S. "Toward Full Equality." Adult Education Journal. V (October, 1946), 162-165.
An exposition of the role of labor education in the post-
war United States.

1166. Vogt, Paul. "Western Labor Responds to Its New Educational Task." Journal of Adult Education. VI (October,
1934), 514-620.
A call to meet the challenge of a growing union membership with new educational aims.

1167. Witte, Edwin E. "Social Objectives of Workers' Education
Today." Proceedings of the National University Extension
Association, Chicago, Illinois, May 2-5, 1948. Boston:
Wright & Potter, 1948, 118-121.
An examination of the importance of labor unions, and
thus the importance of labor education. Since labor education is so important, the aims and goals are defined by the
author who singles out the university's role in labor education.

1168. Woll, Matthew. "A Unionist's View on Adult Education."
Catholic Educational Review. XLIV (February, 1946), 105-
108.
A discussion of the inter-relationship of work, citizenship and democracy and the need for educational programs
geared for workers.

1169. "Workers' Education." Adult Education Journal. V (January,
1946), 53-55.
Five prominent labor educators, representing unions,
universities and private agencies examine the changing nature of labor education in the post-war era.

1170. "Workers' Education: A Symposium." Journal of Adult Education. XI (June, 1939), 301-308.
A report of a workers' education symposium and a description of the three main participants, Hilda Smith, Mark
Starr, and Eleanor Coit's definitions of labor education.

1171. Zander, Arnold S. "Let's Use Workers' Education." American Federationist. L (October, 1943), 28-29.
A criticism of labor education for falling behind adult
education in teaching techniques. Included are some suggestions for rejuvenating the former.

CURRICULUM AND METHODS

1172. Abbott, William L. "Let's Put an End to 'Off-the-Cuff' Workers' Education Research." Adult Leadership. IX (September, 1960), 84-85+.

    The author laments the lack of teaching and reading materials in the field of labor education and calls for universities to get into hard-core research to develop materials for the classroom.

1173. Beeler, Duane and Frank McCallister. Creative Use of Film Education; A Case Study of an Adult Education Program for Union Leaders. Chicago: Roosevelt University Labor Education Division, 1968. 85 pp. ERIC Accession number ED 029261.

    A discussion of the way films can be used in a workers' class. Included are discussions of a number of films frequently used in labor education.

1174. Bendix, D. Librarians Should Attend Trade Unionists Schools." Library Journal. LXXII (January 1, 1947), 58-59.

    To assist industrial workers to utilize the library, the author urges librarians to familiarize themselves with industrial workers.

1175. Blough, Maggie "Case History of a Conference." Labor Education Viewpoints. (Spring, 1964), 13-17.

    A description of the planning of a culminating conference of the union leadership of a particular local union.

1176. "Building the Union." Ammunition. XV (January-February, 1957), 88 pp.

    The entire issue of Ammunition is a special issue written by the education committee of the UAW. It outlines the UAW role in education and includes excerpts from the union's constitution concerning education and explanations for setting up a local education program.

1177. Campbell, Ralph N. "Education and Leadership Development Challenge to Labor Education." Challenges to Labor Education in the 60's: A Symposium. Washington, D.C.: National Institute of Labor Education, 1962, 56-69.

    A comparison of the organizational patterns which characterize labor education and agricultural education. This study raises the question whether labor education can be conducted by a relatively independent educational agency serving the needs of the labor movement.

1178. Carroll, Mollie Ray. "Cooperative Workers' Education." Journal of Adult Education. IX (April, 1937), 184-186.

A description of the methods and materials used by
the Workers' Education Bureau in the labor education programs.

1179. Clowes, Florence M. "Women's Auxiliaries in the SWOC."
Affiliated Schools Scrapbook. I (February, 1939), 34-35.
A description of curriculum and methods used by the
Steelworkers Organizing Committee Women's Auxiliary in
the education of the wives of union members.

1180. Cohn, Fannia. Workers' Education and Labor Leadership.
New York: Workers' Education Bureau, 1935. 4 pp.
An examination of the attributes necessary for labor
leadership and a listing of curricula and methods which
should be used to train labor leaders.

1181. _____. Workers' Education in the World Crisis. New
York: Education Department International Ladies Garment
Workers' Union, 1940. 4 pp.
A discussion of the content of labor education for all
trade union members.

1182. Coit, Eleanor and Orlie Pell. "Group Work in the Workers'
Education Setting." In Charles Hendy, ed., A Decade of
Group Work. New York: Association Press, 1948, 68-76.
A discussion of the use of group work techniques in a
labor education classroom.

1183. Connors, John D. "To Help Us Find Our Way." American
Federationist. LVIII (August, 1951), 18-20.
A discussion of the educational outlook of the AFL,
emphasizing some of the innovative educational techniques
that the Federation uses in the education of its members.

1184. _____. "Is Your Union Showing Movies?" American Federationist. LXII (September, 1955), 10-11.
A discussion of the use of 16mm films and filmstrips
for educational purposes and to increase attendance of members at Union meetings.

1185. Cook, Cara. "The Workers Speak." The Affiliated Schools
Scrapbook. I (February, 1939), 28-30.
The educational benefits of the New York Women's
Trade Union League's organizing groups of workers to tes-
tify for or against pieces of legislation.

1186. Cosgrove, John E. "New Approaches in Labor Education."
American Federationist. LXIV (October, 1957), 12-14.
A discussion of the regional labor school concept with
specific attention given to the curriculum in such a school.

1187. Giles, Harry H. "Implications of These Educational Techniques." Journal of Educational Sociology. XXV (Febru-

ary, 1952), 374-380.
   An examination of the educational techniques being
used by the American Labor Education Service (ALES).

1188. Gilmore, Marguerite. "Workshops in Living History." Adult
   Education Bulletin. III (June, 1939), 26-27.
      A description of the educational methods used to teach
   a history workshop for textile union members.

1189. Golatz, Helmut. "How Much Do They Take Back with Them?"
   Labor Education Viewpoints. (Fall, 1961), 1-3.
      A description of a test to determine how much steel-
   workers learned in the Penn State summer institutes.

1190. Goshkin, Ida. "The Public Library Cooperation with Labor
   Organizations." Wilson Library Bulletin. XVII (December, 1942), 306-309.
      A discussion of the various types of cooperation li-
   braries should offer labor education endeavors.

1191. Hanson, (Cook) Alice. "An Alliance of Labor and Teachers."
   American Teacher. XXVI (February, 1942), 18-19, 24.
      An examination of the role and responsibility of the
   unionized teacher in labor education.

1192. Hoffman, Seth and Molly. "Labor Art Workshop." Adult
   Education Journal. III (October, 1944), 154.
      A discussion of various ILGWU locals which had set
   up art workshops for their members.

1193. "How to Organize Education in Your Local Unions." Ammunition. I (April, 1943), 4.
      An outline of a three step program for establishing
   an educational program in a UAW local.

1194. "ILGWU Radio Stations." Adult Education Journal. V (April,
   1946), 103.
      An announcement of its union's plan to establish a non-
   profit radio station and the educational uses of the station.

1195. In Quest of Knowledge. Washington, D. C. : Communications
   Workers of America, Department of Education, 1964, 32
   pp.
      A handbook which explains how local unions can estab-
   lish their own labor education committee.

1196. Jackman, Herbert. "The Union Educational Film." In J. B.
   S. Hardman and Maurice Neufield, eds. , The House of
   Labor: Internal Operations of American Unions. New
   York: Prentice Hall, 1951, 471-473.
      A discussion of the use of the motion picture as an
   educational device.

1197. Juris, Hervey. "Reaching State and Local Public Employees in the Boondocks." Labor Education Viewpoints. (Fall, 1968), 15-16, 21.
    A discussion of the methods to be used in reaching newly-organized public employees and the types of educational programs they need.

1198. Kalish, A. H. "Ins and Outs of Attracting Labor." Library Journal. LXIX (January 15, 1944), 54-56.
    An examination of the Boston Public Library's educational work with trade unionists in the Boston area.

1199. _____. "Public Libraries Can Serve Unions." American Federationist. L (December, 1943), 29.
    A description of the Boston Public Libraries services to trade unions in the area.

1200. Karlen, Harvey. "Poll Taking and Opinion Survey: A Course of Instruction for Union Members." Adult Education. XIV (Autumn, 1963), 20-25.
    A discussion of an educational program and the methods used to train union members to poll effectively.

1201. Keddie, Wells and Richard E. Ryan. The Impact of the Union Leadership Academy upon the Behavior and Attitudes of Union Members. Philadelphia: Pennsylvania State University Labor Studies Department, 1969. 90 pp.
    A case study of the ULA center in Pennsylvania which examines the impact of the educational program on the worker-student.

1202. Kerrison, Irvine L. H. "Using Films and Filmstrips with Union Groups." Film Forum Review. III (Winter, 1948-1949), 13-16.
    An examination of the use of films and filmstrips in a labor education class.

1203. _____. "Wanted: A Better AV Job in the Labor Field." Educational Screen. XXVIII (October, 1949), 348-350.
    A critique of the materials available for labor groups in the AV field. The author discusses the need for good educational discussion stimulators.

1204. "Labor Speaks." Adult Education Journal. V (April, 1946), 103.
    An examination of a radio educational program conducted by the Wisconsin School for Workers.

1205. Larsen, Margit. "A New Group Strikes." Affiliated Schools Scrapbook. I (February, 1939), 31-33.
    A discussion of the educational values of a strike conducted by department store workers in San Francisco.

1206. Lawrence, Mary. Education Unlimited. Monteagle, Tenn.:
      Highlander Fold School, 1945, 45 pp.
      A pamphlet which describes how to organize a labor
      education program.

1207. Lefranc, Emile. "Workers' Schools and Correspondence
      Courses." American Federationist. XLIII (October,
      1936), 1069-1070.
      A discussion of the use of various models in labor ed-
      ucation to meet its utilitarian goals.

1208. Levit, Grace. "Labor's Big Buzz." Adult Leadership. III
      (May, 1954), 6-7.
      A discussion of the use of buzz groups to encourage a
      large group to participate individually in discussion.

1209. Liveright, Alexander. Union Leadership Training: A Hand-
      book of Tools and Techniques. New York: Harper, 1951,
      265 pp.
      An extensive delineation of various methods and tech-
      niques being used by AFL-CIO unions and universities of-
      fering labor education courses. The work stresses how
      and when to use the various methods.

1210. _____. "Workers' Educators Examine and Approve Infor-
      mal Education Technics." Adult Education Bulletin. XIV
      (June, 1950), 135-140.
      A discussion of the educational techniques used in a
      conference on labor education to encourage student partici-
      pation.

1211. Marquart, Frank. "The Educational Program of Local #3
      United Automobile Workers of America." Affiliated
      Schools Scrapbook. I (February, 1939), 11-12.
      A list of educational techniques for increasing attend-
      ance at general membership meetings.

1212. Maurer, Freda. "The Flexible Workshop." Affiliated
      Schools Scrapbook. I (February, 1939), 12-13.
      A report by the labor education leader of the CIO re-
      gional office in Philadelphia of the ways she manufactured
      a flexible workshop when she was denied a permanent spot
      for one.

1213. McClusky, Howard. "What Lessons Has Adult Education
      Taught Us about Educational Methodology." Challenges to
      Labor Education in the 60's: A Symposium. Washington,
      D.C.: National Institute for Labor Education, 1962, 70-
      79.
      An examination of the various educational methods
      which have been successfully used with adults.

1214. McCurdy, Joseph. "Workers' Education in Baltimore."

American Federationist. XLIII (October, 1936), 1040-
1041.
A discussion of the use of "skits" to bring educational
issues before the union membership.

1215. McKelvey, Jean T.   "Teaching Industrial and Labor Relations." Labor and Nation. IV (November-December,
1948), 33-34.
An overview of the methodology used at the New York
State School of Industrial and Labor Relations at Cornell.

1216. McNally, Miriam E.   "Working with Organized Labor."
Adult Education Journal. IV (July, 1945), 107.
A discussion of library-union cooperation in Denver
and the resulting educational endeavors.

1217. Mire, Joseph.   "Recent Trends in Labor Education." School
for Workers 35th Anniversary Papers. Madison: University of Wisconsin School for Workers, 1960, 50-61.
A discussion of labor education with special emphasis
on students, curriculum, and educational methods.

1218. Mounce, E. W.   "Workers' Education in Missouri." American Federationist. XLII (April, 1935), 419-422.
An examination of the educational methodology of a successful labor education program.

1219. Newmann, H.   "International Collaboration of Workers' Educational Centers on Film." American Federationist.
XLIII (October, 1936), 1067-1068.
This article outlines a method of loaning films between
labor education centers in various countries.

1220. Nockels, Edward M.   "Labor's Experience in Radio." American Federationist. XLIV (March, 1937), 276-281.
A report of labor pioneer radio station WCFL (Chicago Federation of Labor) and the programs it offers.

1221. Nonamker, Catherine.   "Education Through the Portable Classroom." Affiliated Schools Scrapbook. I (February, 1939),
6-7.
A description of organizing labor education classes
around the work schedules of prospective students.

1222. Oko, Dorothy and Bernard Downey. Library Services to Labor. New York: Scarecrow Press, 1963, 313 pp.
A study of the role of public libraries as educational
resources for trade unionists.

1223. "An Outline for a Handbook on Labor Education." Labor Education Viewpoints. (Spring, 1965), 35-45.
An outline describing how to set up a labor education
program.

1224. Ozanne, Dorothy R. "Songs of the Needleworkers." Journal of Adult Education. X (June, 1938), 293-295.
    An account of the musical and dramatic training opportunities open to members of the ILGWU.

1225. Pleysier, A. "Workers Education and Broadcasting." American Federationist. XLIII (October, 1936), 1056-1063.
    A discussion of the role labor should play in determining what is broadcast over the radio for public consumption.

1226. Plunder, Olga Law. "Cultural Activities in the Amalgamated." Affiliated Schools Scrapbook. I (February, 1939), 16-18.
    A discussion of the educational and recreational methods of the Amalgamated Clothing Workers of America.

1227. Posell, Elsa. "Reaching Labor." Wilson Library Bulletin. XV (November, 1940), 213-217.
    An appeal to librarians to interest labor to use the public libraries and to provide material of interest to union members.

1228. Repas, Bob. "How Can Basic Labor Issues Be Tackled." Labor Education Viewpoints. (Winter, 1961), 7-10.
    A description of the educational techniques which can be used to deal with current labor issues.

1229. _____. "Laborites Look at World Issues." Labor and Nation. VII (Fall, 1951), 44-49.
    A discussion of some unique educational methods used to generate workers' interest in international affairs.

1230. Russell, C. Phillips, Ida L. Coker, and Harold Coy. "Labor's Own Group Work--Alias Workers' Education, Participants, Not Targets." Social Work Today. VII (November, 1939), 16-19.
    A series of three articles which examine workers' education as a form of group work, as a way of aiding black women workers, as participant in the WPA.

1231. Schwartz, Milton and Irvine Kerrison. The Learning Process with Applications to Workers' Education. Bulletin #5, Rutgers University IMLR, 1956, 22 pp.
    A pamphlet written for local union officers as a summary of the basic learning process. Key concepts in the psychology of learning have been summarized and integrated into the basic needs of a labor education program.

1232. Schwarztrauber, Ernest E. "Administering Workers' Education." In Theodore Brameld, ed., Workers' Education in the United States. New York: Harper, 1941, 203-229.
    A discussion of the techniques which should be used in administering labor education.

1233. Schwenkmeyer, Freida. "Union Offices as Cultural Centers."
Affiliated Schools Scrapbook. I (February, 1939), 14-16.
          A discussion of ways the union office can widen the
educational horizons of the membership.

1234. Silvey, Ted. "Public Response to the Farand Bill." Labor
Education Viewpoints. (Winter, 1960), 7-13.
          The article depicts how a political issue can be used
to build an educational program.

1235. Simon, Fanny S. Teaching Methods and Techniques in Labor
Education. 2nd ed. Mexico: ORIT, 1968, 237 pp.
          A methodological study for conducting labor education
programs. Although the examples in the book concentrate
on Latin American trade unionists, the various explanations of techniques apply to labor education everywhere.

1236. Smith, Hilda W. "The Student and Teacher in Workers' Education." In Theodore Brameld, ed., Workers' Education
in the United States. New York: Harper, 1941, 181-202.
          A description of the typical student and the needs and
goals they expect from a labor education class. After describing the typical teacher, the author suggests the ways
the students' aspirations can best be met.

1237. _____ and Ernestine Freidmann. "Methods in Workers'
Education." Adult Education Bulletin. I (January, 1937),
3-6.
          The democratic process is the most important element
in labor education, and the authors stress various educational methods which will enhance the democratic nature of
labor education.

1238. Smith, J. C. "Each Man Is an Island " Common Ground.
VII (Summer, 1947), 61-73.
          A description of a class in race relations taught by the
author at the Hudson Shore Labor School.

1239. Starr, Mark. The Eye Route. New York: Education Department ILGWU, 1938. 22 pp.
          An examination of the agencies involved and the meth-
ods to be employed in using visual aids in workers' classes.

1240. _____. "How One Union Uses Films." American Federationist. LVIII (March, 1951), 23-24.
          The author criticizes labor education for being slow in
learning to use and make documentary films. However,
he does note several worthwhile films which can be used
in labor education classes.

1241. _____. "Training for Union Leadership." Labor and Nation. III (November-December, 1947), 45-47.

An examination and critique of various educational methods being used to prepare the next generation of union leaders.

1242. _____. "Workers' Education." Harvard Educational Review. XXI (Fall, 1951), 243-267.
A broad discussion of the goals and methods of labor education in the United States.

1243. Stein, L. S. "An Experiment in Correspondence Training of Trade Union Leaders." Adult Education. I (June, 1951), 176-183.
A discussion of the pro's and con's of correspondence courses as a method of labor education.

1244. "The Teacher in the Labor Movement: A Discussion in Memory of Sam Jacobs." Labor Education Viewpoints. (1960), 17-29.
A discussion of the role and methods used by a teacher in labor education.

INDIVIDUAL ORGANIZATIONS

American Labor Education Service

1245. Algor, Marie. "The Problem Is Tackled as a Union Problem." Journal of Educational Sociology. XXV (February, 1952), 338-341.
A discussion of the work of the American Labor Education Service in joint cooperation with New Jersey unions to combat prejudice and get minority groups and unions together to fight for full employment.

1246. _____. "The New Director Writes of the School." Bryn Mawr Alumnae Bulletin. XXI (March, 1941), 15-16.
A report of the activities of the twenty-first summer school for women workers at the Hudson Shore Labor School. Included in the article are descriptions of studies carried on by the faculty of the summer school.

1247. "ALES." Adult Education Journal. II (January, 1943), 30-31.
An activity report of the work of the American Labor Education Service.

1248. "ALES." Adult Education Journal. II (October, 1943), 162.
An activity report of the educational work of the American Labor Education Service.

1249. Barton, Becky. "Midwestern Trends in Workers' Education." Adult Education Journal. I (January, 1942), 34-36.
A description of the midwest Workers' Education Con-

ference sponsored by the American Labor Education Service.

1250. Coit, Eleanor G. "The American Labor Education Service."
The Highway. XLI (February, 1950), 88-90.
A description of the role of the American Labor Education Service in providing educational benefits for American workers.

1251. _____. "Educational Counselling and Advisory Services to all Types of Unions and Workers' Education Groups and Agencies." Industrial Labor Relations Review. II (January, 1949), 307-309.
A short description of the work of the American Labor Education Service for 1948.

1252. _____ and Andrea Taylor Hourwich. "Workers' Education, Changing Times: The Story of the American Labor Education Service." Yearbook of Workers' Education, 1926-1943. New York: American Labor Education Service, 1943, 12-17.
A report of the activities of the American Labor Education Service.

1253. _____ and Orlie Pell. Labor Education Inter-Group Relations." Journal of Educational Sociology. XXV (February, 1952), 319-320.
A report of the changing activities of the American Labor Education Service which turned its attention to intergroup problems.

1254. "Chicago Labor Education Council." Adult Education Journal. IV (October, 1945), 166.
A discussion of the role of the American Labor Education Service in establishing a Labor Education Council in Chicago.

1255. "Developing International Understanding." Journal of Educational Sociology. XXV (February, 1952), 320-321.
A description of a program developed by American Labor Education Service designed to provide union members with an understanding of international affairs.

1256. Fairchild, Mildred. "The Hudson Shore Labor School in the Summer of 1939." Bryn Mawr Alumnae Bulletin. XIX (December, 1939), 14-15.
A report of the first summer school class held at Hudson Shore, West Point, New York. Some advantages and disadvantages of the new location are included in this article.

1257. _____. "Hudson Shore Labor School in Wartime." Bryn Mawr Alumnae Bulletin. XXIII (May, 1943), 20-22.
A report of how Bryn Mawr's ties with the Summer School for Women Workers has continued despite its move

to Hudson Shore in West Point, New York.

1258. Fincke, William Mann. "The Summer School for Office
Workers." Affiliated Schools Scrapbook. I (March, 1937),
16-19.
    A description of the summer school for office work-
ers.

1259. Gardner, Dorothy. "Affiliated Schools for Workers." Occu-
pation. XV (March, 1937), 530-532.
    An article concerned with the publications of the Af-
filiated Schools which changed its name to the American Labor Education Service.

1260. Graham, Chester A. "Farmer-Labor Understanding--and Ac-
tion--Education Conference of Farmers and Workers."
Journal of Educational Sociology. XXV (February, 1952),
356-362.
    A report of the efforts of the American Labor Educa-
tion Service to enhance mutual understanding and respect
between workers and farmers.

1261. Guernsey, George T. "Experiments in Farmer Labor Cooperative." Journal of Educational Sociology. XXV (February, 1952), 348-356.
    A report of the efforts of the American Labor Educa-
tion Service to provide organized labor with an understanding of the importance of farmer-worker cooperation.

1262. Heaps, David. "The ALES International Project." Thirty
Year History of an Idea. New York: American Labor-
Education Service, 1958, 15-18.
    A report of the educational activities of ALES in the
area of international affairs.

1263. Henson, Francis A. "Exploring Labor Education in International Affairs." Journal of Educational Sociology. XXV
(February, 1952), 331-336.
    A discussion of the needs and methods for educating
workers in international affairs.

1264. Hopkins, William S. "The Pacific Coast School for Workers."
Labor Information Bulletin. VI (August, 1939), 6-7.
    A description of the beginning and functioning of this
labor education project from 1933-1939.

1265. Hourwich, Andrea Taylor. "The American Labor Education
Service." The Woman's Press. XXXV (November, 1941),
459.
    A brief discussion of the educational work done by the
American Labor Education Service.

1266. "Hudson Shore Institute." Adult Education Journal. VII (July,

1948), 148.
An activity report of the labor institutes at Hudson Shore.

1267. "Hudson Shore Labor School." Adult Education Journal. IV (October, 1945), 165-166.
An activity report of the Hudson Shore Labor School.

1268. "Hudson Shore Labor School." Adult Education Journal. V (April, 1946), 103.
An activity report of the Hudson Shore Labor School.

1269. "Hudson Shore Labor School." Adult Education Journal. VI (April, 1947), 93.
A report of the eight-week summer program of the school and a description of the proposed curriculum.

1270. Kohn, Lucile and Eleanor Coit. "The Future of the Idea." Thirty Year History of an Idea. New York: American Labor Education Service, 1958, 19-21.
A descriptive study of the functioning of ALES and its future educational plans.

1271. "Labor Education Service." Journal of Adult Education. XII (April, 1940), 319.
A description of the changing name and organization of the Affiliated Schools for Workers to the American Education Service.

1272. "Labor Education Service." Adult Education Journal. I (January, 1942), 11-12.
An activity report of the American Labor Education Service.

1273. "Labor Education Service." Adult Education Journal. V (July, 1946), 140.
An activity report of the American Labor Education Service.

1274. "Labor Education Service Forms Chicago Council." Adult Education Journal. III (April, 1944), 69.
A report of the efforts of the American Labor Education Service to establish a labor education council in Chicago.

1275. "LES News." Journal of Adult Education. XIII (June, 1941), 319.
A description of a publication of the American Labor Education Service on current materials for workers' classes.

1276. "Labor Schools." Adult Education Journal. I (October, 1942), 146-147.

An activity report of the various labor schools which were in some way affiliated with the American Labor Education Service.

1277. Liveright, Alexander A. "Life-Long Learning in Montana." Adult Education. VI (Spring, 1956), 202-210.
A descriptive explanation of the Montana Farmers Union and the varied educational programs which its members undertake.

1278. Liveright, Alice F. and Helen Kingery. "Workers' Education for White Collar Workers." Yearbook of Workers' Education, 1926-1943. New York: American Labor Education Service, 1943, 32-33.
An examination of the reasons why labor education is needed for white collar workers who are for the most part at least high school graduates.

1279. "Midwest Conference." Adult Education Journal. III (January, 1944), 39.
A report of an American Labor Education Service conference on labor education in the midwest.

1280. "Midwest Conference." Adult Education Journal. IV (January, 1945), 37.
A report of an American Labor Education Service Conference on labor education in the midwest.

1281. "Minnesota Labor Institute." Adult Education Journal. III (April, 1944), 70.
An activity report of a labor institute held in Minnesota.

1282. "Non-Resident Study Project." Adult Education Journal. IV (April, 1945), 76.
An activity report of the educational work carried on by the American Labor Education Service with office workers.

1283. "Office Workers." Adult Education Journal. III (October, 1944), 166.
A report of the summer school for office workers.

1284. "Office Workers Sessions." Social Work Today. VII. April, 1940, 26.
A short description of the Office Workers Summer School to be held in Chicago.

1285. "Office Workers Summer School." Adult Education Journal. IV (October, 1945), 165.
An activity report of the American Labor Education Service's Office Workers Summer School.

1286. Park, Marion Edwards.   "New Director Appointed for Hudson
      Shore Labor School."   Bryn Mawr Alumnae Bulletin.   XXI
      (March, 1941), 15.
              An announcement made by the president of Bryn Mawr
      College concerning the new director of the Hudson Shore
      Labor school, Marie Elliott Algor who replaced Jean Car-
      ter.

1287. Pell, Orlie.   "For White Collar Workers."   Opportunity.
      XXIV (Spring, 1946), 86-87.
              An examination of the educational goals of the Summer
      School for Office Workers.

1288. _____.   "The Idea That Is ALES."   Thirty Year History of
      an Idea.   New York: American Labor Education Service,
      1958, 11-14.
              An historical survey of the development of the ALES
      from its initial days as the Affiliated Schools for Women
      Workers in Industry.

1289. _____.   "Labor Education for World Understanding."   Jour-
      nal of Educational Sociology.   XXIX (November, 1955),
      134-139.
              A report of the American Labor Education Service's
      school on the United Nations and the educational attempts
      to provide workers with an understanding of international
      affairs.

1290. _____.   "Practice in Democracy."   Woman's Press.
      XXXVI (February, 1942), 72+.
              A descriptive study of the Summer School for Office
      Workers.

1291. _____.   "A Labor School on World Affairs."   Adult Lead-
      ership.   IX (February, 1961), 239-264.
              A report on the United Nations School, the School on
      World Affairs, conducted by the American Labor Educa-
      tion Service.

1292. _____.   "Something Is Happening to White Collar Workers."
      Woman's Press.   XXXII (April, 1938), 175-177.
              A description of the growing power of white collar
      workers and the role of the Summer School for Office
      Workers.

1293. _____.   "Summer School for Office Workers."   School and
      Society.   LXV (June 28, 1947), 477-479.
              A short summary of the Summer School for Office
      Workers.

1294. _____.   "Workers Go to School."   School and Society.
      XLV (May, 1937), 754.
              A description of the educational work carried on by

the Affiliated Schools and in particular, the Summer
School for Office Workers.

1295. _____ and Marie S. Algor. "Unions Explore the United
Nations." Adult Leadership. V (January, 1957), 209.
A description of the ALES project on international af-
fairs education which included a study tour of the United
States.

1296. "St. Louis Labor Education Service." Adult Education Journal. VII (January, 1948), 13.
A report of the establishment of a special labor education project in St. Louis started under the auspices of the
American Labor Education Service.

1297. "Schools for Workers." Adult Education Journal. I (July,
1942), 92.
A report of the various schools connected with the
American Labor Education Service.

1298. Sender, Toni. "Labor Education Service." Nation. CLII
(February 1, 1941), 140.
A letter calling attention to the function of the Ameri-
can Labor Education Service.

1299. "Southern School." Adult Education Journal. II (April, 1943),
80.
An activity report of the Southern Summer
School.

1300. "Southern School for Workers." Adult Education Journal.
VI (April, 1947), 93.
An activity report of the Southern Summer School.

1301. "Summer School for Office Workers." Adult Education Jour-
nal. V (October, 1946), 178.
An activity report of the American Labor Education
Service's School for Office Workers.

1302. "Summer School for Office Workers." Adult Education Jour-
nal. VI (October, 1947), 189.
An activity report of the Summer School for Office
Workers.

1303. Taylor, Harold. "The Social Meaning of the Exchange of
Worker-Students." Journal of Educational Sociology. XXV
(February, 1952), 322-327.
A discussion of the exchange of students between coun-
tries and a call for workers to participate in these foreign
exchange programs.

1304. "Washington's Birthday Conference." Adult Education Journal,
VI (April, 1947), 92-93.

A report of the 1947 Washington's Birthday Conference of Teachers in Labor Education.

1305. "Washington's Birthday Conference." Adult Education Journal. VII (April, 1948), 84-85.
A report of the 1948 Washington's Birthday Conference of Teachers in Labor Education.

1306. "Weekend School." Adult Education Journal. III (January, 1944), 39.
A report of educational programs conducted for office workers.

1307. Wertheimer, Barbara. "Labor Educators Analyze Values and Objectives in U.S. Society." Journal of Educational Sociology. XXXIV (March, 1961), 320-323.
This article describes the proceedings and discussion topics of the ALES's annual week-end conference of 1960 conducted in cooperation with Workers' Education Local 189 of the American Federation of Teachers.

1308. Wolfson, Theresa. "The Educational Program of the Resident Session of White Collar Workshops." Journal of Educational Sociology. XXV (February, 1925), 363-373.
A discussion of the development of the American Labor Education Service and particularly, the summer school known as the White Collar Workshop.

1309. _____. "Education Through White-Collar Workshops." Monthly Labor Review. LXXIV (May, 1952), 508-510.
A descriptive study of the history, curriculum, and student body of the American Labor Education Service's White Collar Workshop.

1310. _____. "A New Educational Frontier." Educational Trends. V (May-June, 1937), 25-28.
A discussion of the Summer School for Office Workers held in 1936 at Northwestern University.

1311. _____. "The White Collar Worker Asks Questions." Social Frontier. IV (March, 1938), 184-187.
A brief, historical description of some of the initial problems faced by early workers' schools.

1312. "Workers' Education Conference." Adult Education Journal. VII (January, 1948), 30.
A description of an ALES conference of farmers and labor.

Organized Labor

1313. Allen, Russell. "Resident Study Programs for Union Staff."

In Freda Goldman, ed., Reorientation in Labor Education.
Chicago: Center for the Study of Liberal Education for
Adults, 1962, 61-74. ERIC Accession Number ED 027445.
    A discussion of the failures of some unions to keep up
with national and world affairs, and the author's suggestion for labor education to remedy this problem.

1314. "Amalgamated Pioneers in Field of Labor Education." Butcher
    Workman. LXIV (March, 1958), 2-5, 22.
        A description of a new concept in labor education--the
    invitation to management representatives to attend the un-
    ion educational program so that discussions concerning col-
    lective bargaining problems could be more clearly under-
    stood.

1315. Amidon, Beulah. "Union Teacher." Survey. LXXXVI (De-
    cember, 1950), 549-550.
        A biographical sketch of Mark Starr and a description
    of the union education program he directs.

1316. Baab, Otto J. "As the Arbitrator Sees the Union." Labor
    and Nation. III (May-June, 1947), 34-35.
        A call for trade unions to assume the responsibility to
    educate all of their members regarding the full meaning of
    unionism.

1317. Bacon, Emery F. "The United Steelworkers' Labor Institute."
    Labor and Nation. II (November-December, 1946), 55-57.
        A report of the first Steelworkers' Labor Institute held
    at the Pennsylvania State College in 1946.

1318. Barbash, Jack. The Practice of Unionism. New York:
    Harper & Row, 1956, 269-276, chpt. XII.
        A discussion of the objectives and methods of labor
    education with examination of various programs including
    Trade Unions.

1319. Bennett, Andrew J. "The Hosiery Workers and Education."
    American Federationist. LX (February, 1953), 21.
        A general description of the educational programs of
    the American Federation of Hosiery Workers.

1320. Bernays, Edward L. "Educational Program for Unions."
    Industrial Labor Relations Review. I (October, 1947),
    103-109.
        A management public relations counsel examines the
    role of education in the trade union setting. The author
    believes that industrial peace can be realized if all union
    members receive adequate education in industrial relations.

1321. Birmingham, L. H. and E. H. Johns. "Baltimore Emphasizes
    Education." American Federationist. LX (June, 1953),
    21-22, 28.

A report of the educational activities of the Baltimore
Federation of Labor.

1322. Bloomberg, Warner, Jr.; Joel Seidman and Victor Hoffman.
"The Role of Training Leaders." New Republic. CXLI
(August 24, 1959), 15-19.
A descriptive analysis of how some unions recruit and
educate their upcoming leadership.

1323. Brameld, Theodore. "Workers' Education--A Challenge to
Teachers' Unions." American Teacher. XXVIII (December, 1943), 15, 19.
Because of the growing need for labor education, the
author calls on members of the American Federation of
Teachers to accept responsibility for helping locals establish labor education programs.

1324. Brooks, George W. and Russell Allen. "Union Training Programs of the AFL Paper Unions." Monthly Labor Review.
LXXIV (April, 1952), 395-399.
A descriptive examination of the shop steward training
programs of the unions in the paper industry.

1325. Brooks, George W. and S. Gamm. "A Union Steward Training Program." Industrial Labor Relations Review. IV
(January, 1951), 249-256.
An examination of the shop steward training courses
conducted by the AFL paper makers' unions.

1326. Brotslaw, Irving. "Apprentice Class in Trade Unionism in
Milwaukee Area." Labor Education Viewpoints. (January,
1964), 9-12.
An examination of a labor education class conducted
for the building trades in Milwaukee.

1327. Brown, H. S. "Casting a Little Light in Texas." American
Federationist. LXVI (February, 1959), 9, 29-30.
A descriptive study of the development of the labor
education movement in Texas.

1328. "Building the Union." Ammunition. V (December, 1948),
30-39.
A description of how an education program can assist
workers in building both a better union and a better world.

1329. "California Labor School." Adult Education Journal. IV
(April, 1945), 77.
A report of a union-sponsored school in San Fran-
cisco.

1330. "California Labor School." Adult Education Journal. V
(April, 1946), 102-103.
A brief description of the curriculum of the school.

1331. "California Labor School." Adult Education Journal. V (October, 1946), 178.
    A description of the summer school conducted by the California Labor School for white collar and professional workers.

1332. Close, Kathryn. "Steelworkers with Diplomas." Survey Graphics. XXXVI (November, 1947), 610-611, 614, 660-661.
    A descriptive article about the Steelworkers' Institute held at Penn State University.

1333. Cohn, Fannia. "Address." Report of the Proceedings of the Sixty-Seventh Convention of the American Federation of Labor held at Cincinnati, Ohio, November 15-22, 1948. 510-513.
    A report of the role and activities of labor education in the Workers' Education Bureau.

1334. _____. "Education Department ILGWU." Industrial Labor Relations Review. I (July, 1948), 704-708.
    A short historical sketch of the education department of the ILGWU and a statement on the future prospects of labor education.

1335. _____. "Workers' Education and Labor Leadership." Justice. (September, 1934), 24.
    A discussion of the need for labor leaders to take education courses so they will be better prepared to meet the problems confronting the union.

1336. Connors, John D. "Address." Report of the Proceedings of the Sixty-Third Annual Convention of the American Federation of Labor held at Boston, Massachusetts, October 4-14, 1943. 399-400.
    A report of the activities of the Workers' Education Bureau for the preceding year.

1337. _____. "Address." Report of the Proceedings of the Sixty-Fourth Annual Convention of the American Federation of Labor held at New Orleans, Louisiana, November 20-30, 1944. 560-562.
    An activity report of the Workers' Education Bureau.

1338. _____. "Address." Report of the Proceedings of the Sixty-Sixth Convention of the American Federation of Labor held at San Francisco, California, October 6-16, 1947. 449-451.
    A report of the activities of the Workers' Education Bureau in the field of labor education.

1339. _____. "Labor Education Today and Tomorrow." American Federationist. LXIII (October, 1956), 14-17.

A general description of the function and activity of the AFL-CIO education department.

1340. _____. "The Labor Institute." In J. B. S. Hardman and Maurice Neufeld, eds., The House of Labor: Internal Operations of American Unions. New York: Prentice Hall, 1951, 431-433.
A brief description of the educational role of labor institute

1341. _____. "Report on Workers' Education." Report of the Proceedings of the Sixty-Sixth Convention of the American Federation of Labor held at San Francisco, California, October 6-16, 1947. 449-451.
An activity report of the Workers' Education Bureau.

1342. _____. "Union Activities in Education." Conference Board Management Record. IX (May, 1947), 137-140.
A short description of the various organizations which are active in labor education.

1343. _____. "What's Wrong with the Unions? The Need for Constructive Measures." Sign. XXV (May, 1946), 7-9.
According to the author, good labor education can alleviate certain problems in the trade union movement such as communist infiltration and undemocratic leadership.

1344. _____. "The Workers' Education Bureau." American Federationist. LX (March, 1953), 8-9.
An examination of the historical development of the Workers' Education Bureau tracing its close ties with the American Federation of Labor until the Bureau became the education department of that organization.

1345. _____. "Workers' Education Has a Vital Role to Perform." American Teacher. XXX (March, 1946), 19-20.
A descriptive explanation of the various models labor education has taken and the need to utilize all of these models in classes.

1346. Cosgrove, John E. "Labor Education in Iowa." American Federationist. LXI (April, 1954), 22-23, 30-31.
An examination of the state-wide labor education program in Iowa.

1347. Creason, Joe. "Kentucky Labor Goes to School." Journal of Electrical Workers and Operators. XLV (September, 1946), 333, 360.
A descriptive article of the organization and program of the Kentucky Labor School sponsored by the Kentucky State Federation of Labor.

1348. Davis, R. L. "Organizing for Union Education: How One

Local Union Goes About It." Catering Industry Employee. LIX (July, 1950), 9-10.

A report of the establishment of the education committee of the Cooks Union Local 186 of Boston. The committee was established under the premise that the strength of the union rests in the understanding of the entire membership.

1349. _____. "Education in Our Union." The Catering Industry Employee. LIX (April, 1950), 11.

A description of the educational program being carried out by the Catering Union at the international and local levels.

1350. _____. "First Labor Institute Complete Success." The Catering Industry Employee. LVIII (September, 1949), 9.

Highlights of the first institute for training union members as leaders in workers education at the School for Workers in Madison.

1351. Davis, Walter G. "Labor Education and Effective Unions." American Federationist. LXXXIV (September, 1967), 16-20.

An examination of the needs for substantial training so that the trade union movement will continue to grow and service its membership.

1352. "Democracy in Action. UAW Summer School." Ammunition. II (August, 1944), 12-13.

A description of the various UAW summer schools held throughout the country in 1944.

1353. Douty, Agnes and Lawrence Levin, et al. "Education Package." In J. B. S. Hardman and Maurice Neufeld, eds., The House of Labor: Internal Operations of American Unions. New York: Prentice Hall, 1951, 452-470.

A description of the educational package offered by the Amalgamated Clothing Workers of America. The three programs described are the regional cultural conference, the workers school, and the correspondence courses.

1354. Douty, K. "Baltimore's Education Program." American Federationist. XLII (September, 1935), 949.

A description of the educational program established by the Baltimore Federation of Labor.

1355. Dubinsky, David "Training Future Officers." American Federationist. LIX (April, 1952), 7-9, 30.

A description of the year-long training institute sponsored by the International Ladies Garment Workers' Union.

1356. "Educating the Workers." New Republic XCIII (December, 22, 1937), 185.

An article praising the CIO's impetus toward labor education as well as the AFL's increased support for the WEB.

1357. "Education Councils in Unions." Adult Education Journal. V (April, 1946), 103.
A descriptive report of the UAW education councils.

1358. "Education in the Local Union Is Every Member's Business." The Catering Industry Employee. LVIII (November, 1949), 12.
A short explanation of what union education at the local level entails. The tasks of the union education committee are listed and the tools that this committee needs at the local level are outlined.

1359. "Education's Double Job." Ammunition. I (April, 1943), 3-5.
An explanation of the dual role of labor education in the UAW.

1360. "Education Is Mandatory." Ammunition. XIII (August, 1956), 6-8.
A discussion of the role of labor education in the UAW and why the union constitution states that education shall be a mandatory part of the business of the union.

1361. Elder, Arthur A. "ILGWU Training Institute." Industrial Labor Relations Review. V (January, 1952), 311-314.
A report of the second year-long program of the ILGWU's Training Institute.

1362. Ferleger, Harry "Educating with Labor." American Teacher. XXVII (December, 1942), 6-7.
The chairman of the education committee of the AFT Local 3 discusses the labor education work in progress in Philadelphia, including the establishment of a Labor Education Association for the city.

1363. Fitzpatrick, James L. "AF of T Summer Workshops." American Teacher. XLI (April, 1957), 10, 18.
An examination of curricula and programs of three separate summer workshops conducted by the AFT in cooperation with universities.

1364. _____. "Three Shops for Leadership." American Teacher. XL (April, 1956), 9, 22.
An explanation of the educational goals and functions of the AFT's labor education endeavors.

1365. Flagler, John J. Building the Local Union Education Program. State University of Iowa: Bureau of Labor and Management Information Series, No. 4, 1961, 28 pp.

A pamphlet which explains the administration, curriculum, recruitment, and materials development process in establishing a labor education program at the local union level.

1366. Flanders, J. D. "An American Experiment in Trade Union Education." Highway. XLI (January, 1950), 63-66.
A Britisher examines the educational work of the International Brotherhood of Pulp, Sulphite and Paper Mill Workers, AFL.

1366a. "For Workers." Journal of Adult Education. X (April, 1938), 215-216.
A report of the educational activities of various labor organizations, including the Ohio State Federation of Labor, The Transport Workers Union, and the Richmond [Virginia] Central Labor Council. Also included is a report of the education work of The New Haven Labor College and the AFL-Rutgers Labor Institute.

1367. Godfredson, Svend. "Workers' Education--A People's Movement." Ammunition. II (July, 1944), 17-18.
A description of the education department of the United Packing House Workers of America.

1368. Gorman, Francis J. "Labor and Schools in Contemporary Society." American Teacher. XXI (May-June, 1937), 9-11.
An examination of the role and responsibility of AFT members to contribute to the labor education movement.

1369. Goslin, Ryllis. Growing Up: Twenty-One Years of Education with the ILGWU. New York: H. Wolff Co., 1938, n.p.
A pictorial history of the ILGWU with portions of the pamphlet dedicated to the learning experiences provided by the union.

1370. Habber, S. and H. Stieglitz. "Joint Training for Foremen and Stewards." Conference Board Management Record. XII (November, 1950), 417-419.
An examination of a joint educational endeavor between management and the union to jointly educate stewards and foremen in contract administration.

1371. Hall, Wiley A. "Adult Education Programs of Labor Unions and Other Worker Groups." Journal of Negro Education. XIV (July, 1945), 407-411.
A brief history of the difficulties faced by blacks in trade unions prior to the CIO. This section is followed by a three-part delineation of the educational programs of trade unions.

1372. Hammerton, Albert. "Some Thoughts on Trade Union Education." Free Labour World. (September, 1959), 392-393.

An attempt to determine how any trade union movement can equip its officers and rank and file to handle the
many problems with which the movement is faced.

1373. Hammond, Reese. "New Approaches to Labor Education Explored by Two IUOE Union Leaders." International Oper-
ating Engineers. CV (July, 1961), 17-18.
An examination of a new experiment in labor education conducted with three universities in cooperation with
NILE.

1374. Hastings, W. H. "Developmental Reading for UAW." Journal
of Reading. IX (March, 1966), 253-255.
A report of an intensive course in developmental reading that was given to a selected group of UAW workers at
Purdue University in 1963.

1375. Hawes, Elizabeth. Hurry Up Please, It's Time. New York:
Reynal, 1946, 245 pp.
The author, an international representative of the UAW
education department, cites her experiences in the trade
union movement.

1376. Heaps, David. "Upholsters International Union (AFL) Edu-
cation Department." Industrial Labor Relations Review.
V (April, 1952), 477-478.
A report of the activities and programs of the ed-
ucation department of the Upholsters International
Union.

1377. Henson, F. A. "One Union's Education Program." American
Federationist. LVII (January, 1950), 26-27, 36-37.
An outline of the educational program of the UAW.

1378. Herberg, Will. "Local 22 Reports 1500 Students, 45 Classes."
Justice. (December, 1934), 14.
An account of one local's workers' education project
and a description of how it is run.

1379. "Holyoke Workers Forum." Journal of Adult Education. XII
(April, 1940), 214-215.
A description of an educational forum sponsored jointly
by the U.S. Office of Education and the Holyoke School department.

1380. Huberman, Leo. "Education in the NMU." Ammunition. II
(May, 1944), 11-12.
A description of the goals and procedures of the educa-
tion department of the National Maritime Union.

1381. "ILGWU." Journal of Adult Education. XII (April, 1940), 214.
An activity report of the education department of the
ILGWU.

1382. "ILGWU." Journal of Adult Education. XII (June, 1940),
        322-323.
            An activity report of the education department of the
        ILGWU.

1383. "ILGWU." Adult Education Journal. II (January, 1943), 31-
        32.
            An activity report of the educational work of the ILGWU.

1384. "ILGWU." Adult Education Journal. II (October, 1943), 163.
            An activity report of the educational work of the
        ILGWU.

1385. "ILGWU." Adult Education Journal. III (October, 1944), 167.
            An activity report of the educational work of the ILGWU.

1386. "ILGWU Institutes." Journal of Adult Education. XII (October,
        1940), 414.
            A description of one union educational program.

1387. "ILGWU Program." Adult Education Journal. I (July, 1942),
        92-93.
            A description of the educational program with specific
        reference to the changing emphasis of the union's educa-
        tional program.

1388. "ILGWU Shows Increased Enrollment." Adult Education Jour-
        nal. VI (July, 1947), 157.
            A statistical examination of the increasing yearly en-
        rollment in ILGWU educational program.

1389. "International Union's First Educational Institute Aids Locals."
        The Catering Industry Employee. LVIII (October, 1949),
        11-12.
            A report of the catering employees' first institute for
        intensive union education held at the Wisconsin School for
        Workers. Implications of the first institute for present
        and future educational work of the international union are
        listed.

1390. Jones, Felix C. "Education and the Cement Workers."
        American Federationist. LXIII (July, 1956), 13, 31.
            A description of the education program of the United
        Cement, Lime, and Gypsum Workers International.

1391. _____. "A Smaller Union Tries Education." IUD Digest.
        I (July, 1956), 38-40.
            A description of the educational program of the United
        Cement, Lime, and Gypsum Workers.

1392. Kern, Helmut. "Amalgamated Education Program, What's It
        All About." Butcher Workman. XLIII (May, 1957), 10-
        12, 28.

A description of the activities of the education department of the Amalgamated Meat Cutters & Butcher Workmen of North America.

1393. Kilpatrick, Joan G. "Education by Local Unions." Labor Education Viewpoints. (Winter, 1961), 11-15.
A discussion of the problem of having the local union's education programs administered by outside educational sources.

1394. Kornbluh, Hy. "Survey of Non-University Connected Liberal Education for Trade Unionists." In Freda Goldman, ed., Reorientation in Labor Education. Chicago: Center for the Study of Liberal Education for Adults, 1962, 89-100.
ERIC Accession Number ED 027445.
A discussion of union labor education programs centering on CWA and IBEW Local 3.

1395. Kotrotsios, G. T. "IAM Training for Active Participation in Local Lodges." Monthly Labor Review. LXXIV (June, 1952), 653-657.
A description of the development and scope of the education department of the International Association of Machinists.

1396. "Labor's Best Tool." New Republic. LXXXI (January 30, 1935), 320.
The best tool open to the labor movement for its own growth and development is an active labor education program for its members.

1397. Levin, R. A. "Amalgamated Clothing Workers of America, Department of Education." Industrial Labor Relations Review. III (April, 1950), 469-472.
An examination of the practical and philosophical reason for the Amalgamated Clothing Workers' educational program.

1398. Linton, Thomas. An Historical Examination of the Purposes and Practices of the Education Department of the United Automobile Workers, 1936-1959. Ann Arbor, Michigan: University of Michigan Graduate School of Education, 1965. 334 pp.
An indepth study of the education department of the United Automobile Workers of America comparing the educational goals of the union with the goals of the leadership as the goals and leadership change over a period of twenty some years.

1399. "Louisville Labor Institute." Adult Education Journal. VI (July, 1947), 157.
A description of the education program conducted by the Louisville Labor Institute.

1400. Mayer, C. H. "Education in a Trade Union." Labor Today.
III (December-January, 1964-1965), 2-5.
    A discussion of the use of education in the development
of a United Furniture Workers local union under trustee-
ship for corrupt practices.

1401. Miller, Spencer, Jr. "Address." Report of the Proceedings
of the Fifty-Seventh Annual Convention of the American Federation of Labor held at Denver, Colorado, October 4-15,
1937. 268-273.
    A report of the activities of the Workers' Education
Bureau and its relationship to the American Federation of Labor.

1402. _____. "Address." Report of the Proceedings of the Sixty-
First Annual Convention of the American Federation of Labor held at Seattle, Washington, October 6-16, 1941. 361-367.
    A discussion of the role that labor education plays in
a democracy and a report of the activities of the Workers'
Education Bureau.

1403. _____. "Address." Report of the Proceedings of the Sixty-
Second Annual Convention of the American Federation of
Labor held at Toronto, Ontario, Canada, October 5-14,
1942. 359-361.
    A report of the activities of the Workers' Education Bur-
eau for 1942.

1404. _____. "Labor and Culture." Report of the Proceedings
of the Fifty Eighth Annual Convention of the American Federation of Labor held at Houston, Texas, October 3-13,
1938. 323-327.
    A report to the American Federation of Labor conven-
tion of the educational and cultural activities of the Workers' Education Bureau.

1405. _____. "Labor Education and the World Crisis." Report
of the Proceedings of the Fifty-Ninth Annual Convention of
the American Federation of Labor held at Cincinnati, Ohio,
October 2-13, 1939. 271-275.
    A report to the convention of the American Federation
of Labor concerning the educational activities of the Workers' Education Bureau.

1406. _____. "Labor Institute." Workers' Education. II (June,
1934), 69. Also in American Federationist. XLI (June,
1934), 615-618.
    A discussion of the impact and relationship of the Na-
tional Recovery Act on and to labor education.

1407. _____. "The Strategy for American Labor and Education in
the World Crisis." Report of the Proceedings of the Six-
tieth Annual Convention of the American Federation of Labor held at New Orleans, Louisiana, November 18-29,

1940. 362-366.
    A report of the educational activities of the Workers'
Education Bureau and an examination of the role of education during the second world war.

1408.   . "Workers' Education and Democracy." Report of
the Proceedings of the Fifty-Sixth Annual Convention of the
American Federation of Labor held at Tampa, Florida,
November 16-27, 1936. 350-357.
    A report of the educational activities of the Workers'
Education Bureau.

1409. Nash, Al. "Impact of Adult Education on Taxi Drivers During an Organizing Drive." Adult Leadership. XVI (November, 1967), 183-185.
    A discussion of Taxi Drivers Union Local 3036 AFL-
CIO whose members simultaneously organized a union
while attending a labor education class in Basic Leadership
Training.

1410. "Nick Hyshka Has Been an Educator for Forty Years." Ammunition. V (June, 1947), 2-5.
    A description of the role of Nick Hyshka in the devel-
opment of an educational program of UAW Local 544.

1411. Noe, James E. "Educating Future Leaders." American Federationist. LXX (September, 1963), 23-24.
    A discussion of the need for the leadership training
within the union to insure the success of the labor movement.

1412. "Passing on Labor's Heritage." American Federationist.
LXXII (August, 1965), 22-23.
    A discussion of the development of classes on trade
unionism as a part of the apprentice program of the San
Francisco Bay Counties District Council of Carpenters.

1413. Peoples, Elwood. "Education for Shipbuilding Workers." Ammunition. II (August, 1944), 14-15.
    A description of the education department of the Indus-
trial Union of Marine and Shipbuilding Workers of America,
CIO.

1414. Poole, Edward. "Arizona Goes for Education." American
Federationist. LXVI (January, 1959), 22-24.
    A description of the development of the Arizona Labor
School.

1415. Portman, Lisa. "Reading Courses for Labor Unions." Journal of Reading. X (October, 1966), 29-32.
    A description of a reading improvement class in the
leadership training program of the UAW.

1416. "Program for Education. " <u>Ammunition</u>. II (October, 1944), 12-15.
 The report of the education department to the 1944 UAW Convention.

1417. Rademacher, John. "Training 5000 Postal Union Leaders. " <u>Labor Education Viewpoints</u>. (Spring, 1963), 1-4.
 A description of a shop steward training course prepared for postal union leaders.

1418. Reuther, Victor. "Education on the Local Level. " In J. B. S. Hardman and Maurice Neufeld, eds. , <u>The House of Labor: Internal Operations of American Unions</u>. New York: Prentice Hall, 1951, 446-451.
 A description of the education committee established in the UAW locals.

1419. _____. "Education for Survival. " <u>Ammunition</u>. IV (July, 1946), 4-11.
 A description of the role of education within the United Automobile Workers.

1420. Rogin, Lawrence. "Education for Textile Workers. " <u>Ammunition</u>. II (September, 1944), 27-28.
 A description of the education program of the Textile Workers Union of America.

1421. _____. "UJR Is Not Workers' Education. " <u>Labor and Nation</u>. I (February-March, 1946), 21-222.
 A criticism of the Union Job Relations course which had been thought to be a useful tool in labor education.

1422. _____. "Workers' Education, The New Scope. " <u>Yearbook of Workers' Education, 1926-1943</u>. New York: American Labor Education Service, 1943, 7-8.
 A discussion of the new scope of labor education and its growth among CIO unions.

1423. _____. "Workers Get Ready. " <u>Journal of Educational Sociology</u>. XIX (September, 1945), 43-45.
 A discussion of the experience of a textile worker's local union in New Bedford, Massachusetts in organizing educational classes.

1424. _____ and Joseph Glazer. "The Resident Training Institute. " In J. B. S. Hardman and Maurice Neufeld, eds. , <u>The House of Labor: Internal Operations of American Unions</u>. New York: Prentice Hall, 1951, 434-438.
 A description of the one-week resident training institute sponsored by the Textile Workers Union of America.

1425. <u>Scholar and School--New Targets for Bigotry</u>. San Francisco: California Labor School, 1945, 13 pp.

A polemical pamphlet attempting to disprove the
charges that the California Labor School was communist
dominated.

1426. "School for Washington Workers." Journal of Adult Education.
X (January, 1938), 97.
A description of a labor school established by the
United Federal Workers, CIO.

1427. Schwarztrauber, Ernest E. "Recreation and Study Combine
at AFT Workshop at Madison." American Teacher.
XXXII (May, 1948), 7-9.
A description of the AFT's union summer school held
at the Wisconsin School for Workers.

1428. "Seattle Labor School." Adult Education Journal. V (April,
1946), 102.
A description of the curriculum of the Seattle Labor
School.

1429. "Seattle Labor School." Adult Education Journal. V (October,
1946), 177-178.
A description of the expanded curriculum of the Labor
School.

1430. Sessions, Jack. "The Value of Leadership Education."
American Federationist. LXIX (August, 1962), 22-23.
A report of a recent study which indicated that union
education produced a significant change in the members'
support for the union.

1431. Sexton, Brendan. "Training for Union Leadership." Ameri-
can Federationist. LXXI (August, 1964), 23-24.
A report and evaluation of the United Automobile
Workers' Leadership Studies Center.

1432. Smith, M. Mead. "CIO Training for Active and Effective Local Leadership." Monthly Labor Review. LXXIV (February, 1952), 140-144.
A report of the CIO training program of nationally
sponsored schools geared to increase the activity and effectiveness of local union officers.

1433. _____. "ILGWU Approach to Leadership Training."
Monthly Labor Review. LXXIII (November, 1951), 529-535.
An evaluative description of the first year's class of
the ILGWU's union leadership training school.

1434. Sorenson, Helen and Milo Lathrop. "A New Movement in
Adult Education--The Political Action Committee of the
CIO." Adult Education Bulletin. IX (October, 1944), 6-10.
A description of the political education program con-
ducted by the Political Action Committee of the CIO.

1435. "Spanish for ILGWU." Adult Education Journal. VII (January, 1948), 30.
    A description of the union's classes in English for Spanish-speaking members.

1436. Starr, Emil. "Education for Action." American Federationist. LXV (July, 1958), 21-23, 29-31.
    A brief discussion of the historical development of the educational programs of the Amalgamated Clothing Workers of America.

1437. Starr, Mark. "A Course in Trade Union Training and the Educational Department of the ILGWU." American Federationist. XLIII (June, 1936), 590-592.
    A summary of the aims, methods, and results of a special training course established for officers and active members of the ILGWU in New York City.

1438. _____. "The Days of Our Year." Journal of Adult Education. XIII (October, 1941), 425-428.
    A report by the educational director of the ILGWU on various educational activities of the union during the year.

1439. _____. "The Educational Work of the ILGWU." Journal of Adult Education. IX (January, 1937), 35-39.
    An examination of the philosophical basis of the educational work of the ILGWU.

1440. _____. "The ILGWU--Leaders in Educational Work." Labor and Nation. VI (Summer, 1950), 57.
    A discussion of the newly instituted ILGWU Officers Training program. Also examined in the article is the long educational tradition of the union.

1441. _____. "The ILGWU Program. Twenty-Five Years of Workers' Education." Lithographers Journal. XXVII (August, 1942), 223, 237.
    A report of the activities of the ILGWU Education Department on its twenty-fifth anniversary.

1442. _____. "Labor's Stake in Economic Education. Journal of Educational Sociology. XXIII (March, 1950), 402-408.
    An examination of the educational deficiencies of the public schools vis a vis the labor movement. As a result the author advocates that the labor movement should not only engage in education but should also participate as an active community member in the functioning of public education.

1443. _____. "Meet Them Where They Are." Ammunition. II (June, 1944).
    An examination of the practices of the ILGWU education department.

1444. _____. "Meet Workers' Education Local 189." American
Teacher. XLI (October, 1956), 15-16.
   A short historical synopsis of Workers' Education Local 189, AFT, AFL-CIO which cites its function and future
aspirations.

1445. _____. "New Designs for Union Institute." Adult Leader-
ship. VI (January, 1958), 175, 186.
   A description of new educational techniques used by the
ILGWU at the Union's Officers Training Institute of 1957.

1446. _____. "Preparing Union Leaders for Responsibility."
Journal of Educational Sociology. XVII (March, 1944), 421-
425.
   A description of a new teaching technique in classes
given by the ILGWU in training new unionists about their
rights and duties as members.

1447. _____. "The Tack and Problems of Workers' Education."
In J. B. S. Hardman and Maurice Neufeld, eds., The House
of Labor: Internal Operations of American Unions. New
York: Prentice-Hall, 1951, 423-430.
   A discussion of the role and current trends in labor
education as it is carried on by trade unions.

1448. _____. "A Trade Union Pioneers in Education: The Educational Program and Activities of the ILGWU." American
Federationist. XLIII (January, 1936), 54-60.
   An examination of the role and an outline of the activities of the education department of the ILGWU.

1449. _____. "Training for Union Service." In J. B. S. Hardman
and Maurice Neufeld, eds., The House of Labor: Internal
Operations of American Unions. New York: Prentice-Hall,
1951, 439-445.
   A description of the ILGWU education department.

1450. _____. "Unions Look at Education in Industrial Relations."
Journal of Educational Sociology. XX (April, 1947), 499-
502.
   A plea for educational opportunities to be offered to
workers and designed practically for those in organized labor.

1451. _____. "Workers' Education." American Federationist.
L (June, 1943), 27-28.
   A call for increased union involvement in all facets of
educating its membership.

1452. _____. "Workers' Education--CIO Model." Social Frontier.
IV (January, 1938), 110-113.
   An article praising the CIO's aggressive approach to
workers' education while criticizing the AFL's neglect of

the WPA Workers' Education Programs available to them.

1453. "Textile Workers Union." Adult Education Journal. VI (October, 1947), 188.
A description of the emphasis of the TWUA summer schools and an examination of the curriculum.

1454. Tibbets, Norris and Bertram Gottlieb. "Protecting the Worker on Job 'Standards'." American Federationist. LXXIII (May, 1966), 9-11.
A report and evaluation of the educational programs conducted by the AFL-CIO Union Industrial Engineering Institutes.

1455. "Training Labor Leaders." Adult Education Journal. III (October, 1944), 166-167.
A report of the educational activities of a UAW leadership school conducted at the Highlander Folk School.

1456. "Twenty Years of UAW Education." Ammunition. XIV (April, 1956), 2-6.
A brief history of the development of the UAW education department.

1457. Tyler, Gus. "ILGWU's Training Institute." American Federationist. LXVI (November, 1959), 11-13.
A description of the students and curriculum content of the ILG's Institute for training labor leaders.

1458. "UAW-CIO Education Report." Adult Education Journal. V (July, 1946), 141.
A description of the plans of the UAW to establish summer schools on a regional basis and to encourage a broader use of audio-visual aids.

1459. "UAW-CIO Officers Institute." Adult Education Journal. VII (October, 1948), 196.
A brief description of a twelve-day program conducted by the union to educate the local leadership.

1460. "Union Education." Fortune. XL (September, 1949), 174-175.
An examination of those unions which conduct labor education programs and a discussion of the curriculum content.

1461. "United States: The Education Programme of the United Automobile Workers Union." Labour Education. (February, 1965), 9-10.
Excerpts from the education department's annual report.

1462. United Steelworkers of America. An Experiment in Education. Pittsburgh: Department of Education, United States Steel-

workers of America, 1960, 88 pp.
An historical study of the education department of the
Steelworkers from 1945-1960. The book examines the ad-
ministration, financing, and curriculum with special em-
phasis on a description of the four year program of the
Steelworkers summer schools.

1463. "University Clases for Workers." School and Society.
XLVIII (September 10, 1938), 330.
A short historical synopsis of the development of the
education department of the ILGWU.

1464. Weyler, Edward. "Education for Kentucky's Workers."
American Federationist. LIV (October, 1947), 26-27.
A discussion of the development of Kentucky's workers'
education program and a report of its undertakings.

1465. "What Does the UAW-CIO Education Department Do?" Ammunition. IX (April, 1951), 27-31.
A discussion of the need for and the activities of the
union's education department.

1466. "What Happened Last Year?" Ammunition. V (November,
1947), 13-18.
A report on what the UAW education department was
instructed to do by the convention and then what it actually
accomplished within the year.

1467. Wight, M. A. "Doing Things Together in a Democracy."
American Teacher. XX (November, 1935), 13.
An article which encourages members of the AFT to
get involved in workers' education, since one of the movement's inadequacies is a lack of competent teachers.

1468. Wilensky, Harold L. Intellectuals in Labor Unions: Organizational Pressures on Professional Roles. Glencoe, Illinois: Free Press, 1956, 80-108.
A discussion of the goals and content of various labor
education programs conducted by trade unions.

1469. [No entry.]

1470. Zatinsky, Milton. "Patterns and Power in Labor Education."
Labor Education Viewpoints. (Winter, 1960), 11-13.
A discussion of the reasons for unions having education departments, and an examination of what those departments have in common with union objectives.

1471. Zeller, Jack. "A New Program for UAW Education." Ammunition. III (October, 1945), n.p.
Recommendations by the new education director for
improving the organization of the UAW's education department.

Universities

1472. Adolfson, Torenty H. "University Extension and Industrial Relations in Wisconsin." Journal of Education Sociology. XX (April, 1947), 489.
       A portion of the article examines the philosophy and curriculum of the University of Wisconsin School for Workers.

1473. Ameringer, Oscar. "What Can University Extension Do For Labor?" Proceedings of the National University Extension Association at Oklahoma City, Oklahoma, May 5-7, 1941. Boston: Wright & Porter, 1941, 51-57.
       An analysis of the question, in what and for what are we educating labor?

1474. Archer, Jules. "Labor Trouble Under the Microscope." Survey Graphics. XXXVII (February, 1948), 49-53.
       A descriptive study of the Yale University Labor and Management Center and its combination of educational and research projects to aid labor and management in mutual understanding.

1475. Baisden, Richard N. "How Far May a University Go in an Action Program?" Adult Education. VII (Autumn, 1956), 3-9.
       A discussion of the pitfalls which await a university which gets involved in a controversial project.

1476. Barbash, Jack. Universities and Unions in Workers' Education. New York: Harper, 1955, 206 pp.
       An evaluative report and analysis of the activities of the Inter-University Labor Education committee. The report entails a history of the IULEC and a list of skills and insights developed through the project.

1477. Blaine, Harry R. and Fred A. Teller. "Union Attitudes Toward University Participation in Labor Education." Labor Law Journal. XVI (April, 1965), 237-242.
       A report of a study examining the attitudes of local union presidents toward university participation in labor education.

1478. "The Board of Regents, University of Michigan and Workers' Education Service." School and Society. LXVIII (December 11, 1948), 406-407.
       An announcement of the suspension of the Workers' Education Service released by the Michigan Board of Regents.

1479. Bradley, Phillips. "Labor-Management Relations in the Curriculum." Progressive Education. XXVI (November,

1948), 35-38.
This article presents the need for and some aspects
of a program of instruction in the field of labor management relations for high school students.

1480. _____. "The University's Role in Workers' Education."
Adult Education Journal. VII (April, 1949), 81-90.
An examination of the reasons why the university is a
good resource for having the potentiality of becoming the
most important institution in labor education.

1481. Brotslaw, Irving. "A Philosophy of Labor for Apprentices."
American Federationist. LXX (August, 1963), 23-24.
A report of an educational program conducted by the
Wisconsin School for Workers, the Milwaukee Building
Trades Council, and the Milwaukee Vocational and Adult
School to provide new apprentices a greater understanding
of trade union issues.

1482. Brown, Mark L. "A Pilot Project in Labor Education."
American Federationist. LXXIII (December, 1966), 18-20.
An examination of a pilot project conducted by the Department of Labor Education at Pennsylvania State University to train a group of workers to be able to teach shop
steward training courses.

1483. Carstens, Arthur. "Labor Programs in Universities, the
Next Phase." Proceedings of the Fifteenth Annual Meeting
of the Industrial Relations Research Association. Pittsburgh, 1962, 116-118.
A discussion of the needs of labor education for the
decade of the 1960s. The author also examines the growing problems between unions and universities.

1484. "Classes for Mexican Workers in Michigan Aid Inter-American
Understanding." American Teacher. XXX (January, 1946),
26-27.
A description of a project conducted by the Workers'
Educational Service of the University of Michigan to pro-
mote international labor cooperation.

1485. Connors, John D. "The Attack on Workers' Education in
Michigan." American Teacher. XXXIII (March, 1949),
20-22.
A critical examination of the reasons for the termina-
tion of the University of Michigan's Workers' Education
Service.

1486. _____. "A New Frontier." Adult Education Journal. V
(April, 1946), 73-77. Also in American Teacher. XXXI
(March, 1947), 19-21.
An examination of the increased activities of universi-
ties in labor education. Although the author recognizes

the benefits accompanying university involvement, he cautions trade unionists from allowing the university too much power in planning the educational programs of labor.

1487. _____. "Workers' Education Enters the University." Higher Education. III (May, 1947), 3-5.
A brief summary of the university programs involved in labor education, including Wisconsin, Michigan, Cornell, Harvard, Chicago, and the Jesuit School, Rockhurst.

1488. Cook, Alice H. and Agnes Douty. Labor Education Outside the Unions: A Review of Post-War Programs in Western Europe and the United States. Ithaca: Cornell University Press, 1958. 148 pp.
An examination of the role of non-union institutions in labor education. Only the second part of the book deals with the American experience in this area.

1489. "Cooperates with Labor School." Adult Education Journal. V (July, 1946), 140.
A description of the cooperative effort of the University of California's Extension Division and the California Labor School in conducting educational programs.

1490. Cort, John C. "University of Michigan and General Motors, the Workers' Education Service." Commonweal. XLIX (November 12, 1948), 116-117.
A short polemical article concerning the University of Michigan's reorganization of the Workers' Educational Service.

1491. Day, Ezra. E. "Education in Industrial and Labor Relations." Industrial and Labor Relations Review. III (January, 1950), 221-228.
A discussion of the establishment and goals of the New York State School of Industrial Labor Relations at Cornell University.

1492. Drob, Judah. "University, Education's Possibilities." Labor Education Viewpoints. (Winter, 1961), 21-24.
An examination of the need for union-university cooperation in labor education programs.

1493. Dunlop, John T. and James F. Healy. "The University's Contribution to Advanced Labor Education." Journal of Educational Sociology. XX (April, 1947), 472-477.
An examination of the educational potential which universities can provide for union staff officers.

1494. Eby, Kermit and Frank Fernback. "Unions Look at Education in Industrial Relations." Journal of Educational Sociology. XX (April, 1947), 494-499.
A challenge to higher education to provide and plan

new courses and teaching techniques geared specifically for workers.

1495. Elder, Arthur A. and Elizabeth Irwin. "Course for Workers."
The Nation's Schools. XXXVIII (September, 1946), 52-53.
A description of the beginning of the Workers' Education Service at the University of Michigan.

1496. "Electrical Workers Join in New School Idea." Journal of
Electrical Workers and Operators. XLI (September, 1942),
443-471.
An examination of the Trade Union Fellowship course at Harvard and an announcement that two IBEW members would attend.

1497. Feliz, George C. "Organized Labor: Challenge to Colleges
and Universities." College and University. XXV (April,
1950), 387-402.
An historical examination of the union-university relationships and the development of the labor education movement.

1498. Fernbach, Alfred P. University Extension and Workers' Education. Indiana: National University Extension Association, 1945, 32 pp.
An examination of the historical development of various university labor education programs. Universities examined include Wisconsin, Harvard, Cornell, Pennsylvania State and Virginia.

1499. Finley, N. G. "Virginia University Cooperates with Labor."
Journal of Adult Education. XI (April, 1939), 183-184.
A report of the development of a labor education program at the University of Virginia.

1500. Garman, Phillips. "The Status of Labor Education Programs
within Universities." School for Workers, Thirty-Fifth
Anniversary Papers. Madison: University of Wisconsin
School for Workers, 1960, 62-68.
A discussion of the status with which labor education programs are viewed by the university community.

1501. Golatz, Helmut. "Probing the Institute Glow." Adult Education. XII (Winter, 1962), 116-119.
A statistical examination to determine the amount of learning obtained by steelworkers attending educational programs conducted by Pennsylvania State University.

1502. _____ and Arthur O. Lewis. "Steelworkers in Academe."
Journal of General Education. XV (April, 1963), 18-32.
A study of the experiences that the Pennsylvania State University and the United Steelworkers have gone through in the six years they have jointly sponsored a liberal arts program in labor education.

1503. Graham, Harry. "An Evaluation of Shop Steward Training Courses in the United States." Labour Education. (June, 1970), 17-21. ERIC Accession Number EJ 024166.
A study of the University of Iowa and the difficulties encountered in providing unions with shop steward training courses.

1504. Greene, H. W. "Meeting the Challenge of Workers' Education." School and Society. LXI (May 12, 1945), 317-319.
A report of a conference held at West Virginia State College for the purpose of planning a school of labor education at some college or university in West Virginia.

1505. Hannah, John A. "The People's College." American Federationist. LXVIII (November, 1961), 29-31.
A response by the president of Michigan State University to an attack on the Labor and Industrial Relations Center at that university.

1506. Hartwig, Stella. "I Went to School in Summer." Progressive Education. XXI (April, 1944), 183+.
A description of the thirteen-week educational program for trade unionists conducted at Harvard University.

1507. "Harvard Trade Union Fellowship." Adult Education Journal. VII (July, 1948), 147-148.
A description of the thirteen-week educational program for trade unionists conducted at Harvard University.

1508. "Harvard University Trade Union Programme." Labour Education. (October, 1965), 15.
A historical sketch of the Harvard Trade Union Program.

1509. Hoehler, Fred, Jr. "The Changing Nature of University Labor Education Programs." Proceedings of the Fifteenth Annual Meeting of the Industrial Relations Research Association. Pittsburgh: 1962, 119-122.
A discussion of the changing role of labor education at the university.

1510. _____. "The Programme of Trade Union Education at the Pennsylvania State College." Fundamental Education. IV (July, 1952), 16-18.
A description of the labor education program of Pennsylvania State College during the 1951-52 academic year. In addition the author briefly examines the role of the university in labor education.

1511. _____. "A University Reports on Labor Education." American Federationist. LXVII (March, 1960), 16-18.
An outline of the offerings of the labor education program at Michigan State University.

1512. Ives, Irving M. "The New York School of Industrial and La-

bor Relations." Journal of Educational Sociology. XIX
(September, 1945), 40-42.
A report on the new New York State School of Industrial and Labor Relations, including a description of the
school's program for undergraduates and graduate students.
Information is also included on research and the activities
of the school's extension department.

1513. Johnson, Michael. "Reaching Our Members." American
Federationist. LXI (June, 1954), 18.
A description of labor education project conducted un-
der the auspices of the Inter-University Labor Education
Committee working with ILGWU members in the area of
communications.

1514. Kaplan, Abbott. "Labor-Management Programs." In Mary
L. Ely, ed., Handbook of Adult Education in the United
States. New York: Institute of Adult Education, 1948,
37-41.
An examination of the underlying assumption of university labor-management programs and a discussion of labor's hesitancies with regard to these programs.

1515. Kerrison, Irvine L. H. "Functional Workers' Education in
Michigan." Social Education. X (January, 1946), 29-31.
Also in American Teacher. XXX (December, 1945), 10-12.
A report of the role of the Workers' Educational Serv-
ice of the University of Michigan in the operation of the
CIO summer institute.

1516. _____. Workers' Education at the University Level. New
Brunswick, New Jersey: Rutgers University Press, 1951,
177 pp.
An examination of the need for, the role of, and the
trends in university labor education.

1517. _____ and Herbert A. Levine. "Developing Union Leadership Training: The United Rubber Workers--Rutgers Programs." Adult Education. VIII (Autumn, 1957), 31-36.
A detailed examination of a training program for Rubber Worker leadership by the Rutgers Labor Program.

1518. _____ and _____. Labor Leadership Education: A
Union-University Approach. New Brunswick, New Jersey:
Rutgers University Press, 1960, 188 pp.
A detailed explanation of the need for an intermediate
university labor education program. The authors then describe the administration and curriculum of a four year,
non-credit extension program known as the Union Leadership Academy.

1519. Kramer, Leo. "AFSCME and the Harvard Trade Union Program." Labor Education Viewpoints. (Spring, 1962), 13-17.

A description of the Harvard Trade Union Program
and the impact of the program on trade union graduates.

1520. Levine, Herbert A.   "Comments on Union-University Cooperation. Labor Education Viewpoints. (Winter, 1960), 3-5.
A discussion of the need for union-university cooperation in the development of university labor education programs.

1521. Liveright, Alexander A.   "A Summary of Problems and Directions. " In Freda Goldman, ed. , Reorientation in Labor
Education.   Chicago: Center for the Study of Liberal Education for Adults, 1962, 111-117.   ERIC Accession Number ED 027445.
A description of the basic guidelines aimed at developing union-university cooperation for all university labor
education programs.

1522. "The Massacre of the Shmoo." Ammunition.   VI (November,
1948), 5-9.
A description from the UAW's perspective on the role
of General Motors in the closing of the Workers' Education Service at the University of Michigan.

1523. McCallister, Frank W.   "A College for Everybody." Ameri-
can Federationist.   LVIII (August, 1951), 25-27.
A description of the labor education offerings at
Roosevelt College.

1524. _____.   "Roosevelt College, Labor Education Division. "
Industrial Labor Relations Review.   IV (July, 1951), 631.
A report of the recent activities of the Labor Educa-
tion Division at Roosevelt College.

1525. "Michigan." Adult Education Journal.   IV (April, 1945), 76.
A description of a Workers' Education Service of-
fered at the University of Michigan for trade union
groups.

1526. "Michigan Workers' Education Program. " Adult Education
Journal.   VIII (January, 1949), 32.
A report of the closing of the Michigan Workers' Education Service and a description of the controversy which
caused the closing.

1527. "Michigan's Workers' Education Service Dismantled. " Adult
Education Journal.   VIII (April, 1949), 117-118.
In the wake of the controversy of the reorganization
of Michigan's Workers' Education Service, the newly established program which lacked organized labor's backing
is dismantled for lack of student interest.

1528. Miller, Spencer, Jr.   "Labor Educating Itself. " American

Federationist. XLVII (September, 1940), 18-20.
An examination of the educational benefits derived by labor in university programs which adhere to the concept of union-university cooperation. Singled out as an outstanding example of this cooperation is the Rutgers Labor Institute.

1529. _____ . "Workers' Education." Proceedings of the National University Extension Association at Oklahoma City, Oklahoma, May 5-7, 1941. Boston: Wright & Potter, 1941, 152-160.
An updating of the role of university extension in the field of labor education since the author first addressed the association in 1924.

1530. _____ and Ruth Taylor. The Pioneer Institute of Labor. New York: Workers' Education Bureau, 1945. 40 pp.
An historical examination of the development of the Rutgers Labor Institute from its inception in 1931.

1531. Mire, Joseph. "Developments in University Labor Education Programs." Monthly Labor Review. LXXIX (July, 1956), 793-795.
A description of university labor education programs, curriculum, methodology, administration and financing.

1532. _____ . Labor Education: A Study Report on Needs, Programs, and Approaches. Chicago: Inter-University Labor Education Committee, 1957. 200 pp.
The final report submitted by the board of directors of the Inter-University Labor Education Committee to their funding source, the Fund for Adult Education. The report explains how the IULEC promoted cooperative educational programs between trade unions and the participating eight universities.

1533. _____ . "The University and the Unions in Workers' Education." Adult Education. V (Summer, 1955), 232-236.
An examination of the educational needs for the labor movement and the role university labor education programs should play in aiding them to achieve their needs.

1534. New Jersey State Law Creates Industrial Relations Institute." Labor Information Bulletin. XV (May, 1948), 8.
A brief description of the beginning of the year round labor and management education program instituted at Rutgers University under the name Institute of Management and Labor Relations.

1535. O'Donnell, Joseph P. "Union Training with a Harvard Accent." American Federationist. LXXI (June, 1964), 23-24.
A description of the curriculum and methods used by

the Harvard Trade Union Program in its training of union leaders.

1536. Ozanne, Robert. "The University of Wisconsin's School for Workers." American Federationist. LXV (August, 1958), 16-18, 31.
An historical description of the philosophy, students, and curriculum of the School for Workers.

1537. _____. "The Wisconsin Idea in Workers' Education." School for Workers, Thirty-Fifth Anniversary Papers. Madison: University of Wisconsin School for Workers, 1960, 41-49.
An examination of the historical development of the School for Workers.

1538. Parks, Donald S. "Labor Leadership Training." Personnel Journal. XXIII (October, 1944), 154-158.
A description of the program offered by the University of Toledo to prepare trade unionists to be competent in labor relations.

1539. "Plans Adult Extension Program." Adult Education Journal. V (April, 1946), 103.
A description of the New York State School of Industrial Relations plans to create short term non-credit courses for union and management groups.

1540. Posey, Thomas E. "Workers' Education: A Challenge to Negro College," Journal of Negro Education. XVI (January, 1947), 112-145.
Because of the increased black membership in the CIO it is becoming necessary for blacks to gain the benefit of labor education and preparation for union leadership. The author calls on black colleges to fill the gap and provide labor education programs for black trade unionists.

1541. "Programs in Labor Relations." Occupations. XXIV (January, 1946), 240-241.
A listing and description of university programs in labor relations and labor education.

1542. "Program for Organized Labor." Education for Victory. II (November 1, 1943), 9-10.
A description of a new service developed by Wayne State University specifically to serve organized labor.

1543. "Progress in Labor Education." The Carpenter. LXXIII (August, 1953), 8-11.
A description of the work of the Inter-University Labor Education Committee and the work that it does.

1544. Raffaele, Joseph A. "Labor-Management Group Education."

LXVIII (March, 1948), 415-423.
   An examination of the need for joint labor-management
educational programs to provide the framework for industrial harmony.

1545. "Report of the Committee on Workers' Education." Proceed-
      ings of the National University Extension Association, De-
      troit, Michigan, April 23-26, 1946. Boston: Wright &
      Potter, 1946, 157-158.
         A summary of the activities of various universities
      and colleges in the area of labor education.

1546. "Report of the Committee on Workers' Education." Proceed-
      ings of the National University Extension Association,
      Chicago, Illinois, May 2-5, 1948. Boston: Wright & Pot-
      ter, 1948, 171.
         A short report of the Committee of Workers' Educa-
      tion.

1547. Report and Recommendation: Commission of Inquiry on the
      Workers' Educational Service of the University of Michi-
      gan. Detroit: Michigan Committee on Civil Rights, 1949,
      11 pp.
         The findings and recommendations of a committee of
      inquiry which examined the circumstances surrounding the
      closing of the Workers' Educational Service of the Univer-
      sity of Michigan.

1548. "Rhode Island." Adult Education Journal. IV (January, 1945),
      38.
         A brief discussion of the educational goals of the state
      federation of labor and the cooperation with the state
      university.

1549. Richardson, L. J. "Workers' Education." Proceedings of the
      National University Extension Association, St. Louis, Mis-
      souri, May 13-15, 1937. Boston: Wright & Potter, 1937,
      62-64.
         A description of the workers' education program con-
      ducted by the University of California.

1550. Rittenhouse, E. "School with a Purpose: An Education Pro-
      gram for Labor-Management." Journal of Higher Educa-
      tion. XXI (October, 1950), 360-362.
         A capsule overview of the work and programs of New
      York's School of Industrial and Labor Relations at Cornell.
      Facets of the school emphasized in this article are its
      philosophy, school library, student work-training program,
      and the work of the extension division.

1551. "Rutgers Labor Institute." Adult Education Journal. IV
      (October, 1945), 166.
         A report of the activities of the fifteenth annual Rut-

gers Labor Institute.

1552. "Rutgers Labor-Management Institute." Adult Education Journal. VII (July, 1948), 148.
An examination of the goal of the new Rutgers Institute of Management and Labor Relations. The goal will be
the enhancement of labor-management harmony.

1553. "San Diego Institute." Adult Education Journal. IV (January,
1945), 37-38.
An announcement and description of a three-day institute to be held jointly by the college and the WEB.

1554. "The School for Workers at the University of Wisconsin."
School and Society. XLVI (December 11, 1937), 750.
A summary report of the activities of the School for Work-
ers in its first year as a permanent statewide workers school.

1555. Schwarztrauber, Ernest E. "School for Workers." American
Federationist. LVII (March, 1950), 12+.
A discussion of the twenty-five year history of the
University of Wisconsin School for Workers.

1556. _____. "University of Wisconsin School for Workers."
World Association Adult Education Bulletin. XLIV (February, 1946), 1-11.
An examination of the factors at play in America which
delayed university interest in the field of workers education and an explanation of why Wisconsin was the lone pioneer in the field.

1557. _____. The University of Wisconsin School for Workers.
Madison, Wisconsin: School for Workers, 1949, 40 pp.
An historical examination of the first twenty-five years
of the school.

1558. _____. "University of Wisconsin School for Workers."
Industrial and Labor Relations Review. III (July, 1950),
542-547.
A report on the historical development, curriculum
content, and philosophical basis of the School for Workers.

1559. _____. "University of Wisconsin School for Workers Industrial Relations Institute for Church Leaders." Religious Education. XLIII (September-October, 1948), 301-303.
A description of the sixth annual Industrial Relations Institute for church leaders held at the School for Workers.

1560. _____. "Wisconsin and Workers' Education." American
Federationist. XLVI (June, 1939), 624-629.
An examination of state financing for labor education
and its implications for the movement.

1561. _____. "Workers' Education in the University of Wiscon-
      sin." Labor Information Bulletin. VI (May, 1939), 5-7.
           A description of the newly instituted year-round labor
      education program at the University of Wisconsin.

1562. _____. "Workers' Education Threatened in Wisconsin."
      American Teacher. XXIII (May, 1939), 25-26.
           A description of the action of the state government in
      cutting the funds for the year-round program in labor edu-
      cation at the school.

1563. _____. Workers' Education: A Wisconsin Experiment.
      Madison: University of Wisconsin Press, 1942.
           A history of the Wisconsin School for Workers, exam-
      ining its establishment, philosophy, and curriculum. Also
      included is an evaluation of statewide financing of labor
      education from public funds.

1564. Shoemaker, Alice. "Educate and Organize." American
      Teacher. XXI (January-February, 1937), 22-26.
           An examination of the impact of the Wisconsin School
      for Workers on students once they returned to their com-
      munities.

1565. "Shorter Courses for Workers." Journal of Adult Education.
      XIII (January, 1941), 93.
           An examination of a changing trend in labor education,
      especially at Wisconsin, for short term courses.

1566. Slichter, Summer H. "Harvard Man Comments on Trade Un-
      ion Courses." Journal of Electrical Workers and Opera-
      tors. XLI (November, 1942), 539, 576.
           A description of the Harvard Trade Union program
      and an examination of how the program began.

1567. Smith, Russel A. The Role of the University in Labor and
      Industrial Relations: Report and Recommendations. Ann
      Arbor: University of Michigan, 1956   182 pp.
           An appraisal of the role of the University in Labor
      and Industrial Relations analyzing many operational prob-
      lems.

1568. Starr, Mark. "Communications Re: Education in Industrial
      and Labor Relations." Industrial and Labor Relations
      Review. III (July, 1950), 575-580.
           A comment on an article written by Edmund Ezra Day
      in the January 1950 issue of Industrial and Labor Relations
      Review. Starr discusses the functioning of industrial and
      labor relations programs in general, and the Cornell
      school in particular.

1569. _____. "Labor Leadership." Teachers College Record.
      XL (April, 1939), 615-624.

An examination of the role of University educators in the education of workers for leadership roles in their unions.

1570. _____. "Higher Education for Labor Leadership?" American Federationist. LII (January, 1945), 23-24.
The author warns that labor leadership education must be controlled by the labor movement which should determine what is taught and by whom.

1571. _____. "Labor Needs Learning ... and Vice Versa." Frontiers of Democracy. IX (October, 1942), 22-24.
An examination of the growing cooperation at a number of levels between organized labor and universities.

1572. "Statewide School for Workers." Journal of Adult Education. X (January, 1938), 97.
A short description of the first statewide school for workers established by the University of Wisconsin.

1573. Towell, Howard. "Education for Labor Leadership." Lithographers Journal. XXX (May, 1945), 92, 122.
An examination of the labor education program conducted by the University of Toledo.

1574. Ulriksson, Vidkunn. "School for Workers ... Pioneer in Workers' Education." Lithographers Journal. XXXI (September, 1946), 367, 418.
A short historical examination of the Wisconsin School for Workers.

1575. _____. "The Scope, Functions, and Limitations of University Workers' Education Programs." and "Comments." Industrial and Labor Relations Review. V (January, 1952), 221-235.
A description of many difficulties present in university labor education with a discussion of some of the roles of labor education at the university.

1576. Underhill, H. Fabian. "Does Your University Need a Labor Institute?" Educational Record. XXX (October, 1949), 422-433.
An examination of why union members may be opposed to attending university labor education programs.

1577. _____. "University Labor Relations Center." Labor and Nation. IV (November-December, 1948), 5.
A discussion of why union leadership as well as university officials oppose university labor education.

1578. "Union Men Take to the Campus." Business Week. (August, 13, 1966), 64-66.
An examination of various union summer schools held

on university campuses. It is suggested that 20,000 potential labor leaders went to these summer schools to improve their skills in trade unionism.

1579. "Universities and Unions Get Together." Butcher Workmen.
LX (January, 1954), 18-19.
An historical examination of the development of labor
education in the United States with special reference to
the role of universities in the field.

1580. Walsh, J. R. "Labor Looks at Education." Progressive Education. XXI (April, 1944), 169.
A call for labor union members to play a bigger role
on local school boards and to participate in labor education programs at local universities.

1581. Ware, Carolyn F. Labor Education in Universities: A Study
of University Programs. New York: American Labor Education Service, 1946. 138 pp.
A study of the nature and extent of labor education
programs carried on by universities.

1582. _____. "Trends in University Programs for Labor Education, 1946-1948." Industrial and Labor Relations Review.
III (October, 1949), 54-69.
An update of the author's book which continues her examination of the university in labor education.

1583. "Wisconsin School for Workers." Education for Victory. III
(September 4, 1944), 8-9.
A short description of the summer offerings of the
School for Workers, listing the unions participating and the
topics examined.

1584. Witte, Edwin E. "The University and Labor Education."
Industrial and Labor Relations Review. I (October, 1947),
3-17. Excerpts also in Monthly Labor Review. LXV (July,
1947), 36-40.
A lengthy examination of the role and definitions of
labor education at the university.

1585. Wohlking, Wallace. "Labor and Business in Community Development." Adult Education. VI (Autumn, 1955), 33-39.
A description of a labor education project in Olean,
New York, sponsored by Cornell with funds from a grant
of the IULEC.

1586. Wood, Richard H. "Education in Labor-Management Relations: A Rutgers Extension Program in Action." Adult
Education. II (February, 1952), 99-107.
The author discusses establishing extension programs
in labor-management relations, and uses the Rutgers Institute of Management and Labor Relations as an example.

1587. Woods, Baldwin M., and Abbott Kaplan. "Areas and Service
      of University Extension in Industrial Relations Programs."
      Journal of Educational Sociology. XX (April, 1947), 484-
      489.
         An examination of the question, should there be sepa-
      rate classes for rank and file laborers and management
      personnel when it comes to university programs.

1588. "Workers' Schools." Survey. LXXVI (December, 1940), 365.
         An examination of a change in policy at the school
      for Workers concerning classes of shorter duration.

Federal Government Support

1589. "AFT Resolution Calling for WPA Workers' Education Pro-
      gram." Adult Education Journal. I (October, 1942), 146.
         A report of the AFT Convention which went on record
      as supporting federal support for a labor education pro-
      gram.

1590. Alderman, L. R. "The WPA Program." Journal of Adult
      Education. IX (April, 1937), 187-188.
         This article contains comments on the workers' educa-
      tion branch of the WPA with a statistical summary of stu-
      dent participation.

1591. Asch, Nathan. "WPA Adult Education." American Federa-
      tionist. XLV (April, 1938), 386-390.
         A broad description of the WPA educational programs
      including its labor education offerings.

1592. Coit, Eleanor. Government Support of Workers' Education.
      New York: American Labor Education Service, 1940.
      72 pp.
         Although the study is based upon government support
      of labor education in Denmark and Sweden, the author sug-
      gests methods to make government financial support a re-
      ality in American labor education.

1593. _____. "Workers' Education and Government Support."
      Adult Education. (British), VIII (June, 1936), 263-266.
         A description of the pros and cons of government fund-
      ing for labor education in the Scandinavian countries and
      the implications of such a move for the United States.

1594. "Education Bill." Business Week. (April 24, 1948), 116-
      120.
         An examination of the plight of the Labor Education
      Extension Bill in Congress.

1595. "Education for Freedom of Collective Bargaining." Labor
      Information Bulletin. XIII (March-April, 1946), 2, 4.

A discussion of the response of the Department of Labor to the mushrooming growth of labor education in the United States.

1596. Eiger, Norman. "Toward a National Commitment to Workers' Education: The Rise and Fall of the Campaign to Establish a Labor Extension Service, 1942-1950." Labor Studies Journal. I (September, 1976), 130-150.
An historical examination of the attempt to pass a labor education extension bill during the latter part of the 1940's.

1597. Fuller, L. R. "Workers' Education." Proceedings of the National University Extension Association, St. Louis, Missouri, May 13-15, 1937. Boston: Wright & Potter, 1937, 64-66.
A description of the offerings of the WPA labor education program in St. Louis. The author also attempts to answer why workers go to labor education programs but not to general adult education programs.

1598. Hedges, M. H. "Workers' Education Before the U.S. Congress." Public Affairs. XI (July, 1948), 146-148.
A discussion of the Labor Education Extension Bill.

1599. Kuenzli, Irvin R. "AFL Acts on Crucial Educational Problems." American Teacher. XXIII (April, 1949), 5-6.
A sub-section of this large article deals with federal aid to labor education. The fears of the AFL concerning the labor education extension bill are reported.

1600. "Labor Department Starts Education Service." Labor Information Bulletin. XIII (November, 1946), 4-5.
A description of a labor department service which aids in organizing labor education classes for unions and universities.

1601. "Labor Education." Adult Education Journal. II (January, 1943), 31.
A discussion of the expansion of the curriculum in labor education outside the more traditional areas of economics and labor problems under the WPA.

1602. "Labor Extension Bill." Business Week. (October 6, 1945), 106-109.
An examination of the findings of a conference on labor education which developed a plan for the establishment of a national labor education extension service.

1603. "Labor Extension Bill." Adult Education Journal. VII (January, 1948), 30.
A discussion of the aims and purpose of the Labor Education Extension Bill.

215   Individual Organizations

1604. "Labor Extension Bill (1948)." Industrial and Labor Relations Review. I (July, 1948), 657-663.
       The text of S-1390, the Labor Education Extension Bill, presented to the second session of the eightieth Congress.

1605. "Labor Extension Service Bill." Adult Education Journal. VII (October, 1948), 196-197.
       A report of the status of the Labor Education Extension Bill in the 80th Congress.

1606. "Many Labor Courses Aided by Department." Labor Information Bulletin. XIV (May, 1947), 7.
       A description of the labor department's recruitment of teachers for courses in collective bargaining taught to union representatives.

1607. Miller, Spencer, Jr. "The Problems of Federal Aid." American Teacher. XXIV (April, 1940), 60-61.
       A critical examination of some of the faults of the WPA Workers' Education Service.

1608. Peters, Ronald and Jeanne M. McCarrick. "Roots of Public Support for Labor Education, 1900-1945." Labor Studies Journal. I (Fall, 1976), 109-129.
       A general overview of the historical development of the use of public funds for the advancement of labor education.

1609. "Plowing a New Field." The Nation. CXLVI (February 19, 1938), 201.
       A discussion of the cooperative efforts in labor education between the WPA Workers' Education Project and the UAW, CIO.

1610. "Seek Labor Education Service." Adult Education Journal. V (October, 1946), 177.
       A description of the activities of the National Committee for the Extension of Labor Education.

1611. Smith, Hilda W. "New Directions for Workers' Education." Journal of Adult Education. XII (April, 1940), 162-166.
       An examination of the educational needs of workers discovered through the efforts of the WPA's Workers' Service Program.

1612. _____. "The National Experiment in Adult Education." Bryn Mawr Alumnae Bulletin. XIII (December, 1933), 8-10.
       A description of the author's attempts to get federal monies for workers' education through the Federal Emergency Relief Administration.

1613. _____. "Workers' Education, A Plea for Government Sup-

port." Yearbook of Workers' Education, 1926-1943. New
York: American Labor Education Service, 27-28.
   A discussion of the need to have a full-time labor
extension service funded by the federal government.

1614. _____. "WPA Schools Serve Wage Earners." Journal of
Electrical Workers and Operators. XXXV (April, 1936),
157.
   A descriptive examination of the educational activities
of the WPA and of its workers' education program.

1615. _____. "Workers' Education under the WPA." World Association Adult Education Bulletin. XVI (February, 1939),
1-19.
   An overview of the activities, teaching methods, and
physical facilities of the workers' education program of
the WPA.

1616. _____. "Workers' Service Program of the Works Project
Administration." Adult Education Bulletin. VI (October,
1941), 9-10.
   A description of the activities of the Workers' Service Program of the Works Project Administration.

1617. _____. "Workers Want to Know." American Teacher.
XXIV (April, 1940), 8-10.
   A brief review of the activities of the Workers' Serv-
ice Program of the WPA in 1939.

1618. United States House of Representatives. Hearings Before
Subcommittee #1 of the Committee on Education and Labor.
HR 6202 and HR 6249, 80th Congress, April 13-May 19,
1948.   375 pp.
   Testimony of the hearings conducted on the proposed
Labor Education Extension Bill.

1619. _____. Hearings Before a Special Subcommittee of the
Committee on Education and Labor.   HR 1380, 81st Con-
gress, July 26-28, 1949, 273 pp.
   Testimony of the hearings conducted on the proposed
Labor Education Extension Bill.

1620. United States Senate.   Hearings Before a Subcommittee on Labor and Public Welfare.   S 1390, 80th Congress, second
session, February 16-20,1948, 304 pp.
   Testimony of the Senate hearings on the proposed Labor Extension Bill.

1621. "Workers' Education, Why?" Journal of Electrical Workers
and Operators. XLVI (July, 1947), 259-260.
   An account of the proposed Labor Extension Bill and
why it is needed.

1622. "Workers' Service Program of the WPA." Journal of Adult
      Education. XII (January, 1940), 104.
            A brief descriptive report of the workers' education pro-
      gram conducted by the WPA.

Catholic Labor Schools

1623. Barrenechea, M. "Where the Catholic Labor School Stands."
      Social Order. VI (May, 1956), 222-224.
            A brief examination of the past aims of Catholic labor
      schools and a report of the general trends of the schools
      in 1956.

1624. Brown, Leo. "Catholic Sponsored Labor Management Educa-
      tion." Journal of Educational Sociology. XX (April,
      1947), 510-512.
            A description of curriculum, students, and finances
      of labor education in Catholic schools.

1625. Carey, Philip. "Catholic Labor Schools. Arbitration Jour-
      nal. II (Summer, 1947), 169-171.
            An examination of the general goals of Catholic labor
      schools.

1626. "Catholic Labor Schools." America. LXIII (September 28,
      1940), 686.
            An editorial lauding the role of Catholic labor schools
      for providing a solid Christian education for adult workers.

1627. "Catholic Labor Schools." Catholic Digest. VIII (November,
      1943), 77-79.
            An examination of the philosophical basis of the Cath-
      olic labor school.

1628. "Cincinnati." Adult Education Journal. IV (January, 1945), 38.
            A description of a new labor school founded at Xavier
      College.

1629. Corley, Francis J. "Education for Workers: Catholic Labour
      Schools in the United States." Irish Monthly. LXXVI
      Part I (July, 1948), 296-302. Part II (August, 1948),
      368-372.
            A two-part article examining the historical develop-
      ment and present operation of Catholic labor schools in
      the United States.

1630. Cort, John C. "Teaching the Workers: What Labor Schools
      Can and Can Not Do." Commonweal. XXXIX (April 7,
      1944), 618-622.
            An examination of the role of Catholic labor schools
      with a delineation of their limitations.

1631. Darby, Thomas J.   Thirteen Years in a Labor Schools History of the New Rochelle Labor School.   St. Paul, Minnesota: Fathers Rumble and Curthy, 1953.
        An historical study of a Catholic labor school in New Rochelle, New York, and its efforts to combat the suspicions of the American Federation of Labor that the church was attempting to divide workers along religious lines.

1632. Davitt, T. E.   "Labor Schools: A Positive Help to Workers, Catholic Social Program Is Curriculum of Wage Earners." America.   LX (December 10, 1938), 224-225.
        An examination of the development of Catholic labor schools.

1633. DeWeaver, Norman C.   "ACTU School for Spanish-Speaking." America.   XCIII (August 6, 1955), 451-453.
        A description of the work of the New York Chapter of the Association of Catholic Trade Unions in establishing labor schools for Spanish-speaking workers.

1634. Dobson, Philip E.   "The Xavier Labor School, 1938-1939." Woodstock Letters.   LXVIII (1939), 266-279.
        An activity report of the expansion of the Xavier Labor School for 1938-1939 to provide greater educational services for organized labor in the New York City area.

1635. Donnelly, J. F.   "Working with Workers."   Ecclesiastical Review.   CXIII (July, 1945), 1-15.
        A study of the organization of a Catholic labor institute, the procedures it followed, and how it was received by organized labor and industry.

1636. "Education for Workers by Institute Method."   Journal of Electrical Workers and Operators.   XLV (November, 1946), 415, 434.
        A descriptive report of the annual labor education program for women workers entitled "Institute in Industry" held at the National Catholic School of Social Service.

1637. Fagan, Gerard.   "Where Workers Are Taught to Think." Catholic Digest.   XIII (December, 1948), 77-79.
        A short descriptive article reporting on the work of the Xavier Labor School and its Director, Father Philip Carey.

1638. Fitzgerald, Mark J.   "Labor School Program."   Catholic Mind.   LIII (July, 1955), 419-424.
        A description of the five types of Catholic institutes involved in the labor school field.

1639. Justin, Brother.   "The Study of Industrial and Labor Relations in Catholic Colleges."   Industrial and Labor Relations Review.   III (October, 1949), 70-75.

A discussion of the philosophy and goals of Catholic colleges which offer programs in industrial and labor relations.

1640. Keane, Edmund. "Experiment in Social Education: Rockhurst College, Kansas City, Missouri." Irish Monthly, LXXVIII (February, 1950), 62-67.
A description of the goals, curriculum and student body of the labor school conducted at Rockhurst College.

1641. "Labor and Education and Effort." Commonweal. XXXIV (September 12, 1941), 485.
A report of an address by Father John C. Friedl before the Omaha Central Labor Union, outlining the educational offerings of the labor school at Rockhurst College.

1642. "Labor Schools." America. LXXI (September 30, 1944), 615.
A brief description of Catholic labor schools.

1643. McKeon, Richard. "The School of Social Sciences: St. Joseph's College, Philadelphia, Pennsylvania." The Woodstock Letters. LXVII (1938), 103-120.
An historical study of labor education in the United States examining the role of radical political parties and then contrasting the role Catholic labor schools play in the field.

1644. McLaughlin, Vincent J. "Labor School Takes Inventory." Commonweal. XXXI (January 12, 1940), 261-262.
A statistical study of the student body at the Association of Catholic Trade Unionists (ACTU) labor school at New Rochelle College.

1645. Murphy, Francis X. "Go to the Workingman ... How to Run a Labor School." America. LXXVIII (March 27, 1948), 713-714.
A description of the nuts and bolts of starting and successfully running a labor school.

1646. Ramsay, Anne M. "Workers' Education 1945: The Present State of Labor Schools." Commonweal. XLI (April 6, 1945), 614+.
An examination of the changing objectives of labor education and their effects on Catholic labor schools.

1647. Riordan, Leo. "Schools for Temper Keeping." Catholic Digest. XXII (May, 1958), 45-49.
A description of the role of the Institute of Industrial Relations of St. Joseph's College and the role of its director Father Dennis J. Comey.

1648. "Rockhurst College Offers Full Labor Courses." Journal of

Electrical Workers and Operators. XLV (September, 1946), 332.

A description of the organization of the 1945-1946 academic year at the labor school of Rockhurst College.

1649. Smith, William J. "Are Labor Schools Passe?" Social Order. VII (December, 1957), 446-452.

An examination of the criticism which was being leveled at Catholic labor schools.

1650. _____. "Catholic Labor Schools." Catholic Mind. XLVII (July, 1949), 392-397.

An examination of the curriculum and spiritual doctrines in Catholic labor schools.

1651. _____. "The Crown Heights School of Catholic Workmen." The Woodstock Letters. LXVII (1938), 235-244.

An historical examination of the purposes and practices of the Crown Heights School for organized labor in Brooklyn, New York.

1652. _____. "There Is a Need and Future for the Labor School." America. LXIV (February 1, 1941), 455-456.

Even though there are failures in the Catholic labor schools, the author makes a case for expanding the schools because they are the strongest weapon in Catholic life to enhance social reform.

1653. Weinberg, Jules. "Catholic Labor Schools." Commonweal. XLIX (November 3, 1948), 92.

An examination of the role of the Xavier Labor School as a training ground for union leaders.

1654. "Workers' Center in Cincinnati." Journal of Adult Education. XII (April, 1940), 214.

Discusses Workers' Center in Xavier University, Ohio.

GENERAL, HISTORICAL AND DESCRIPTIVE STUDIES

1655. Adam, Thomas R. The Workers' Road to Learning. New York: American Association of Adult Education, 1940. 162 pp.

An examination of the varied organization and programs involved in labor education in the United States.

1656. Adams, James T. Frontiers of American Culture. New York: Charles Scribner & Son, 1944. Chapt. X: Adult Education for Workers, 202-220.

After defining "workers" the author examines the early stages of adult education including a brief description of the WEB.

1657. Brameld, Theodore. "Workers' Education in America. "
      Educational Administration and Supervision. XXXII
      (March, 1947), 129-140.
          The author places the organizations involved in work-
      ers' education into three types and then describes each type.

1658. Cheyney, Alice S. "Workers' Education in the United States. "
      International Labor Review. XXXII (July, 1935), 39-59.
          An examination of the relationship between organized
      labor and workers' education.

1659. Coit, Eleanor G. "Some Contrasts in Workers' Education in
      the Country and Abroad." Woman's Press. XXXI (May,
      1937), 210-211.
          An examination of labor education in the United States
      in contrast to the movement in Denmark and Sweden.

1660. _____. "The Worker Accepts Responsibility for Educa-
      tion. " In Warren Seyfert, ed. , Capitalizing Intelligence--
      Eight Essays on Adult Education. Cambridge: Harvard
      University, 1937. 15 pp.
          An examination of the trends in labor education as
      well as the various organizations involved.

1661. _____. "Workers' Education." In Mary L. Ely, ed. ,
      Handbook of Adult Education in the United States. New
      York: Institute of Adult Education, 1948, 30-36.
          A discussion of the role, scope and method of study
      used in labor education in the United States. The article
      also examines the difficulties which beset the movement
      and suggests some solutions.

1662. _____ and John D. Connors. "Agencies and Programs in
      Workers' Education. " Journal of Educational Sociology.
      XX (April, 1947), 520-528.
          A list and description of various labor education pro-
      grams conducted by national agencies, labor unions, and
      local groups.

1663. _____ and Orlie A. H. Pell, Irvine Kerrison, and Larry
      Rogin. "Workers' Education. " Adult Education. III (No-
      vember, 1952), 19-25.
          The separate examination of various areas of labor
      education. Coit and Pell develop the idea that labor edu-
      cation has come of age having become an integral part of
      the labor movement. Kerrison examines the historical de-
      velopment of the movement since World War II focusing
      on this education as a deterrent to totalitarianism. Rogin
      traces the history of the movement from 1933 with spe-
      cial emphasis on the role of the university.

1664. _____ and Mark Starr. "Workers' Education in the United
      States. " Monthly Labor Review. XLIX (July, 1939), 1-21.

An examination of the current trends in labor education and a delineation of the activities of various agencies
in the field.

1665. Connors, John D.   "Spring Conference is Held in Washington." American Federationist. LXI (May, 1954), 19-20.
A report of the proceedings of the conference with
some examination of the role of labor education.   At this
conference it was announced that the WEB would officially
be known as the Department of Education of the AFL.

1665a. Cook, Alice (Hanson).   "Workers' Education on the March."
American Teacher. XXIII (April, 1939), 15.
A survey of the field of workers' education and a discussion of how the AFT membership can cooperate in the
program of education.

1666. Edelman, John W.   "Workers' Education." Education for
Victory. III (April 20, 1945), 16.
A discussion of the extent of labor education both in-
side and outside of the labor movement.

1667. Elder, Arthur A.   "A Note on the Progress of Workers' Education in 1947." Monthly Labor Review. LXVI (April,
1948), 406-408.
A general activity report of the states of labor education
in the United States.   Union university and government activity
in the field is mentioned.

1668. [No entry.]

1669. Hansome, Marius.   "The Development of Workers' Education."
In Theodore Brameld, ed., Workers' Education in the
United States.   New York: Harper, 1941, 48-66.
An historical study of the development of workers' ed-
ucation in the United States.

1670. Hardman, J. B. S.   "The Challenge and the Opportunity."   In
Theodore Brameld, ed., Workers' Education in the United
States.   New York: Harper & Row, 1941, 3-14.
An examination of the reasons why workers' education
developed so slowly in the United States.

1671. Hewes, Amy.   "Workers' Education in the United States."
International Labor Review. LXXVI (November, 1957),
423-445.
An historical examination of the development of labor
education since 1935.

1672. McCallister, Frank.   "Labor Education, a Growing Institution." American Teacher. XLVI (February, 1962), 13-
14, 22.
A study of the development of labor education with

some hopes given for the future.

1673. Miller, Spencer, Jr. "Labor and Public Education." In
      Theodore Brameld, ed., Workers' Education in the United
      States. New York: Harper & Row, 1941, 25-47.
          Although the chief aim of the article is the examina-
      tion of public education, some space is given to an analy-
      sis of various labor education programs.

1674. _____. "Twenty Years of Workers' Education." American
      Federationist. XLVIII (April, 1941), 14-15, 31.
          A brief historical examination of the labor education
      movement by tracing the activities of the WEB.

1675. _____. "Twenty Years of the Workers' Education Bureau."
      Labor Information Bulletin. VIII (June, 1941), 8-9.
          An historical study of the WEB and an examination of
      its influence on labor education.

1676. _____. "Twenty Years of Workers' Education in the
      U.S.A." World Association Adult Education Bulletin. #27.
      (November, 1941), 19-21.
          A study of the role of the WEB as a background to
      the development of labor education.

1677. _____. "Workers' Education." In Fred S. Hall, ed.,
      Social Work Yearbook, 1935. New York: Russell Sage
      Foundation, 1935.
          A descriptive study of the various labor education pro-
      grams in 1935.

1678. Mire, Joseph. "Adult Education in Labor Unions." In Mal-
      colm S. Knowles, ed., Handbook of Adult Education in the
      United States. Washington, D.C.: Adult Education Asso-
      ciation of the United States, 1960, 286-301.
          An examination of the status, trends, and development
      of labor education since 1945.

1679. Myers, James. Do You Know Labor? New York: The John
      Day Co., 1943. Chapt. X: "Workers' Education," 195-
      201.
          A statement on the function and benefit of labor educa-
      tion, with a descriptive list of the various unions and other
      organizations with education programs.

1680. Rogin, Lawrence. "Changes During Labor Education's 43
      Years." Labor Education Viewpoints. (Fall, 1959), 3-9.
          An historical study of the development of labor educa-
      tion from 1916-1959.

1681. _____. "Survey of Workers' Education." Thirty Year His-
      tory of an Idea. New York: American Labor Education
      Service, (1958), 4-10.

An historical survey of the development of labor education in the United States.

1682. Rowden, Dorothy. "Workers' Education." Social Work Yearbook. New York: Russell Sage Foundation, 1939, 26-28.
A description of the various forms which labor education in America has taken.

1683. Smith, Hilda W. "Workers' Education." Social Work Yearbook. New York: Russell Sage Foundation, 1937, 551-554.
A survey of the types of organizations involved in labor education.

1684. Starr, Mark. "The Current Panorama." In Theodore Brameld, ed., Workers' Education in the United States. New York: Harper & Row, 1941, 89-113.
A description of the labor education programs of various national organizations such as unions, the WEB, and the WPA.

1685. _____. "Higher Education and Organized Labor." Current History. XXIX (September, 1955), 168-172.
An assessment of the current situation in labor education and a description of the various programs in the field.

1686. _____. Labor Looks at Education. Cambridge: The League for Industrial Democracy, 1947. 51 pp.
A study of labor's attitude toward education generally. Several references to labor education are included.

1687. _____. "Trade Union Education Survey." Labor and Nation. VII (Fall, 1951), 55-80.
A survey and description of all the active labor education programs in the United States.

1688. _____. Workers' Education Today. New York: League for Industrial Democracy, 1941. 48 pp.
A description of the field of labor education in the United States with special emphasis on the rule of unions.

1689. Stein, Rose M. "Workers' Education--Today's Challenge." Harvard Business Review. XVIII (Winter, 1940), 207-214.
An examination of the status of labor education in the late 1930's in the United States.

1690. "Wartime Developments in Workers' Education." Monthly Labor Review. LXI (August, 1945), 301-318.
A study of the steady increase of agencies involved in labor education during the war years.

1691. Wolfson, Theresa. "The Recent Social Climate." In Theo-

dore Brameld, ed., Workers' Education in the United
States.   New York: Harper & Row, 1941, 67-88.
 An examination of the social, economic, and political
causes which assisted the labor education movement.

1692. "Workers' Education." In Mary L. Ely, ed., Handbook of
 Adult Education in the United States. New York: Institute of Adult Education, 1948, 489-501.
  An alphabetically arranged list with a description of
 the agencies involved in labor education.

1693. "Workers' Education Notes." Adult Education Journal. VIII
 (July, 1949), 189.
  An activity report of various organizations involved in
 labor education.

1694. Zatinsky, M.   "Three Agencies, One Job." Adult Education.
 I (April, 1951), 152-153.
  An examination of three different organizations involved in labor education: unions, universities, and independent schools.

                         MISCELLANEOUS

1695. Adam, Thomas R.   "Against Separation." Journal of Adult
 Education.   XI (April, 1939), 117-122.
  A criticism of labor education's exclusive character,
 only being for workers. Argues that such a trend is
 harmful for a "Free Society."

1696. Allen, Russell.   "The Professional in Unions and His Educational Preparation." Industrial Labor Relations Review.
 XVI (October, 1962), 16-29.
  A brief discussion of the need for and description of
 education for professional union staff members.

1697. "An American Pioneer." World Association Adult Education
 Bulletin.   #29 (May, 1942), 19.
  A eulogy for Thomas E. Burke, president of the WEB
 since 1929.

1698. Barkas, Benjamin.   "Labor Education and the Philadelphia
 Public Schools." Adult Education Bulletin. XIII (April,
 1949), 115-119.
  A description of the educational programs established
 by unions for their members in cooperation with the Philadelphia public schools.

1699. _____.   "The Labor Education Association, Philadelphia
 Industrial Area." Industrial Labor Relations Review.
 VI (January, 1953), 285-287.

A report of the history and activities of the Philadelphia Labor Education Association.

1700. Friedlander, Etta. "Education in the Workers' School of New
York." Social Research. VII (February, 1940), 92-101.
An examination of the role of labor education as a
student-centered operation.

1701. "Georgia People's School." Adult Education Journal. VI
(April, 1947), 93.
A description of the course offerings of the school.

1702. "Georgia People's School." Adult Education Journal. VII
(January, 1948), 30.
A description of the curriculum of the Georgia
People's School.

1703. "Georgia Workers' Education Service." Adult Education Journal. V (October, 1946), 178.
A description of the groups involved and the funding of
the Georgia Workers' Education Service.

1704. Gidlow, Elsa. "A New Kind of College." Current History.
LII (December 24, 1940), 22-24, 31-32.
A description of a labor college established by the Par-
affine Companies, Inc., for its union and company leaders
to study problems together.

1705. Jensen, G. "Careers in Adult Education." Adult Leadership.
X (February, 1962), 228-229, 249-250.
An examination of the requirements and salaries available in adult education jobs. One section deals with labor
education.

1706. Kerrison, Irvine L. H. "What Every Teacher Should Know."
Education. LXXII (April, 1952), 550-556.
An examination of some vital information for labor education teachers, and a call for teachers to keep up with
changes in the field.

1707. Lawrence, Mary. Education Unlimited. Monteagle, Tennessee: Highlander Folk School, 1945.
A handbook and manual for labor education in the south.

1708. McCallister, Frank. "Organizing Statewide Education Center."
Labor and Nation. III (May-June, 1947), 39-40.
A description of the organization, financing, and staff
of the Georgia Workers' Education Service.

1709. Miller, Seymour Michael. "New York Chapter Discusses Resident Schools." Labor Education Viewpoints. (Winter,
1961) 32-33.
A discussion of the pros and cons of resident workers'

schools vs. non-residential schools.

1710. Miller, Spencer, Jr. "Tribute to a Great American." American Federationist. XLVIII (December, 1941), 24-25.
A eulogy for Thomas Burke with a brief discussion of his role in the development of labor education.

1711. Pell, Orlie. "Jobs in Workers' Education." Adult Education Journal. IX (April, 1950), 66-73.
A discussion of the nature of jobs in labor education with notes on qualifications for getting such jobs.

1712. "Savannah Workers' Program." Adult Education Journal. VI (October, 1947), 193.
A discussion of the changing administration at the workers' program in Savannah, Georgia.

LABOR STUDIES

PHILOSOPHY AND GOALS

1713. Bacon, Emery F. "Achieving Excellence in Labor Education."
School for Workers Thirty-Fifth Anniversary Papers.
Madison: University of Wisconsin School for Workers,
1960, 69-78.
An examination of what the author believes to be excellence in labor studies and how the worker and society
will benefit from a broad liberal education.

1714. Boyle, George. "Defining Labor Education Needs." Adult
Leadership. XVIII (March, 1970), 278-280, 292.
A discussion of the worker's need to have a more liberal education rather than just the traditional "tool" courses.

1715. Brickner, Dale. "Labor Education: Some Questions of Scope
and Credibility." Labor Studies Journal. I (May, 1976),
60-76.
With the increase in the unionization of higher education, the author examines the role of the university labor
educator in the organization effort.

1716. Eby, Kermit. "The 'Drip' Theory in Labor Unions." Antioch Review. XIII (March, 1953), 95-102.
A discussion of the educational goals which the author
feels should be adopted by the American labor movement.

1717. _____. "Workers' Education for What?" Antioch Review.
XI (Summer, 1951), 185-192.
An examination of what the author believes the purpose
of labor studies should be.

1718. Goode, William. "Labor Education, Need for Revival." Nation. CCXV (September 4, 1972), 141-143.
After examining some of the weaknesses in labor studies, the author suggests some solutions for strengthening
the movement.

1719. Jacobs, Samuel. "An Approach to Workers' Education."
Adult Education. IX (Winter, 1959), 80-89.
After a discussion of the reasons why education does
not prepare an individual for this changing world, the

author delves into the need for coordination of educators
to get important questions to workers through education.

1720. Kornbluh, Hy. "Reading the Lower Fifth." Labor Education
Viewpoints. (Spring, 1964), 1-7.
A discussion of the need to broaden the role of labor
studies at the university to reach the "lowest fifth" of the
working class.

1721. Lens, Sidney. "What Happened to Ideas and Idealism?" Labor Education Viewpoints. (Fall, 1959), 9-14.
The author discusses where he thinks the goals and
objectives of labor studies have gone wrong.

1722. London, Jack. "Labor Education and the University." In
Freda Goldman, ed., Reorientation in Labor Education.
Chicago: Center for the Study of Liberal Education for
Adults, 1962, 11-24.
A discussion of a new approach for labor studies so
the discipline can meet the real needs of the labor move-
ment.

1723. _____. "A Reappraisal of Labor Education." Adult Education. VII (Winter, 1957), 103-111.
A critical examination of the field of labor studies,
and a call for the movement to give a truly liberal education.

1724. _____. "What Is Liberal Education for Workers?" Labor
Education Viewpoints. (Spring, 1963), 13-16.
An appraisal of the pitfalls of an educational program
which is only practical. The article calls for the liberali-
zation of labor studies programs.

1725. _____. "Workers' Education." Adult Leadership. IX
(March, 1961), 177-282.
An examination of the continuing need for labor studies
programs because of our changing society.

1726. Lynd, Staughton. "What's Wrong with Workers' Education?"
American Teacher. LVII (December, 1972), 16.
A scathing critique of the labor studies movement as
institutionally dependent and pedagogically regressive.

1727. Miller, Robert. "New Dimensions in Union Education." Labor Today. IV (October-November, 1965), 21-24.
An analysis of the role labor studies should play in re-
directing the labor movement.

1728. Millgate, Michael. "An English View of Workers' Education
in the United States." Adult Education. VIII (Spring, 1958),
162-174.
The author describes and analyzes the goals of the type

of education he feels should be offered to American workers.

1729. Nash, Al. "What's Right with Workers' Education." American Teacher. LVII (December, 1972), 17.
      An examination of some of the new innovations in labor studies such as the United Automobile Workers of America's Family Education Center at Black Lake, and D.C. 37's College in New York City.

1729a. "189 Symposium on Goals of Labor Education." Labor Education Viewpoints. (Spring, 1964), 23-32.
      A discussion of both short term and long term goals of AFT Local 189 and labor studies in general.

1730. Robinson, James W. "Effects of the Social and Economic Environment on Workers' Education: United States and British Examples." Adult Education. XIX (Spring, 1969), 172-185. ERIC Accession Number EJ 006960.
      An examination of the central philosophy which undergirds the educational movements for workers in the United States and Great Britain.

1731. Senn, Peter R. Liberal Education for Trade Union Leaders: Problems and Prospects for a University Labor Program. Chicago: Union Research and Education Prospects University College, University of Chicago, 1958, 100 pp.
      An analysis of the problems involved in establishing a college level educational program for union leaders. The authors discuss many aspects of the program including its goals and objectives.

1732. [No entry.]

CURRICULUM AND METHODS

1733. Abbott, William L. "Labor Education Is the Key to Training Community Educators." Adult Leadership. XVIII (September, 1969), 86, 101-102.
      Since Labor Studies is attempting to reach poor, industrial workers educationally, it can be expected that the same educational methods could be used to train community educators.

1734. Applebaum, Leon and Higdon Roberts. "An Analysis of Participants in a Long-Term Adult Education Program." 40 pp. ERIC Accession Number 018768.
      A final report to the Department of Health, Education, and Welfare of a study to determine the reasons why trade unionists dropped out of a long-term adult education program at Ohio State University.

1735. Barbash, Jack. "A New Approach to Teaching Labor Courses. " Industrial Relations. IV (October, 1964), 18-22.
     An examination of a method for teaching current labor
problems in a labor studies class.

1736. _____. "The Public Responsibility of Unions in Respect
to Their Internal Affairs: Educational Implications. " Labor's Public Responsibility. Madison: NILE, 1960, 90-
105.
     An examination of the educational implications for
gaining union democracy.

1737. Chamberlain, Neil W. "Emphasizing the Labor Factor. " Industrial Relations. IV (October, 1964), 33-36.
     An examination of the content of labor courses and
some suggestion for modifications and alternatives.

1738. Connors, Terrence. "Impressions of a Joint Stewards-Fore-
man Class in Human Relations. " Labor Studies Journal.
I (May, 1976), 52-59.
     A study of a class in human relations where both la-
bor and management students were in the same class.

1739. Cook, Alice (Hanson). "Education of Workers for Public Responsibility in Community and Political Affairs. " Labor's
Public Responsibility. Madison: NILE, 1960, 146-167.
     An examination of the ways in which union groups can
be educated to participate in community and political areas
more effectively.

1740. Craypo, Charles. "Workers in Common Predicament: Labor
Education in an Era of Conglomerate, Multinational Enterprises. " Labor Studies Journal. I (May, 1976), 3-16.
     An examination of the need to educate organized work-
ers to be informed about the problems of multinational
corporations.

1741. Daws, Lee. "What Is Programmed Instruction?" Labor Education Viewpoints. (Fall, 1968), 12, 22.
     A description and definition of programmed instruction
and how it differs from standard instruction.

1742. Golatz, Helmut J. "Adult Education a New Approach. " American Federationist. LXXVII (August, 1970), 16-18.
     An examination of the use of sensitivity training as an
educational method in labor studies.

1743. Hampel, Paul. "Teaching Methods for Labor Education. "
Labor Education Viewpoints. (Fall, 1968), 7-9, 23.
     A listing of various methods for teaching labor studies.

1744. Joray, Paul and Keith Knauss. "The Use of Video-Tape Re-
cording in Labor Studies: Implementation in Collective

Bargaining Courses." Labor Studies Journal. I (May, 1975), 19-26.

A discussion of the use of video tape equipment for labor studies courses.

1745. Leys, Wayne A. R. "Education for Labor's Public Responsibility." Labor's Public Responsibility. Madison: NILE, 1960, 1-15.

An examination of the use of the Socratic method to teach labor about its public responsibility.

1746. _____ and Peter R. Senn. Teaching Ethics and Labor Education. Washington, D.C.: NILE, 1962, 88 pp.

A manual for labor studies teachers to use as an aid in developing proficiency in the case method of teaching "rights, duties, loyalties, and ideals."

1747. "Meeting Individual Needs." Labor Education Viewpoints. (Spring, 1964), 19-21.

An examination of methods of teaching which are conducive to meeting workers' needs.

1748. Myers, Charles. "Two Neglected Areas in Traditional Labor Courses." Industrial Relations. IV (October, 1964), 29-32.

A discussion of two areas which are usually neglected in a traditional labor course ... comparative economic development and the role of management.

1749. Myerson, C. "Applying Labor Education Techniques to the Problem of School Integration." Labor Education Viewpoints." (Fall, 1961), 5-11.

A discussion of the methods of education in a black, working class community.

1750. Odell, Charles E. "An Urgent Need: Education for Retirement." American Federationist. LXXIII (September, 1966), 21-24.

An examination of various unions' pre-retirement education programs.

1751. Portman, Lisa. "Teaching Reading, a Double Pronged Task." Labor Education Viewpoints. (Fall, 1968), 14.

A discussion of the task of teaching the worker-student to read and then getting him to use the skill.

1752. Role of the University in Labor Education: Proceedings of a Conference. Amherst: Labor Relations and Research Center, University of Massachusetts, 1965. 43 pp.

An appraisal of the role of the university in the expanding area of labor studies.

1753. Ross, Arthur M. "Labor Courses: The Need for Radical

Construction." Industrial Relations. IV (October, 1964),
1-17.
    An examination of labor courses and labor textbooks
is given in which the author cites general deficiencies in
the latter.

1754. Schultz, George P. "Labor Courses Are Not Obsolete."
    Industrial Relations. IV (October, 1964), 23-28.
        An examination of the relevance of labor courses at
    the university.

1755. Segal, Ben D. "The Educational Implications of Labor's
    Public Responsibility in Public Affairs, Civil Liberties,
    Civil Rights, and International Affairs." Labor's Public
    Responsibility. Madison: NILE, 1960, 168-185.
        An examination of the need for and the extent of la-
    bor education in the areas listed.

1756. United Automobile Workers, Department of Education. "Crea-
    tivity in Adult Education." Adult Leadership. XIV (No-
    vember, 1965), 159-160+.
        A report of the new programs and projects which won
    the UAW Education Department an award for "unusual cre-
    ativity in adult education" in Michigan.

1757. Wertheimer, Barbara M. "Blueprint for Community Action:
    A Suggested Frontier for Workers' Education." Adult
    Leadership. X (December, 1961), 168-170.
        An examination of a "new frontier" for labor educa-
    tion in the area of community action programs.

1758. _____. "Labor Explores the Arts; A New Program of
    Cornell's School of Industrial and Labor Relations."
    Adult Leadership. XVII (May, 1968), 5-6+.
        A description of an educational program for trade un-
    ionists in the area of cultural arts.

1759. Young, Holgate. "Can the Labor Movement Be Turned On?"
    Labor Education Viewpoints. (Fall, 1968), 13.
        A discussion of the use of audio-visual aids in labor
    studies classes.

1760. [No entry.]

INDIVIDUAL ORGANIZATIONS

National Institute of Labor Education (NILE)

1761. Miller, Seymour Michael. "Notes from a Short Visit to a
    Long-Term Residential School." Labor Education View-
    points. (Spring, 1963), 17-19.

A report of one observer's impressions of and recommendations for a ten-week NILE residential program.

1762. Mire, Joseph. "Liberal Education for Union Staff." Adult
        Leadership. IX (December, 1960), 181-182.
              A report of an educational program for union staff
        members conducted by NILE.

1763. _____. "Training for Executive Staff in Labor Unions."
        Monthly Labor Review. LXXXV (March, 1962), 261-263.
              A report and evaluation of three NILE-sponsored ten-
        week residential programs for union staffers.

1764. _____. "Union Officials Mesh Theory and Practice: Three
        Residential Study Institutes for Union Staff." American
        Federationist. LXVIII (October, 1961), 28-29.
              An examination of the educational experiences re-
        ceived by paid union staff members in a ten week institute.

1764a. National Institute of Labor Education. Madison: NILE, 1960.
        32 pp.
              A short description of the history, philosophy and edu-
        cational activities of NILE.

1765. Rogin, Lawrence. "The Changing Nature of Trade Union Edu-
        cation." American Federationist. LXVIII (June, 1961),
        2-5.
              A discussion of the projects conducted under the aus-
        pices of NILE.

1766. "Union Leaders Go Back for Liberal Education." Business
        Week. (August 25, 1962), 68-69.
              A report on the experimental labor studies project con-
        ducted jointly by NILE and the University of Michigan.

1767. Young, Holgate. "The Meeting in Madison." Labor Education
        Viewpoints. (Winter, 1960), 21-25.
              A report of a NILE conference on Labor's Public Re-
        sponsibility.

Organized Labor

1768. "AFL-CIO Labor Studies Center." American Labor. IV
        (May, 1970), 35-41.
              An examination of the initial steps which led to the es-
        tablishment of a labor college for the AFL-CIO.

1769. Allen, Russell. "The Educational Implications of Labor's Pub-
        lic Responsibility in Collective Bargaining." Labor's Pub-
        lic Responsibility. Madison: NILE, 1960, 42-56.
              An examination of the role of collective bargaining and
        the educational implications for labor education.

1770. _____. "Impact of Trade Union Education Efforts on Recurrent Education." In Selma J. Mushkin, ed. , Recurrent Education. Washington, D.C.: National Institute of
Education, 1973, 213-220.
An examination of the relationship of recurrent education to trade union education efforts.

1771. Bacon, Emery F. "World of Ideas, Fourth Year Institute
United Steelworkers." In Freda Goldman, ed. , Reorientation in Labor Education. Chicago: Center for the Study
of Liberal Education for Adults, 1962, 43-50. ERIC Accession Number ED 027445.
An examination of the Steelworkers' four-year summer
school which is held in cooperation with Penn State University.

1772. Beirne, Joseph. "Unionists Must Prepare for a Different Future." Adult Leadership. X (January, 1962), 195-196,
216.
An address to the staff of the Communications Workers of America which stresses the need for education within the trade union movement.

1773. Confer, Steven H. "A Second View of Union Summer Schools."
Adult Leadership. XXI (September, 1972), 85-86.
A reply to Higdon Robert's article on union summer
schools which appeared in the November 1971 Adult Leadership. The author examines the quality of curriculum
and instruction in union summer schools and makes suggestions for improvements.

1774. Gottlieb, Bertram. "CWA Staff Training: The Conceptual Approach to Problem Solving." Labor Education Viewpoints.
(Spring, 1963), 5-6.
A rationale and description of the staff training program of the Communications Workers of America.

1775. Gray, Lois. "Training of Labor Union Officials." Labor
Law Journal. XXVI (August, 1975), 472-477.
A discussion of the need for union leadership training
with examples of different programs which are conducted
throughout the country.

1776. "A Half Century of Workers' Education." American Teacher.
LVII (December, 1972), 13-14.
A description of Local 189 and a discussion of its his-
torical development and present activities.

1777. Hutchinson, Bud R. "Breakthrough in Staff Training." American Federationist. LXXI (February, 1964), 19-21.
A description of the staff training program for all new
staff members of the Communication Workers of America.

1778. Jacobsen, Carolyn J. "An Expanding Role for Labor's College." American Federationist. LXXXI (October, 1974), 13-19.
A report of the activities and growth of the AFL-CIO Labor Studies Center.

1779. _____. "New Plateau for Labor's College." American Federationist. LXXX (January, 1973), 11-16.
An examination of the goals and curriculum of the AFL-CIO Labor Studies Center.

1780. "The Labor Studies Center--Year One." American Federationist. LXXVII (November, 1970), 22-24.
A description of the first year's activities of the AFL-CIO Labor Studies Center.

1781. "Labor Union Goes to College: D.C. 37 Campus." Saturday Review of Education. I (March, 1973), 65.
A description of the efforts of the American Federation of State, County, and Municipal Employees District Council 37's attempts to establish a degree-granting college for their union members.

1782. Levine, Herbert A. Labor Unions and Adult Education. Monograph #6. The New Jersey Association for Adult Education, 1963. 6 pp.
An examination of the role of labor education as a division of adult education. The author discusses the various educational services which should be available to the trade union movement.

1783. Nash, Al. "The Walter and May Reuther UAW Family Center." Free Labour World. (May, 1973), 14-16.
An illustrated article describing an experimental labor studies endeavor by the UAW at Black Lake, Michigan.

1784. _____ and May Nash. Labor Unions and Labor Education. University Park, Pa.: University Labor Education Association, 1970, 24 pp.
An analytical examination of why trade unions maintain a very narrow scope in the educational programs for their membership.

1785. "The New AFL-CIO Labor Studies Center." American Federationist. LXXVI (April, 1969), 19-24.
An examination of the goals and principles of the new Labor Studies Center established by the AFL-CIO.

1786. Roberts, Higdon. "Union Summer Schools--A Light Dose of Costs Benefits." Adult Leadership. XX (November, 1971), 181-182+. ERIC Accession Number EJ 145692.
A computation of a cost-benefit analysis of the traditional union summer school. Based upon this analysis,

the author suggests money-saving alternatives for unions interested in education.

1787. Rogin, Lawrence. "Staff Training with a Southern Accent." American Federationist. LXXII (September, 1965), 19.
A description of a staff training program for southern union officials, co-sponsored by the AFL-CIO Education and Civil Rights Department and NILE.

1788. Sexton, Brendan. "Staff and Officer Training to Build Successful Unions." Industrial Relations. V (February, 1966), 83-96.
An examination of the historical development of labor education and a study of the movement's current form in various unions.

1789. Sexton, Patricia Cayo. "Organizing a Labor College." Dissent. XX (Summer, 1973), 349-352.
A description of a unique, innovative college established by the American Federation of State, County, and Municipal Employees' District Council 37 in conjunction with New Rochelle College.

1790. "Teamsters Open a Labor School to Process Their Local Talent." Business Week. (September 27, 1969), 61.
A report on the opening of a labor institute in Miami, Florida, by the International Brotherhood of Teamsters. Included is a description of the goals and curriculum of the school.

1791. "Where It All Began." American Teacher. LVII (December, 1972), 14.
An historical examination of local 189 from its beginnings at Brookwood Labor College in 1921.

1792. Widick, B. J. "Staff and Officer Training to Build Successful Unions." Industrial Relations. VI (October, 1966), 116-117.
A rejoinder to the Brendan Sexton Article which appeared in the February 1966 issue of Industrial Relations.

1793. Young, Holgate. "Building and Education System in the Labor Movement." Labor Education Viewpoints. (Fall, 1961), 13-20.
A discussion of the practicality of labor studies in the labor movement.

1794. _____. "The Future of Education in Unions." Labor Education Viewpoints. (Spring, 1963), 7-12.
A discussion of an attempt to broaden the number of students reached in union education classes.

Universities

1795. Applebaum, Leon and Higdon Roberts. "An Approach to Lo-
      cal Trade Union Leadership Training." Adult Leadership.
      XVI (February, 1968), 299-300+. ERIC Accession Num-
      ber ED 018768.
            An historical description of the Labor Education and
      Research Service at Ohio State University.

1796. Boyle, George. "Goals of Unions and Universities in Labor
      Education." Labor Studies Journal. I (Fall, 1976), 157-
      161.
            An examination of the newly developing role of labor
      studies at the university level and what this will mean for
      the more traditional concept of university extension work
      in labor education.

1797. Brickner, Dale. "Blue Collar Scholars." American Federa-
      tionist. LXXI (April, 1964), 20-22.
            A description of a long-term resident labor education
      program at Indiana University.

1798. Eiger, Norman. "A Hot Bed of Learning." Education and
      Training. XVI (April-May, 1974), 108-109.
            A description of the educational activities of the Rut-
      gers University Labor Education program.

1799. Gould, Anne L. "Liberal Arts for Labor, The University of
      California." In Freda Goldman, ed., Reorientation in La-
      bor Education. Chicago: Center for the Studies of Liber-
      al Education for Adults, 1962, 25-42. ERIC Accession
      Number ED 027445.
            An examination of the University of California's at-
      tempt to provide a broad-based liberal arts program for
      trade unionists.

1800. Gray, Lois. "Labor Studies Credit and Degree Programs, a
      Growth Sector of Higher Education." Labor Studies Jour-
      nal. I (May, 1976), 34-51.
            An analysis of the extent of development in the labor
      studies discipline. The data was gathered in a national
      survey sponsored by the Universities and College Labor
      Education Association.

1801. Hutton, Carroll. "Extending and Expanding Labor Education."
      Labor Education Viewpoints. (Spring, 1962), 19-20.
            An examination of the role of the state university in
      extension labor studies' programs.

1802. Kelley, S. C. "The University and Labor Education." Labor
      Education Viewpoints. (Spring, 1962), 3.
            An examination of the debate between union and univer-

sity labor educators as to the role of the university in labor studies.

1803. Kerrison, Irvine L. H. "Institute Labor Program, Rutgers University." In Freda Goldman, ed., Reorientation in Labor Education. Chicago: Center for the Study of Liberal Education for Adults, 1962, 51-60. ERIC Accession Number ED 027445.
    A description of the Rutgers University offerings for labor.

1804. Levine, Herbert A. "Labor Education on the American University Campus." International Labour Review. CII (November, 1970), 497-506.
    After a broad survey of the field of labor studies, the author examines the need for union-university cooperation for successful labor studies programs.

1805. _____. "Union-University and Inter-University Cooperation in Workers' Education in the United States." The Role of Universities in Workers' Education. Geneva: International Labour Organization, 1974, 172-201. ERIC Accession Number ED 068838.
    An examination of union-university cooperation as the major variable in the establishment of a university labor studies program. Also included is an historical case study of the Rutgers University Labor Program.

1806. _____. "Will Labor Educators Meet Today's Challenge?" Industrial Relations. V (February, 1966), 97-106.
    An examination of the objectives of university labor studies programs with a definition of the changing patterns of the movement, and a description of the Rutgers program.

1807. MacKenzie, John. "The Role of the University and College Labor Education Association in Promoting Orderly Expansion of University Labor Education." Labor Studies Journal. I (May, 1976), 27-33.
    An examination of the role of a national organization of university and college labor studies programs in establishing new labor studies offerings.

1808. McCallister, Frank. "Innovation--Long Term Leadership Education." American Federationist. LXXIII (March, 1966), 22-24.
    A description of the labor studies program at Roosevelt University and the four year leadership training program which the school also sponsored.

1809. McConnell, John W. "The Role of a Labor Relations Center." American Federationist. LXXII (November, 1965), 22-24.
    A discussion of the need for and the ideal role of a university labor relations center.

1810. Orr, Charles A. "University Sponsored Labor Education in the United States." Labor Law Journal. XXI (June, 1970), 365-373.

A comparison of American university labor studies programs with examples in other parts of the world.

1811. Rayback, Joseph G. "The Union Leadership Academy in Pennsylvania." Labor Education Viewpoints. (Spring, 1962), 9-11.

An examination of the purposes, principles, and curriculum of a four-year program for union leaders conducted by Pennsylvania State University.

1812. Roberts, Higdon, Dale Brickner and H. Haines Turner. "An Education Evaluation of Local Union Leadership Training." Adult Leadership. XVIII (February, 1970), 251-252, 263-265. ERIC Accession Number 015600.

A report of the findings of a questionnaire sent out by the University of Indiana to evaluate the teaching effectiveness of its labor studies program.

1813. Robinson, James W. "Trends in Labor Education--Missouri and the Nation." Business and Government Review. VIII (March-April, 1966), 19-25.

A description of the goals of labor studies and the various programs and institutes offered by different organizations and universities, including the University of Missouri.

1814. Ruhig, Theodore. "Summer Institute on Labor and World Affairs." Adult Leadership. XI (June, 1962), 47-48.

A report on the activities of the fifteenth annual session of the Steelworkers Institute held at the University of Kansas.

1815. Schwartz, Edward. "Training Union Leaders." Change. VI (February, 1974), 18-21.

An examination of the union leadership academy as a university experiment in reaching a group of people traditionally deprived of the benefits of higher education.

1816. Witte, Edwin E. "Labor Education and the Changing Labor Movement." School for Workers, Thirty-Fifth Anniversary Papers. Madison: University of Wisconsin School for Workers, 1960, 36-40.

An examination of the changing objectives of the University of Wisconsin School for Workers.

Community Colleges

1817. Bilanow, Alex. "A Growing Partnership. Unions and Community Colleges." RWDSU Record. (February, 1973), 13.

An examination of the growing partnership between the

trade union movement and the community college.

1818. Brickner, Dale. "National Allies--Organized Labor and Com-
      munity Colleges." Organized Labor and Community Col-
      leges. Report of the American Association of Community
      and Junior Colleges--United Auto Workers and AFL-CIO
      Assembly. Washington, D.C., December 8-10, 1975, 9-
      14.
          A report on the assembly of a conference on the role
      of community colleges in the education of organized labor.

1819. Connally, John and Herbert A. Levine. "Symbiosis, Organ-
      ized Labor and the Community College." Changing Educa-
      tion. (June, 1971), 10-11. ERIC Accession Number
      EJ 039975.
          A discussion of the new role which many community
      colleges are assuming by moving into the field of labor
      studies.

1820. Golatz, Helmut. "Have You Tried Labor Education?" Junior
      College Journal. XLII (March, 1972), 28-29. ERIC Ac-
      cession Number EJ 051669.
          A description of the purposes and practices of a labor
      studies program with a discussion of how a community col-
      lege can become involved in the field.

1821. Good, Wallace E. "Labor Studies in the Community College."
      ERIC Accession Number ED 097089.
          An examination of the development of a labor studies
      program at El Camino Community College. Included is the
      curriculum and student recruitment.

1822. Gray, Lois. "Organized Labor and Community Colleges."
      Organized Labor and Community Colleges. Report of the
      American Association of Community and Junior Colleges--
      United Automobile Workers and the AFL-CIO Assembly,
      December 8-10, 1975, Washington, D.C., 3-8.
          An examination of the need for and proposed role of
      community colleges in the field of labor studies.

1823. Gross, Alan. "The Community College and the Workers, An
      Opportunity Open to Question." Phi Delta Kappan. LV
      (May, 1974), 624-626.
          An English professor at Macomb County Community
      College in California discusses the need for making post
      secondary education more attractive to workers.

GENERAL, HISTORICAL AND DESCRIPTIVE STUDIES

1824. Abbott, William. "Needed More Liberalism." Labor Educa-
      tion Viewpoints. (Winter, 1960), 5-10.

An examination of the history of liberal education in the labor movement.

1825. Eiger, Norman. "Labor Education--A Past and Future View." The New Jersey Adult Educator. (Winter, 1975), 13-15.
    A brief historical synopsis of the development of labor studies.

1826. Gray, Lois. "The American Way in Labor Education." Industrial Relations. V (February, 1966), 53-66.
    A discussion of the historical development of labor studies in America.

1827. Rogin, Lawrence. "Labor Unions." In Robert M. Smith, George F. Aber, and J. R. Kidd, eds., Handbook of Adult Education. New York: The Macmillian Co., 1970, 301-313.
    A discussion of the sources and goals of labor studies in the United States.

1828. _____ and Marjorie Rachlin. Survey of Adult Education Opportunities for Labor: Labor Education in the United States. Washington, D.C.: National Institute of Labor Education, 1968, 275 pp. ERIC Accession Number ED 023061.
    A general survey of the status of labor studies in the United States. This examination describes both union and university involvement in the field as well as tracing the movement's historical development.

1829. Smith, Hilda W. "Labor Education: Past, Present, Future." Labor Education Viewpoints. (Fall, 1968), 6, 23.
    A discussion of the need to maintain an historical perspective when planning future labor studies programs.

1830. Tift, Katherine. "Labor Education in the U.S., a Survey." Labor Education Viewpoints. (Fall, 1968), 1-5, 22.
    An examination of the historical development of labor studies in the United States.

MISCELLANEOUS

1831. Bacon, Emery F. "Achieving Excellence in Labor Education." C. Scott Fletcher, ed., Education for Public Responsibility. New York: W. W. Norton, 1964, 88-98.
    After a discussion of some of the major areas of concern in American industrial life, the author suggests that these problems be examined and that solutions to these problems begin to be implemented through education in a labor studies program.

1832. Brickner, Dale. "Long Term Resident Programs: Cinderella or Stepsister." Labor Education Viewpoints. (Spring, 1965), 1-7.

A discussion of the pros and cons of long-term resident labor studies programs.

1833. Czarnecki, Edgar R. "The Need for Selectivity in Labor Education." Adult Leadership. XVIII (April, 1970), 313-314. ERIC Accession Number EJ 019817.

A short discussion endorsing a plan for restricting the students entering the field of labor studies in order to develop motivated students who direct community action.

1834. Hagburg, Eugene C. "Labor Education Participants." Adult Leadership. XV (April, 1967), 353-355.

A report of a study which examined the characteristics of students who attend labor studies programs.

1835. Levine, Herbert A. and Milton M. Schwartz. "Personnel Frontiers: Labor Leadership." Personnel Administration. XXVIII (January-February, 1965), 44-47.

A report of a study which compared leadership characteristics between management and union groups involved in education programs at Rutgers University.

1836. Linton, Thomas E. "Reality and Distortion in the Articles on Labor Education." Adult Leadership. XV (June, 1966), 45-46.

A critical examination of the authors and articles in the area of labor education.

1837. London, Jack and Robert Wenkert. "Obstacles to Blue Collar Participation in Adult Education." Labor Education Viewpoints. (Spring, 1965), 13-28.

An examination of the reasons why fewer blue collar workers participate in adult education programs than do white collar workers.

1838. Suarez, Joan. "Job Forecasts in the Field of Labor Education." Labor Education Viewpoints. (Fall, 1968), 17, 21.

A discussion of the impact of the "Great Society" on jobs in the field of labor education.

1839. Tracy, Laura. "Reminiscences of a Pioneer." American Teacher. LVII (December, 1972), 15.

In celebration of Hilda Smith's eighty-fourth birthday, a short biographical sketch is presented of one of labor studies first pioneers.

ARCHIVES AND ORAL HISTORIES

ARCHIVAL COLLECTIONS

Amalgamated Clothing Workers of America
    1840. Papers of the Department of Education

Barnard College Library
Wollman Library
Broadway & 118th St.
New York, N.Y. 10027
    1841. Barnard Summer School for Women Workers
    1842. Virginia Gildersleeve papers

Elmer Holmes Bobst Library (Tamiment Library)
New York University
70 Washington Sq. So.
New York, N.Y. 10012
    1843. The Rand School of the Social Sciences
    1844. Algernon Lee papers
    1845. Mark Starr papers
    1846. J. B. S. Hardman papers
    1847. Extensive collection of pamphlets and publications on
          workers' education, 1900-1960, including materials on the
          Jefferson School of Social Science.

Bryn Mawr College, Archives
Merriam Coffin Canaday Library
Bryn Mawr, Pa. 19010
    1848. Bryn Mawr Summer School for Women Workers in Indus-
          try
    1849. M. Carey Thomas papers
    1850. Marion Park papers

Catholic University Library
John K. Mullen of Denver Memorial Library
620 Michigan Ave., N.E.
Washington, D.C. 20017
    1851. Richard L. Deverall papers

Columbia University Library (Nicholas Murray Butler Library)
535 W. 114th St.
New York, N.Y. 10027
    1852. Harry J. Carman papers. ILGWU Workers' Schools
    1852a. Abraham Epstein--several files on workers' education

including Brookwood and The Workers' Education Bureau.

Duke University
William R. Perkins Library
Manuscript Department
Durham, N.C.   27706
   1853. The Socialist Party of America papers--one box on labor
          education miscellaneous; some material on the American
          Labor Education Service and the Workers' Education Bur-
          eau of America.
   1854. The Southern Summer School for Women Workers in In-
          dustry
   1855. The Highlander Folk School papers
   1856. Lucy Randolph Mason papers 1917-1954.   Some other ma-
          terial on the Highlander Folk School and the Southern
          School for Workers in Richmond, Va.

International Ladies Garment Workers Union
   1857. Papers of the Department of Education

Library of Congress
Manuscript Division
Washington, D.C.   20540
   1858. Margaret Drier Robins papers
   1859. National Women's Trade Union League papers

The University of Michigan
Labadie Collection
711 Hatcher Library--South
Ann Arbor, Mich.   48104
   1860. Highlander Folk School--scattered papers from 1945-
          1955; fairly complete yearly reports of activities from
          1956-1960.
   1861. Commonwealth College, Mena, Arkansas--"Historical
          notes, 1922-1931 Commonwealth College," an 154-page
          typescript by F. M. Goodhue, with supplements, later
          letters, and clippings.
   1862. California Labor School papers, San Francisco, donated
          by Holland Roberts.   These papers may be identical with
          his donation to the Wisconsin State Historical Society.

Minnesota Historical Society Collection
690 Cedar Street
St. Paul, Minn.   55101
   1863. Minneapolis Central Labor Union papers--some material
          on workers' education.

National Archives Library
Pennsylvania Ave. & Eighth St. N.W.
Washington, D.C.   20408
   1864. Federal Emergency Relief Administration
   1865. Works Progress Administration

New York Public Library
Fifth Ave. & 42nd St.
New York, N.Y.
    1866. Fannia M. Cohn papers, correspondence, notes, writings, speeches. 19 boxes.
    1867. Rand School of the Social Sciences--mainly the papers of Alexander Trachtenberg, the director of the Department of Labor Research, 1916-1923. 2 boxes.

New York State Department of Labor Library
2 World Trade Center
New York, N.Y.   10047
    1868. New York City chapter of the National Women's Trade Union League

New York State School of Industrial and Labor Relations
Cornell University
Martin P. Catherwood Library
Ithaca, N.Y.   14850
    1869. American Labor Education Service--Pearl L. Willen Memorial. 125 boxes.
    1870. American Federation of Teachers, Local 189 Workers' Education Local--Correspondence 1939-1956.
    1871. Workers' Education Bureau of America--miscellaneous. 3 boxes.
    1872. Affiliated School for Workers, Inc.   Pamphlets prior to 1955.
    1873. Brooklyn Labor Lyceum Association--1896 pamphlets and publications.
    1874. Committee for the Extension of Labor Education
    1875. Highlander Folk School
    1876. Hudson Shore Labor School
    1877. International Workers' Order
    1878. Inter-University Labor Education Committee
    1879. Labor Education Association
    1880. Mark Starr, Union Education Survey
    1881. Trade Union Educational League
    1882. Alice Hanson Cook papers 1952-1955.   Cornell's Inter-University Labor Education Committee papers.

Ohio Historical Society
Archives Library
Interstate 71 and 17th Ave.
Columbus, Ohio   43211
    1883. Elmer Fern Cope papers 1927-1965--union official United Steelworkers of America, organizer of unemployed workers, some labor education.

Oregon Historical Society Library
1230 SW Park Ave.
Portland, Ore.   97205
    1884. Labor Temple, Portland, Oregon--Records 1918-1965; Correspondence and financial records 1918-1957; clippings

1923-1965. 29 boxes.
1885. WPA Workers' Education

University of Oregon Library
Eugene, Ore.   97403
   1886. Farmers Educational and Cooperative Union of America
       --Oregon Southern Idaho Division; Correspondence 1929-
       1933 of Leonard H. McBee, president and Betty M. Kap-
       pany, secretary.   500 items.

The Pennsylvania State University
The University Libraries (Pattee Library)
University Park, Pa.   16802
   1887. Records of labor education institutes and conferences
       held at Pennsylvania State University, 1946-1972.
   1888. Clinton S. Golden papers.   17 boxes.
   1889. E. J. Lever Papers.   21 boxes unorganized.
   1890. United Steelworkers of America Education Department
       files.   91 boxes unorganized.

Presbyterian Historical Society Collection
425 Lombard St.
Philadelphia, Pa.   19147
   1891. Labor Temple, New York, Records 1908-1966.

Radcliffe College
Schlesinger Library
3 James St.
Cambridge, Mass.   02138
   1892. National Woman's Trade Union League--records from
       1904 to 1949.
   1893. Special Services Committee, Ann Arbor Michigan papers
       on American Labor Education Service and the Committee
       on the Extension of Labor Education.
   1894. Hilda Worthington Smith papers 1835-1959.   Contains pa-
       pers on the Affiliated Schools, Barnard and Bryn Mawr
       Summer School for Women Workers, Hudson Shore, Vine-
       yard Shore, the Works Service Project of the Federal
       Emergency Relief Administration, and the Works Progress
       Administration Workers' Education project.

Franklin D. Roosevelt Library
Hyde Park, N.Y.   12538
   1895. Hilda Worthington Smith papers

Rutgers University Labor Education Center
James B. Carey Library
Ryders Lane and Clifton Ave.
New Brunswick, N.J.   08903
   1896. Rutgers University Inter-University Labor Education Com-
       mittee project--correspondence and reports.   1 box.
   1897. Bryn Mawr Summer School for Women Workers--Hudson
       Shore, Affiliated School for Workers, Barnard Summer

School for Women Workers, Vineyard Shore.   4 boxes.
(Duplicates of some of the originals which are located
at the Wisconsin State Historical Library.)
1898.   National Committee for the Extension of Labor Educa-
tion--some materials on the New Jersey Committee.   1
box.   (Duplicates of some of the originals which are located at the Wisconsin State Historical Library.)
1899.   AFL-Rutgers Labor Institute--some file material in archives at Alexander Library, Rutgers; other files on
microfilm 1931-1956.
1900.   Rutgers Labor Education Program--annual reports 1947-
present.
1901.   American Labor Education Service--annual reports and
pamphlets (duplicates; originals at Cornell).

Smith College
Sophia Smith Collection
Neilson Library
North Hampton, Mass.   01060
1902.   Eleanor Coit papers
1903.   American Labor Education Service
1904.   YWCA Industrial Department papers

Southern Illinois University at Carbondale
Morris Library
Carbondale, Ill.   62901
1905.   International Ladies Garment Workers Union--Southwest-
ern Region office, St. Louis, Missouri, Education director's records, 1937-1964.

Swarthmore College
McCabe Library
Swarthmore, Pa.   19081
1906.   Brookwood Labor College--one box located in the papers
of A. J. Muste.

Talladega College
Savery Library
627 W. Battle St.
Taladega, Ala.   35160
1907.   Adam D. Beitel papers 1945-1960.   Includes some material on the Highlander Folk School.

Temple University
Urban Archives Center
Berks and 13th St.
Philadelphia, Pa. 19122
1908.   Amalgamated Clothing Workers of America, Philadelphia
Joint Board.   Education Department Records, 1915-1970.
1909.   Benjamin Barkas--Philadelphia Committee for the Ad-
vancement of Labor Education and Philadelphia Labor
Education Association, 1930-1967.

Tennessee State Library and Archives
Seventh Ave. N.
Nashville, Tenn. 37219
 1910. Highlander Folk School, Monteagle, Tennessee records
   from 1932-1961.

University of Vermont
Guy W. Bailey Library
Wilbar Collection
Burlington, Vt. 05401
 1911. Sarah Norcliffe Cleghorn papers--some material on Brook-
   wood Labor College and the Manumit School at Pawling,
   New York.

Wayne State University
Archives of Labor History
5210 Second St.
Detroit, Mich. 48202
 1912. Selma Burchardt 1911-1967--Secretary AFL Education
   Committee, 1929-1953; some material on workers' education and Washington Trade Union College.
 1913. Charlmers W. Ellison 1926-1938--Bryn Mawr Summer
   School for Women Workers in Industry--University of Wisconsin Summer School for Women Workers in Industry--
   Pittsburgh Labor College.
 1914. Edward Connor--some papers on Works Project Administration's Workers' Education Project.
 1915. Charles Orr--Workers' Education at Universities, 1950-
   1967.
 1916. Walter Reuther--some material on Workers' Education.
 1917. Brookwood Labor College File 1923-1937
 1918. Mark Starr and Helen Norton Starr--ILGWU education materials, 1920-1956.
 1919. AFT Miscellaneous Office files 1916-1961; some workers'
   education.
 1920. Michigan CIO's Education Department general files, 1946-
   1955. Files of summer schools and training institutes,
   1946-1954.
 1921. Carroll Hutton papers--1948-1963, Director of Education
   Region 3 of the United Automobile Workers of America.
 1922. Nicholas Hyshka--Director of Education United Automobile
   Workers of America Locals 80 and 544, Detroit, Michigan.
 1923. Arthur Elder--University of Michigan, Workers' Education
   Service.
 1924. Katherine Pollack Ellickson--Brookwood correspondence
   and papers, 1929-1968.
 1925. Father Raymond S. Clancy--organized workers schools for
   the Association of Catholic Trade Unions.
 1926. Dorothy Hubbard Bishop--Supervisor Works Progress Administration Workers' Education Project, Michigan Division
 1927. Wayne County AFL-CIO education committee papers, 1963-

1967.
1928. Stuart Brock papers
1929. Arthur Calhoun papers
1930. Otto Pragan papers
1931. Frank Marquart--United Automobile Workers of America
        education director, Detroit, Michigan, 1936-1950.
1932. CIO Department of Education--record from 1945-1955;
        office files of George T. Guernsey Associate Director in
        charge of education.
1933. Samuel Jacobs papers--1939-1957 some labor education.
1934. George Lyons--United Automobile Workers of America,
        Local 174, Education Committee papers, 1947-1957.
1935. Leon Cousens papers 1930-1936--course materials, study
        guides and other materials pertaining to Cousens' study
        at the Brookwood Labor College.
1936. Merlin Bishop papers 1936-1937--Director of Education,
        United Automobile Workers of America.
1937. John Edelman papers 1926-1963 some material on labor
        education.
1938. Donald Montgomery--many materials on union institutes
        and educational conferences 1943-1955.
1939. Oscar Paskel United Automobile Workers, Local 227, edu-
        cation for civil rights.

Wisconsin State Historical Society Library
816 State St.
Madison, Wisc. 53706
1940. Ernest E. Schwarztrauber papers 1884-1953.   Included are
        papers on the Portland Labor College and the Wisconsin
        School for Workers.
1941. American Labor Education Service (incorrectly titled)
        contains: The Bryn Mawr Summer School for Women
        Workers in Industry 1921-1939; The Hudson Shore Labor
        School, 1939-1951; The Vineyard Shore School for Women
        Workers, 1929-1933; Barnard Summer School for Work-
        ers, 1927-1934; The Affiliated School for Workers; the
        National Committee for the Extension of Labor Education,
        1945-1950.
1942. Alice Shoemaker--miscellaneous papers, 1950-1969; First
        director of the Wisconsin School for Workers--recollec-
        tions of the school, events and people associated with it.
1943. Jefferson School of the Social Sciences--papers from 1942-
        1956; correspondence, annual reports, minutes of the ex-
        ecutive committee and materials concerning the 1953-1954
        Justice Department suit.
1944. Milwaukee Labor College papers
1945. Textile Workers of America--files of the Education De-
        partment.
1946. Margaret Drier Robins papers
1947. Morris Hillquit--some papers on the founding of the Rand
        School of the Social Sciences.
1948. Samuel Sigman--papers on Appleton Labor College.
1949. Edwin Witte--some papers on the School for Workers.

ORAL HISTORIES

Columbia University Libraries
535 W. 114th St.
New York, N. Y. 10027
    1950. A. J. Muste
    1951. Benjamin McLaurin--University of Wisconsin School for
           Workers and Brookwood Labor College

Schlow Memorial Library
100 E. Beaver Ave.
State College, Pa.   16801
    1952. Frank Fernbach--Brookwood Labor College--Steelworkers.
    1953. Frank Fernbach and Hilda Smith on the Labor Education
           Extension Bill.
    1954. Ernestine Friedmann--YWCA--NWTUL--Bryn Mawr
           Summer School--Barnard.
    1955. Hilda Smith--Bryn Mawr
    1956. Lee B. Stanley--Brookwood
    1957. American Federation of Teachers, Local 189--Nelson
           Cruikshank, Ernestine Friedmann, Dorothy Oko, Oliver
           and Ester Peterson, Hilda Smith and Mark Starr.
    1958. Hilton Hanna--International Vice President Amalgamated
           Meatcutters and Butcher Workmen; Works Progress Ad-
           ministration Workers' Education Project, Atlanta, Geor-
           gia--Ernestine Friedmann.
    1959. Mark and Helen Starr--Brookwood Labor College
    1960. Sarah Fredgant--ACWA Education Department, Philadel-
           phia
    1961. Bonnie Siegal--ILGWU--Allentown & Harrisburg Educa-
           tion Department--Hudson Shore Labor School.

Wayne State University
5210 Second St.
Detroit, Mich.   48202
    1962. United Auto Workers--discussion of the function of labor
           education in building a union.
    1963. Len De Caux--Brookwood Labor College student.

AUTHOR INDEX

Abbott, William L. 1101, 1172, 1733, 1824
Adam, Thomas R. 1655, 1695
Adams, Frank 317, 317a
Adams, James T. 1656
Adler, Felix 1
Adolfson, Torenty H. 1472
Agger, Eugene E. 801
Alderman, L. R. 1590
Algor, Marie S. 1245, 1246, 1295
Allen, Devere 3
Allen, Russell 1102, 1313, 1324, 1697, 1769, 1770
Ameringer, Oscar 1473
Amidon, Beulah 981, 1315
Anderson, Frank 1010
Anderson, Gust 837, 838
Applebaum, Leon 1734, 1795
Archer, Jules 1474
Asch, Nathan 1591
Atkinson, Glen 320

Baab, Otto J. 1316
Bacon, Emery F. 1317, 1713, 1771, 1831
Baisden, Richard N. 1476
Baldwin, Roger 323
Bancroft, Gertrude 581
Barbash, Jack 1318, 1476, 1735, 1736
Barghorn, Fred 98
Barkas, Benjamin W. 77, 99, 1698, 1699
Barrenechea, M. 1623
Barton, Becky 1249
Bascom, Lelia 100
Bauerman, G. F. 101
Beard, Charles 4, 234, 466, 1011
Beck, Gustav F. 839, 840
Beeler, Duane 1173

Beirne, Joseph 1772
Bendix, D. 1174
Bennett, Andrew J. 1319
Bennett, Toscan 324
Berg, Jacob 5
Bernays, Edward L. 1320
Bestor, Arthur E. 982
Bilanow, Alex 1817
Birmingham, L. H. 1321
Bishop, Dorothy Hubbard 914
Blaine, Harry R. 1477
Blanshard, Paul 102, 103, 467, 841, 842
Blechschmidt, Richard 104
Bloomberg, Warner J. 1322
Blough, Maggie 1175
Bohn, William E. 952
Bonner, Marion 587
Borchardt, Selma 915
Bowerman, George 105, 106
Boyle, George 1714, 1796
Bradley, Phillips, 235, 916, 1479, 1480
Brainard, Theodore 107
Brameld, Theodore 1103, 1104, 1323, 1657
Brickner, Dale 1715, 1797, 1812, 1818, 1832
Brooks, George W. 1324, 1325
Brophy, John 6
Brotslaw, Irving 1326, 1481
Brougham, H. B. 355, 356
Brown, H. S. 1327
Brown, Leo 1624
Brown, Mark L. 1482
Browne, Waldo 1012
Bruere, Robert W. 588
Brunson, H. L. 7, 236, 237, 238
Budenz, Louis F. 1067
Budish, Jacob M. 108, 109, 468, 844, 845, 846
Bugniazet, G. M. 8
Burnham, Grace 110

SUBJECT INDEX

Academic Freedom 285, 382, 383, 421, 428, 1122
Action Programs 1475
Administration 28, 32, 136, 553, 1232, 1657; trade union control 15, 145, 488, 531
Adult Education 2, 18, 62, 63, 64, 170, 1130, 1213, 1782
Adult Learning Theory 138, 151, 155, 1231, 1835
Advertising Workers' Classes 103, 188
Affiliated Schools for Workers in Industry, Inc. 572, 573, 574, 575, 576, 604, 612, 615, 616, 621, 624, 625, 631, 647, 663, 671, 689, 690, 697, 738, 762, 1872, 1894, 1897, 1941; activities of graduates 617; educational department 577, 618, 648; experimental projects with federal funds 613; job histories of women workers at summer schools 752; organization and administration 772 (See also individual summer schools--Barnard, Bryn Mawr, Pacific Coast, Southern, Vineyard Shore, and Wisconsin)
American Association of Adult Education 1098, 1146
American Federation of Labor (AFL) 94, 96, 466, 467, 489, 507, 516, 535, 536, 538, 539, 1016, 1128, 1452; committee on education 501, 1912; department of education 1665
American Federation of Labor--Congress of Industrial Organization (AFL-CIO), education department 1339, 1787; labor studies center 1768, 1778, 1779, 1780, 1785
American Fund for Public Service see Foundations--Garland Fund
American Labor Education Service (ALES) 1187, 1245, 1247, 1248, 1250, 1251, 1262, 1265, 1270, 1272, 1273, 1275, 1276, 1286, 1289, 1291, 1294, 1297, 1298, 1853, 1869, 1893, 1901, 1903; change from Affiliated Schools for Workers 1259, 1271, 1288; midwest workers education conference 1249, 1279, 1280; Washington's birthday conference (cooperation with AFT Local 189) 1304, 1305, 1307 (see also office workers, summer school for)
Amherst College Classes for Workers 836, 887, 888, 889
Appleton Labor College 1948
Arizona Labor School 1414
Art Workshop 578, 579
Atomic Age 1117
Audio Visual Aids 219; film 113, 1173, 1184, 1196, 1202, 1203, 1209, 1219, 1235, 1239, 1240, 1759; strip films 1202; video tape 1744
Automobile Workers, United (UAW) 1176, 1193, 1211, 1328, 1359, 1360, 1374, 1375, 1377, 1398, 1415, 1416, 1419, 1455, 1456, 1458, 1459, 1461, 1465, 1466, 1471, 1609, 1756, 1851, 1921, 1922, 1931, 1936, 1939, 1962; Family Education Center (Black Lake) 1729, 1783; Leadership Studies Center 1431; local edu-

unions and councils)
Burchardt, Selma 1912
Burke, Thomas E. 1697, 1710
Buzz groups 1208, 1209, 1235

Calhoun, Arthur 1929 (see also Brookwood Labor College, discharge of)
California, University of Workers' Education Service 804, 811, 812, 813, 815, 817, 818, 831, 1489, 1549; liberal arts for labor 1799; state funding 814
California Labor School (San Francisco) 1329, 1330, 1331, 1425, 1862
Carey, Philip 1637
Carman, Harry J. 1852
Carpenters and Joiners, International Brotherhood of 1412
Case Methods 1746
Catholic Labor Schools 381, 1623, 1624, 1625, 1626, 1627, 1629, 1630, 1632, 1635, 1638, 1639, 1642, 1646, 1649, 1650, 1652 (see also individual Catholic labor schools)
Catholic School of Social Science, National 1636
Catholic Trade Unions, Association of (ACTU) 1644, 1925; New York Chapter 1633
Cement, Line and Gypsum Workers International, United 1380, 1381
Central Labor bodies 467, 500, 555 (see also individual central labor bodies)
Chautauquas see Labor Chautauquas
Chicago, University of 1139, 1487
Chicago Central Labor Body 1220
Chicago Labor Education Council 1254, 1274
Chicago School of Civics and Philanthropy 1100
Chicago Trade Union College 848
Children 42, 140, 1070
Church Leaders see Institute for Church Leaders
Cincinnati, University of 807, 821
Citizenship, education for 1112, 1133, 1168, 1755
Civil Rights and Liberties 1755, 1939
Clancy, Raymond 1925
Class Consciousness see Workers' consciousness
Cleghorn, Sarah 1911
Clerical Workers see Office Workers, Summer School for
Cleveland Labor College 903
Clothing Workers of America, Amalgamated (ACWA) 464, 468, 504, 517, 564, 841, 1023, 1226, 1353, 1397, 1436; department of education 1840; friction with the Workers' Education Bureau 297; Philadelphia Joint Board 1908, 1960
Cohn, Fannia 1866
Coit, Eleanor 663, 1902
Collective Bargaining Training 1744
Colleges 20, 22, 221, 380, 808 (see also universities)
Colorado 499
Colorado Labor College 849, 866, 871, 873, 898, 907

Colorado State Federation of Labor 499
Columbia University 737, 751
Comey, Dennis 1647
Commonwealth College 359, 360, 362, 363, 364, 365, 366, 367,
369, 379, 380, 391, 402, 404a, 405, 412, 413, 443, 462, 1861;
closing 368, 440; problems with Arkansas legislature 319,
321; student strike 448; condemned as "Marxist institution"
381
Communications education 1513
Communications Workers of America (CWA) 1195, 1394, 1772,
1774, 1777
Communist Party 1343 (see also New Workers' School; Workers'
School)
Community 1124, 1143, 1739; action 1757; education 1733
Community Colleges 1817, 1818, 1819, 1820, 1822 (see also indi-
vidual community colleges)
Company Unionism 1067, 1071
Conferences 107, 179, 934, 1072, 1073, 1080, 1083, 1089, 1175
Congress of Industrial Organizations (CIO) 1422, 1432, 1452; New
Jersey 1245; Philadelphia Regional Office 1212; political edu-
cation 1434; department of education 1932
Connor, Edward 1914
Consumer Cooperative Movement 173, 1082
Cook, Alice Hanson 1882
Coordinating Agencies see Workers' Education Bureau; Affiliated
Schools
Cope, Elmer Fern 1883
Cornell University see New York State School for Industrial and
Labor Relations
Correspondence Courses 81, 100, 152, 213, 941, 1243
Cousens, Leon 1935
Creative Arts 1192
Crown Heights School 1651
Cruikshank, Nelson 1957
Cultural Activities 38, 65, 70, 1226, 1233, 1758; education 72,
143
Curriculum 24, 28, 122, 132, 148, 157, 168, 180, 206, 226, 494,
1181, 1186, 1209, 1215, 1217, 1235, 1737, 1748, 1753, 1754,
1756 (see also individual courses)

Dance 195
De Caux, Len 1963
Democracy, Education for 4, 23, 25, 62, 95, 209, 1129, 1132,
1134, 1157, 1168, 1237, 1290, 1352, 1402, 1408, 1663; student
1095
Denver Labor College 499, 690, 855, 856
Department of Labor 1595, 1606; Labor Education Service 1600
Depression 76, 486, 1092
Deverall, Richard L. 1851
Discussion 118, 134, 135, 184, 194, 207, 208, 209, 218
Dogmatic Training see Propaganda
Drama 112, 114, 119, 158, 174, 175, 177, 190, 197, 198, 435,

1059, 1060, 1061, 1062, 1063, 1064, 1065, 1066, 1068, 1081,
1318; labor education 1655, 1656, 1657, 1658, 1659, 1660,
1661, 1662, 1663, 1664, 1665, 1665a, 1666, 1667, 1669, 1670,
1671, 1672, 1673, 1677, 1678, 1679, 1680, 1681, 1682, 1683,
1684, 1686, 1687, 1688, 1689, 1691, 1692, 1693, 1694; labor
studies 1825, 1826, 1827, 1828, 1829, 1830
General Motors 1490, 1522
Georgia Workers' Education Service 1701, 1702, 1703, 1708, 1712
Gildersleeve, Virginia 1842
Girls' Clubs, National League of 926, 948
Gleason, Arthur 1069, 1084
Golden, Clinton 1888
Government Support 984, 985, 1073, 1592, 1593, 1608 (see also
Federal Emergency Relief Administration; Department of Labor;
Works Progress Administration)
Graphic Arts 200
Group Dynamics 184, 1182, 1230
Guernsey, George 1932

Hana, Hilton 1958
Hardman, J. B. S. (Salutsky) 1846
Harvard Trade Union Fellowship Program 1127, 1487, 1493, 1496,
1498, 1507, 1508, 1519, 1535, 1566
Health Education 110, 230
Highlander Folk School 317, 317a, 388, 394, 395, 396, 397, 398,
399, 400, 401, 405, 406, 453, 1455, 1707, 1855, 1856, 1860,
1875, 1907, 1910
Hillquit, Morris 1947
History, teaching of 1188
Holyoke Labor College 900
Holyoke Workers' Forum 1379
Homogeneous vs. Heterogeneous Groupings 130
Hosiery Workers, American Federation of 1319, 1506
Hotel, Restaurant and Bartenders Union 1348, 1349, 1350, 1358, 1389
Hudson Shore Labor School (for before 1939 see Bryn Mawr Sum-
mer School for Women Workers in Industry) 1238, 1246, 1256,
1257, 1266, 1267, 1268, 1269, 1876, 1894, 1897, 1941, 1961
Hutton, Carroll 1921
Hyshka, Nick 1410, 1922

Indiana, University of 1797, 1812
Indoctrination 1133
Industrial Justice 27, 38, 68
Industrial Labor Relations 1152, 1215, 1491, 1494, 1567, 1568,
1639
Industrial Peace, Education for see Labor-Management Harmony,
Education for
Industrial Unionism 1067
Institute for Church Leaders 1559
Institutes see Labor Institutes
Instructional Methods see Teaching Techniques